THE GUITAR COLLECTION
TONY BACON

CHAPTER 01
FLATTOPS PAGE 6

CHAPTER 02
HOLLOWBODIES PAGE 66

03

04

THE GUITAR COLLECTION
FOREWORD

I started out building my own guitars – or screwing them together might be a better way of describing it – so I know how hard it is to make a great guitar. In the 80s in the electric guitar world, Eddie Van Halen epitomized a new movement where lots of players suddenly said, "OK, we'll do it ourselves." They said, "Yes, I did put this together in my garage – and so what? Listen to how good it sounds." And people did listen. I guess that's how I got associated with Ibanez and eventually collaborated with them to make my JS guitars.

This crucial mix of the guitarist's playing input and the major maker's production knowledge comes up again and again in this exciting new book. Here you'll find some of the greatest guitars ever made, and all presented in their historical and musical contexts in a way that I think you'll find really informative. And it's a joy to hear for the first time on vinyl a rare version of 'Smoke On The Water' by RockAid Armenia, which includes Brian May, David Gilmour, Ritchie Blackmore, Tony Iommi, and Alex Lifeson.

All the big names are here, and some of the smaller, and idiosyncratic ones too. This is what keeps music – and guitar playing – moving forward all the time. Some days we may want to go back, to reflect on the older tools, but eventually we have to use the modern tools. It's a constant search, a continual craving for new sounds, for new techniques, for new tones and timbres. No two guitars are alike, in the same way that no two musicians are exactly the same. This book celebrates those differences in great pictures and absorbing text.

Früher habe ich meine eigenen Gitarren gebaut – oder besser gesagt, die Einzelteile zusammengeschraubt. Deshalb habe ich auch vor Gitarrenbauern größten Respekt. In den 1980er-Jahren verkörperte Eddie Van Halen eine neue Generation von E-Gitarristen. Daraufhin legten viele Musiker selbst Hand an und sagten: „Okay, dann bauen wir einfach selbst eine." Sie pflegten zu sagen: „Ich hab die in meiner Garage gebaut, na und? Hör mal, wie gut die klingt." Und die Leute hörten zu. So kam vermutlich der Kontakt mit den Leuten von Ibanez zustande, mit denen ich später meine JS-Gitarren gebaut habe.

Diese essentielle Mischung aus dem Spiel des Gitarristen und dem großen Konstruktionswissen des Gitarrenbauers ist in diesem spannenden, neuen Buch immer wieder Thema. Man erfährt hier viel Wissenswertes über die besten Gitarren aller Zeiten in ihrem jeweiligen historischen und musikalischen Kontext. Außerdem ist es eine wahre Freude, erstmals eine seltene Vinyl-Version von „Smoke On The Water" von RockAid Armenia zu hören, eingespielt von Brian May, David Gilmour, Ritchie Blackmore, Tony Iommi und Alex Lifeson.

In diesem Buch sind neben den bekannten Größen auch einige seltenere, nur Insidern geläufige Namen vertreten. Genau das ist es, was die Musik und das Gitarrenspiel ständig weiter vorantreibt. An manchen Tagen wünschen wir uns die alten Instrumente zurück, doch irgendwann kommen wir ohne die modernen nicht mehr aus. Es bleibt die ständige Suche, das ständige Verlangen nach neuen Techniken, Tönen und Klangfarben. Keine Gitarre gleicht der anderen, so wie auch zwei Musiker nie genau gleich klingen. Dieses Buch feiert eben diese Unterschiede mit großartigen Bildern und fesselnden Texten.

JOE SATRIANI

CHAPTER 01
FLATTOPS

What is a guitar? It's worth starting this book with a definition: a guitar is a plucked stringed instrument, often featuring a waisted body with incurved sides, a neck with frets, and a headstock with tuners. It can be an acoustic box or an electric plank. As we'll discover, there are many variations on those basic themes, and this potential diversity is one of the joys of the guitar. It has a delightful simplicity, but also it can stand about as much complexity as you care to throw at it.

There are two broad types of acoustic guitar: the flattop and the archtop. In this first section, we'll look at the flattop guitar. Usually it has a hollow wooden body with a flat top – hence the name – and a round soundhole. Two further broad divisions are the nylon-string classical guitar and the steel-string folk guitar, although those two names are general and not specific. As ever with the guitar, players adapt instruments to their own purposes and use guitars in all manner of styles and types of music.

The earliest guitars were flattop instruments. Experts disagree, not least on what to call a guitar and which instruments qualify as guitars, but there is little evidence of a proper guitar existing much before the 15th century. One of the oldest survivors dates from around 1590. The ones before were played and enjoyed – and then were lost to history. We still recognise these early instruments as guitars. They have that incurved waisted body, they have strings (although fewer or more than the standard six we have become used to), they have a neck and a headstock, and they have a flat top with a soundhole.

The "classical" guitar as we know it today began to emerge in the 19th century, with the Spanish maker Antonio de Torres most responsible for its early development. He introduced a bigger but not heavier body with wider bouts – the two curves above and below the waist – and he established a fan-shaped system of strutting underneath the top to help the guitar achieve good projection of tone and volume.

Steel-string flattops started to appear in greater numbers during the 20s and 30s as makers listened to guitarists who wanted their instruments to maintain a place in bigger ensembles. Martin, one of the earliest and still one of the best-known American makers, began to brace their flattops more strongly, to fit a tougher bridge, and to strengthen the necks to take the greater strain of steel strings.

Makers began looking for further ways to increase the volume and projection of the flattop acoustic guitar, and a number of solutions were proposed, including bigger bodies, the resonator guitar with its internal loudspeaker-like fitments, and pickups and amplification. Today, the flattop is a fixture in many types of music, from classical to celtic, and in the hands of everybody from country strummers on the festival stage to hopeful singer-songwriters on YouTube.

Was ist eigentlich eine Gitarre? Es ist sinnvoll eine Definition voranzustellen: Eine Gitarre ist ein besaitetes Zupfinstrument mit tailliertem Korpus, geschwungenen Zargen, einem Hals mit Bünden und einer Kopfplatte mit Stimmmechaniken. Generell unterscheidet man zwischen akustischen Gitarren mit Hohlkörper und elektrischen Gitarren mit massivem Korpus. Auf den folgenden Seiten wird deutlich, dass es viele Varianten dieser zwei Gitarrengrundarten gibt. Genau diese Vielfalt macht die Gitarre zu etwas ganz Besonderem. Das Instrument besticht einerseits durch seine erfreuliche Einfachheit und bietet andererseits so viel Komplexität, wie man ihm zu entlocken vermag.

Es gibt zwei Arten von Akustikgitarren: Flattops und Archtops. Das erste Kapitel beschäftigt sich mit der Flattop-Gitarre. Diese besteht in der Regel aus einem hölzernen Hohlkörper mit einem Schallloch und einer flachen Decke – daher der Name. Zwei weitere Varianten sind die klassische Gitarre mit Nylonsaiten und die Westerngitarre mit Stahlsaiten. Beide Bezeichnungen sind jedoch schon deshalb recht grob, da Gitarristen die Instrumente ihren Bedürfnissen anpassen und diese auf alle möglichen Arten und für jede nur denkbare Musikrichtung einsetzen.

Die ersten Gitarren waren Flattop-Instrumente. Experten sind sich uneinig darüber, welche Instrumente als Gitarre bezeichnet werden können. Es gibt kaum Hinweise darauf, dass vor dem 15. Jahrhundert nennenswerte Gitarren existierten. Eines der ältesten noch erhaltenen Instrumente stammt aus der Zeit um 1590. Sicherlich gab es frühere Vorgänger, die sich dann allerdings irgendwo in der Geschichte verloren. Dennoch verfügten auch die frühen Instrumente über die meisten Merkmale einer modernen Gitarre. Sie wiesen einen ähnlich geschwungenen Körper auf, waren besaitet (mal mit mehr oder weniger als 6 Saiten, die heute standardmäßig verwendet werden), hatten einen Hals, eine Kopfplatte sowie eine flache Decke mit Schallloch.

Die „klassische" Gitarre, wie wir sie heute kennen, hat ihren Ursprung im 19. Jahrhundert. Die frühe Entwicklung ist maßgeblich vom spanischen Gitarrenbauer Antonio de Torres beeinflusst. Er entwarf einen größeren Korpus, wobei das Gewicht gleich blieb. Diesen versah er mit größeren Bügen – die zwei Umrissrundungen ober- und unterhalb der Taille. Außerdem entwickelte er eine fächerförmige Verstrebung unter der Decke, die der Gitarre zu besserer Projektion in Klang und Lautstärke verhalf.

Flattop-Gitarren mit Stahlsaiten kamen vermehrt in den 1920er- und 1930er-Jahren auf. Damit entsprachen Gitarrenbauer dem Wunsch vieler Gitarristen, die ihre Instrumente in größeren Ensembles einsetzen wollten. Martin, einer der ersten und immer noch einer der bekanntesten amerikanischen Gitarrenhersteller, begann, die Flattop-Gitarren stärker zu verstreben. Außerdem verwendete man robustere Stege und verstärkte die Hälse, damit diese der hohen Spannung der Stahlsaiten standhielten. Zudem suchten Gitarrenbauer nach weiteren Möglichkeiten, um die Lautstärke und Projektion der akustischen Flattop-Gitarren zu erhöhen. Lösungen hierfür gab es einige: u.a. die Verwendung größere Korpusse, die Resonator-Gitarre mit lautsprecherähnlichen Resonatoren im Inneren des Korpus sowie Tonabnehmer und Verstärker. Heutzutage ist die Flattop-Gitarre eine feste Größe in vielen Musikrichtungen, von klassischer bis zu keltischer Musik. Man sieht sie überall, ob bei Country-Bands auf Festivals oder in YouTube-Videos von Nachwuchskünstlern.

PACO DE LUCIA was one of the great flamenco guitarists. He modernised the traditions of flamenco and he took the flattop nylon-string guitar into new areas, before his death at age 66 in 2014.

PACO DE LUCIA war einer der größten Flamenco-Gitarristen. Er modernisierte das traditionelle Flamenco-Spiel und wagte sich mit seiner klassischen Konzertgitarre in neue musikalische Gefilde vor, bevor er 2014 im Alter von 66 Jahren starb.

FIVE-COURSE GUITAR

GUITARS and women have been used as images to sell many things through the years. This 18th century French poster is an early example that combines the two – with a good example of a six-string guitar of the era – in an attempt to make us eat more biscuits.

Bilder von GITARREN und Frauen halten schon seit Jahren als Werbemotive her. Dieses französische Werbeplakat aus dem 18. Jahrhundert ist ein frühes Beispiel, bei dem gleich beides miteinander kombiniert wird – samt einem schönen Exemplar einer sechssaitigen Gitarre aus der Zeit. Ob die Leute danach wirklich mehr Kekse gegessen haben?

EARLY GUITARS

UNKNOWN MAKER FIVE-COURSE GUITAR

A rare survivor, probably thanks to its elaborate workmanship, this is a very early guitar. It has five courses – a course is a single, double (as here), or even triple string – and this format developed around the middle of the 16th century from the earlier "treble" four-course instrument. Tunings suggested by the surviving music varies widely. This guitar has been restored: the top has been replaced and it has a rebuilt neck, which over its long life has once been cut down, but the beautiful central "rose" in the soundhole is original.

Vermutlich dank der aufwändigen Handarbeit ist diese sehr frühe Gitarre eine der wenigen erhaltenen aus dieser Zeit. Sie besitzt fünf Chöre – ein Chor ist eine einzelne, doppelte (wie hier) oder sogar dreifache Saite – und dieses Format entwickelte sich etwa Mitte des 16. Jahrhunderts aus einem früheren Instrument mit vier Chören. Die heute noch existierende Musik deutet darauf hin, dass die Gitarre auf unterschiedlichste Weise gestimmt werden konnte. Dies ist ein restauriertes Modell: die Decke wurde aus- getauscht und ein neuer Hals eingesetzt, der jedoch mit der Zeit verkürzt wurde; die wunderschöne Schallloch-Rosette ist noch original.

SALOMON FIVE-COURSE GUITAR

Jean-Baptiste DeHaye Salomon made this guitar in Paris, and it has been modified with two extra tuners in the centre of the headstock and an extra bridge channel, to provide the guitar potentially with six courses. There is no more room on the neck, so the extra string probably ran free on the bass side, over an extended nut. As with most early guitars, the frets are tied-on gut. By the middle of the 18th century, tuning began to settle to A/D/G/B/E, in other words the same as generally used for the top five strings of the modern guitar.

Jean-Baptiste DeHaye Salomon baute diese Gitarre in Paris. Sie erhielt später zwei zusätzliche Wirbel in der Mitte der Kopfplatte und einen extra Brückenkanal, um die Gitarre auf sechs Chöre erweitern zu können. Weil auf dem Hals kein Platz mehr war, verlief die zusätzliche Saite vermutlich lose auf der Bass-Seite über einen verlängerten Sattel. Wie bei den meisten frühen Gitarren, wurden die Bundstäbchen meist um den Hals gewunden. Bis Mitte des 18. Jahrhunderts wurden Gitarrensaiten vorwiegend auf A/D/G/H/E gestimmt, d. h. so wie die fünf oberen Saiten der modernen Gitarre in Standardstimmung.

DIONISIO AGUADO was a Spanish composer and guitarist who in the early 19th century wrote several pioneering books that taught readers how to play the guitar. In this illustration, which was designed to show correct posture and an ideal playing position, he plays a typical instrument of the period.

DIONISIO AGUADO war ein spanischer Komponist und Gitarrist, der Anfang des 19. Jahrhunderts mehrere wegweisende Bücher verfasste, um Lesern das Gitarrenspielen beizubringen. In dieser Illustration, die die korrekte Haltung und eine ideale Spielposition darstellt, spielt er ein typisches Instrument aus der Zeit.

THIS ENGRAVING was published in London around 1860, and it includes a guitar that appears to be from an earlier period, with several courses on a neck with tied-gut frets. The title is Love, and so we can assume the artist's efforts were focussed on matters other than contemporary guitar trends.

DIESER STICH eines Londoner Künstlers stammt von 1860. Zu sehen ist u. a. eine Gitarre, die noch älter scheint, mit mehreren Chören an einem Hals mit geknoteten Bundstäbchen aus Darm. Der Titel des Werks lautet Liebe. Man kann also davon ausgehen, dass dem Künstler andere Dinge wichtiger waren als aktuelle Gitarrentrends.

c. 1804 — PAGÉS SIX-COURSE GUITAR

PAGÉS SIX-COURSE GUITAR

Around the end of the 18th century, makers began to move from five to six courses, with an extra low course tuned to E. From there a simple change was made, at first in Italy and France, to six single strings, and the result looked closer to what we now recognise as the modern flat-top guitar. This six-course guitar was made in Cádiz in Spain by Josef Pagés. It has 12 full-size metal frets leading to shorter "treble" frets on the body.

Gegen Ende des 18. Jahrhunderts begannen Gitarrenbauer, nicht mehr fünf sondern sechs Chöre zu bauen, mit einem extra tiefen Chor, der auf E gestimmt wurde. Dies wurde nur minimal geändert, zunächst in Italien und Frankreich: Von sechs Chören zu sechs einzelnen Saiten. So sah die Gitarre schon fast aus wie die moderne Flat-top-Gitarre. Dieses Instrument mit sechs Chören wurde von Josef Pagés in Cádiz gebaut. Sie besitzt 12 komplette Bünde mit Bundstäbchen aus Metall, die zu kürzeren „Diskant"-Bünden auf dem Korpus führen.

c. 1835 — MARTIN STAUFFER-STYLE

1836 — UNKNOWN MAKER PANORMO

MARTIN STAUFFER-STYLE

Before he emigrated to America from Germany, C.F. Martin Sr. worked for guitar-maker Johann Stauffer of Vienna, and Stauffer's ideas and styles influenced the early instruments that Martin built upon setting up his workshops, at first in New York City and, in 1839, in Nazareth, Pennsylvania, where the company is still based today. The scroll-shape headstock with the six tuners along one side, the "moustache" bridge, and the relatively large upper bout of this early Martin guitar are all reminiscent of Stauffer's instruments. Successive generations of the Martin family have run the business ever since, the most recent being Chris Martin IV, who became chairman of the board in 1986.

Bevor C. F. Martin Senior von Deutschland nach Amerika auswanderte, arbeitete er für den Wiener Gitarrenbauer Johann Stauffer. Stauffers Ideen und Stil beeinflussten Martins frühe Instrumente, die er während der Errichtung seiner Werkstätten in New York und Nazareth, Pennsylvania (1839) baute, wo das Unternehmen noch heute seinen Sitz hat. Der schnecken-förmige Kopf mit den sechs Wirbeln an einer Seite, der Schnurrbart-Steg und der relativ große Oberbug dieser frühen Martin-Gitarre – all das erinnert an Stauffers Instrumente. Die Geschäfte wurden bisher stets von Nachkommen des Martin-Klans übernommen, seit 1986 heißt der Vorstandsvorsitzende Chris Martin IV.

PANORMO

The son of an Italian violin maker, Louis Panormo ran a busy workshop in London. This guitar shows how Panormo included elements from the best contemporary instruments. He regularly fitted metal geared machine-heads rather than tuning pegs, and he was one of the few makers outside Spain who used fan strutting in the bodies of his guitars, a scheme later popularised by Torres. The guitar has a fine ebony fingerboard that is slightly radiused, or gently curved, unlike the flatter boards common at the time but today seen by most players as a necessity.

Der Sohn eines italienischen Geigenbauers, Louis Panormo, hatte eine gut gehende Werkstatt in London. Diese Gitarre zeigt, wie Panormo Elemente aus den besten Instrumenten der damaligen Zeit mit einfließen ließ. Er verwendete regelmäßig Mechaniken aus Metall anstelle von Wirbeln, und er war einer der wenigen Gitarrenbauer außerhalb Spaniens, der den Korpus seiner Gitarren mittels Fächerbeleistung baute, eine Methode, die Torres später bekannt machte. Die Gitarre hat ein feines Griffbrett aus Ebenholz, das, anders als die flacheren Griffbretter dieser Zeit, leicht abgerundet bzw. gewölbt ist, was heute von den meisten Gitarristen als Notwendigkeit betrachtet wird.

MARTIN 0-42

By the time this guitar was made, Martin had made a clear break from its earlier Stauffer-influenced guitars and was developing its own designs and ideas. Style 42 was Martin's fanciest of the period and Size 0 a relatively large guitar for the time, a little over 13 inches wide. It has three "snowflake" inlays, typical of Style 42 in this period, and 1898 marked the year from which all Martins were given serial numbers, at first stamped on the top of the headstock but soon shifted to the neck block inside the body. The company still used ivory for binding, nut, and bridge, including the saddle, moving to ebony bridges and synthetic ivory binding by the 1910s. It was not until the 30s that Martin began to brace its guitars for use with steel strings.

Als diese Gitarre entstand, hatte sich Martin bereits eindeutig von den früheren Stauffer beeinflussten Gitarren distanziert. Nun entwickelte man eigene Designs und Ideen. Die Style 42 war Martins ausgefallenstes Modell und die Size 0 war mit 33 Zentimetern Breite eine recht große Gitarre für damalige Verhältnisse. Sie besitzt drei, für Style 42 damals typische, "Schneeflocken"-Inlays. Ab 1898 erhielten alle Martin-Gitarren Seriennummern, die zunächst oben auf der Kopfplatte angebracht wurden, kurze Zeit später jedoch an den Halsblock im Korpus verschoben wurden. Das Unternehmen verwendete weiterhin Elfenbein für Randeinfassung, Sattel und Steg; ab 1910 benutzte man Stege aus Ebenholz und Randeinfassungen aus künstlichem Elfenbein. Erst in den 1930er-Jahren begann Martin, Gitarren mit Verbalkung zu versehen, um sie mit Stahlsaiten bespannen zu können.

JOAN BAEZ headed the protest-singer movement in the USA during the Vietnam War. She often played a small-body Martin 0-45 from the late 20s, an instrument with distinctive abalone inlay around the edges. Martin issued a Baez signature model in the 90s.

Folk-Sängerin JOAN BAEZ führte mit ihren Protestliedern die Anti-Vietnamkriegsproteste in den USA an. Sie spielte häufig auf einer kleinen Martin 0-45 aus den späten 1920er-Jahren, ein Instrument mit charakteristischer Zierringeinlage aus Abalone. In den 1990er-Jahren brachte Martin ein Baez Signature-Modell heraus.

BOHMANN HARP GUITAR

The idea for a harp guitar originated in
Europe at the end of the 18th century,
when a revival led to a vogue for all things
classical. This included hybrid instruments
that merged guitar and lyre (the lyre guitar)
and harp and guitar (the harp guitar).
Joseph Bohmann emigrated from Berlin to
Chicago in the 1870s and set up business
as an instrument maker, producing mostly
violins, guitars, and mandolins. His mandolins were among the earliest made in the
United States. This remarkable instrument
has strings inside the body as well as the
multiple ones seen on the two necks, and
the internal strings can be muted with the
lever on the body (which is, sadly, not some
kind of early vibrato arm). It seems almost
certain this must have been a special order
rather than a production item.

*Die Idee für eine Harfengitarre stammt
aus Europa, als Ende des 18. Jahrhunderts
plötzlich alles Klassische wieder in Mode
kam. Dazu gehörten auch Hybrid-Instru-
mente – z. B. die Lyragitarre, eine Mischung
aus Gitarre und Lyra und die Harfengitarre,
eine Mischung aus Harfe und Gitarre.
Joseph Bohmann, der in den 1870er-Jahren
von Berlin nach Chicago auswanderte, eröffnete ein Geschäft als Instrumentenbauer
und produzierte hauptsächlich Violinen,
Gitarren und Mandolinen. Seine Mandolinen gehörten zu den ersten, die in den USA
hergestellt wurden. Dieses bemerkenswerte
Instrument hat neben mehreren Saiten an
zwei Hälsen auch Saiten auf der Korpus-
innenseite. Die inneren Saiten können mit
dem Hebel am Korpus stumm geschaltet
werden (leider kein frühes Tremolo).
Die Gitarre war vermutlich eine Sonderanfertigung und kein massenproduziertes
Instrument.*

c. 1910 – BOHMANN
HARP GUITAR

JOAN
BAEZ

PACO DE LUCIA was born near Cádiz in Spain. He revolutionised the modern idea of flamenco, combining past heritage with the freshness of the present. Sometimes he went further, moving beyond the genre to the new. He often played guitars by Domingo Esteso's nephews, the Conde Hermanos. He died in 2014.

PACO DE LUCIA wurde in der Nähe von Cádiz in Spanien geboren. Er revolutionierte das moderne Konzept von Flamenco-Musik, indem er das traditionelle Erbe mit modernen Elementen vereinte. Manchmal ging er noch weiter und wagte sich über das Genre in neue musikalische Gefilde hinaus. Er spielte häufig Gitarren von Domingo Estesos Neffen, die unter dem Namen Conde Hermanos firmieren. Paco de Lucia starb 2014.

FLAMENCO

ESTESO

Flamenco is the folk music of the gypsies of Andalusia in southern Spain, combining cante (song), baile (dance), and toque (guitar playing). The percussive guitar style includes rhythmic tapping of the top of the instrument, which is often protected by a plastic golpeador or tap plate. Flamencos are much lighter compared to classical guitars, have a low string action to aid percussion and speed, and usually have friction pegs rather than machine-head tuners. Domingo Esteso trained at Manuel Ramírez's workshop in Madrid, and following Manuel's death in 1916 he set up in his own right, producing fine instruments until his own death in 1937. His nephews, the brothers Faustino and Mariano Conde, took over, starting afresh in the early 40s after the Spanish Civil War with a third brother, Julio Conde – the Hermanos Conde. Since 2010, Felipe Conde, son of Mariano Conde, has headed the workshop.

Flamenco ist die traditionelle Musik Andalusiens – eine Kombination aus Gesang (cante), Tanz (baile) und Instrumentalspiel (toque). Zu der perkussiven Spielweise gehört rhythmisches Schlagen auf die Gitarrendecke, die oft durch ein Golpeador (ein Schlagbrett aus Kunststoff) geschützt ist. Flamenco-Gitarren sind viel leichter als klassische Gitarren, haben eine tiefe Saitenlage, die Perkussivschläge und höheres Tempo unterstützt, und besitzen meist Wirbel anstelle von Stimmmechaniken. Domingo Esteso lernte bei Manuel Ramírez in Madrid. Als Ramírez 1916 starb, machte er sich selbstständig und baute bis zu seinem Tod 1937 großartige Gitarren. Seine Neffen, die Brüder Faustino und Mariano Conde, übernahmen sein Geschäft und wagten nach dem Spanischen Bürgerkrieg zu Beginn der 1940er-Jahre einen Neuanfang mit ihrem Bruder Julio Conde – Hermanos Conde. Seit 2010 wird die Werkstatt von Felipe Conde, dem Sohn von Mariano Conde geleitet.

1934 — ESTESO

c. 1931 – NATIONAL **STYLE O**

c. 1935 – DOBRO **NO. 100**

RESONATOR GUITARS

NATIONAL STYLE O

As well as the tricone style, National produced single-cone resonator guitars, such as this Style O. Visible here and also on the Model 35 are the vivid decorations that National sandblasted on to the bodies of some of its models. National founder John Dopyera left and with his two brothers formed Dobro at the end of the 20s, and George Beauchamp was fired, partly for helping to set up the company that would make Rickenbacker guitars. Following resurrections of National-brand resonator guitars in the 50s and 60s, with varied success, a new company, National Reso-Phonic, was started in 1989 and continues to produce a wide range of instruments today.

Neben den Tricone-Gitarren baute National auch Gitarren mit einem Resonator, wie z. B. diese Style O. Hier und am Modell 35 gut erkennbar ist der mit einem Sandstrahler aufwändig verzierte Korpus. National-Gründer John Dopyera verließ das Unternehmen und gründete mit seinen beiden Brüdern Ende der 1920er-Jahre die Firma Dobro. George Beauchamp wurde vor die Tür gesetzt, u. a. weil er beim Aufbau der der Firma geholfen hatte, die später Rickenbacker-Gitarren herstellte. Nach Comebacks der National-Resonatorgitarren in den 1950er- und 1960er-Jahren, jeweils mit gemischtem Erfolg, wurde 1989 eine neue Firma, National Reso-Phonic, gegründet, die noch heute eine Vielzahl unterschiedlicher Instrumente baut.

When MARK KNOPFLER's shining National guitar appeared in 1985 on the front cover of the hugely successful Dire Straits album Brothers In Arms, it sparked a revival of interest in resonator instruments. Knopfler has enjoyed a successful solo career since Dire Straits finally split in the mid 90s.

Als MARK KNOPFLERS glänzende National-Gitarre 1985 das Cover des höchst erfolgreichen Albums Brothers In Arms von den Dire Straits zierte, löste dies ein wiederauflebendes Interesse an Resonatorgitarren aus. Knopfler startete nach Auflösung der Dire Straits Mitte der 1990er-Jahre eine erfolgreiche Solokarriere.

DOBRO NO. 100

Resonator guitars were invented in California in the late 20s. They had resonating aluminium cones suspended inside the body, which acted like loudspeakers, increasing the volume and projection of the instrument. The two main brands were National and Dobro, and their early history is complicated. Dobro was formed by three ex-National men, John, Ed, and Rudy Dopyera, who made their company name by combining DOpyera BROthers. "Dobro" is often used generically to mean a resonator guitar, irrespective of the brand. The instruments are often played with strings high off the neck, on the lap and with a slide. This Model 100 is typical of the early single-cone wooden-body Dobro guitars, with a sound different to the usually metal-bodied Nationals. Gibson bought the Dobro name in the 90s and continues to produce the instruments.

Resonatorgitarren wurden Ende der 1920er-Jahre in Kalifornien erfunden. Sie besaßen Resonatoren aus Aluminium, die im Korpus aufgehängt wurden und ähnlich wie Lautsprecher die Lautstärke und die Tragfähigkeit der Gitarre verstärkten. Die beiden Haupthersteller waren die National Stringed Instrument Corporation, kurz National, und Dobro, doch ihre Geschichte ist kompliziert. Dobro wurde von drei ehemaligen National-Gründern, John,

Ed und Rudy Dopyera, ins Leben gerufen. Der Name Dobro setzt sich zusammen aus DOpyera und BROthers. „Dobro" ist oft der allgemein verwendete Begriff für Resonatorgitarre, ungeachtet der Marke. Resonatorgitarren werden häufig auf dem Schoß und mit einem Slide oder Bottleneck gespielt. Diese Dobro 100 ist eine typische, frühe Resonantorgitarren mit einem Holzkorpus, die anders klingt als die für National typischen Metallkorpus-Gitarren. In den 1990er-Jahren kaufte Gibson den Namen Dobro und stellt die Gitarren bis heute her.

NATIONAL MODEL 35

National was established in California in the mid 20s, at first to produce a metal-body banjo invented by John Dopyera. Dopyera and his partner George Beauchamp devised a system with aluminium resonators suspended inside a guitar's metal body to produce extra volume and a distinctive sound. This Model 35 has National's classic tri-cone design, incorporating three separate resonator cones and a large T-shape cover. The strings' vibration across the bridge moves an internal T-bar, which in turn vibrates the cones, which resonate and amplify the guitar's sound.

National wurde Mitte der 1920er-Jahre in Kalifornien gegründet, um eine Erfindung von John Dopyera herzustellen: ein Banjo mit Metallkorpus. Dopyera und sein Partner George Beauchamp nutzten dafür Resonatoren aus Aluminium, die im Metallkorpus der Gitarre aufgehängt wurden und für mehr Lautstärke sowie einen charakteristischen Klang sorgten. Die National 35 ist eine für National typische Tricone-Gitarre mit drei einzelnen Resonatoren und einem großen T-förmigen Bügel. Die Vibration auf dem Steg bewegt einen T-förmigen Balken im Inneren, der wiederum die Resonatoren zum Schwingen bringt. Diese verstärken dann den Klang der Gitarre.

JERRY DOUGLAS is an American lap-steel virtuoso known for his session work and solo records. James Taylor called him the "Muhammad Ali of the Dobro". He has played on recordings by everyone from Dolly Parton to Lynyrd Skynyrd, and he reached a wide audience with his appearances on the Transatlantic Sessions TV shows and tours.

Der US-Amerikaner JERRY DOUGLAS ist ein grandioser Lap-Steel-Gitarrist und sowohl als Sessionmusiker als auch für seine Soloalben bekannt. James Taylor nannte ihn den „Muhammad Ali der Dobro". Er war auf den Alben sämtlicher Künstler vertreten, von Dolly Parton bis Lynyrd Skynyrd, und erreichte mit seinen Auftritten in der Serie Transatlantic Sessions sowie auf seinen Touren ein breites Publikum.

SON HOUSE was a blues performer, born Eddie James House Jr in rural Mississippi around 1902. He played slide guitar on a metal-bodied National resonator guitar, which lent his playing a brittle, haunting tone. He was rediscovered during the 60s blues boom, and he died in Detroit in 1988.

SON HOUSE wurde 1902 im ländlichen Mississippi geboren und hieß mit bürgerlichem Namen Eddie James House Jr. Der Blues-Gitarrist spielte Slide-Gitarre auf einer National Resonatorgitarre, deren Metallkorpus seinem Spiel eine spröde, eindringliche Note verlieh. Als der Blues in den 1960er-Jahren wieder auflebte, wurde seine Musik neu entdeckt. Son House starb 1988 in Detroit.

SON
HOUSE

1860 — TORRES
FIRST EPOCH

A LUTHIER enjoys the Mexican sun as he fixes strutting to the underside of a few guitar tops.

EIN GITARRENBAUER genießt die Sonne Mexikos während er Verstrebungen einiger Gitarrendecken repariert.

CLASSICAL GUITARS

TORRES FIRST & SECOND EPOCH

In the 19th century, the guitar began to develop into what today we call the classical guitar. The maker most responsible for this development was a Spaniard, Antonio de Torres. He was born near Almeria and worked in Seville (his "first epoch", 1852–1869) and in Almeria ("second epoch", 1875–1892). Torres's primary theory was that the guitar's top was the key to its sound, and he developed a fan-strutting pattern for the underside of the top, domed the lower bout, shifted the bridge further up the body, and used relatively thin woods. The combination produced strong but not heavy guitars with a responsive, rounded sound, and an elegant plain look. His ideas for an integrated guitar were widely adopted in Spain and abroad.

Im 19. Jahrhundert entwickelte sich die Gitarre allmählich zur klassischen Gitarre, wie wir sie heute kennen. Der Gitarrenbauer, der diese Entwicklung maßgeblich mit geprägt hat, war der Spanier Antonio de Torres. In der Nähe von Almeria geboren, arbeitete er zunächst in Sevilla („erste Epoche" 1852–1869) und dann in Almeria („zweite Epoche" 1875–1892). Torres vertrat die Theorie, dass die Decke für den Klang einer Gitarre enorm wichtig ist. Und so baute er eine Fächerbeleistung für die Deckenunterseite, wölbte den Unterbug, versetzte den Steg weiter nach oben und verwendete relativ dünne Hölzer. Diese Kombination brachte starke, aber dennoch leichte Gitarren hervor, die einen runden, responsiven Klang besaßen und dabei schlicht aber elegant aussahen. Seine Ideen für eine integrierte Gitarre wurden in Spanien und darüber hinaus übernommen.

1985 — ROMANILLOS
LA BUHO

JULIAN BREAM has been a great ambassador for classical guitar since his concert debut in his early teens. He was born in London in 1933, and during a long career he encouraged composers to write for the guitar, helping to create the modern repertoire. He has played guitars by Hauser, Bouchet, Romanillos, Rubio, and others.

JULIAN BREAM wurde 1933 in London geboren. Seit seinem Konzert-debüt in Jugendtagen galt er als wichtiger Vertreter der klassischen Gitarre. Er ermutigte Komponisten im Laufe seiner langen Karriere, Werke für Gitarre zu schreiben und trug so zur Entstehung eines modernen Repertoires bei. Er spielte u.a. Gitarren von Hauser, Bouchet, Romanillos und Rubio.

HAUSER I

Based in Munich, Hermann Hauser made a variety of stringed instruments. At first, in the 1900s, he made some guitars in an older, non-Spanish style, but he soon adopted the styles and ideas of Torres. Andrés Segovia once declared the Hauser as "the greatest guitar of our times". Hauser died in 1952, and his son and grandson, both named Hermann, continued the business: Hermann II continued to make instruments until his death in 1988; Hermann III is still active and so is his daughter, Kathrin.

Der Münchner Hermann Hauser stellte verschiedenartige Saiteninstrumente her. In den 1900er-Jahren baute er zunächst Gitarren in einem älteren, nicht-spanischen Stil, übernahm jedoch bald die Ideen und Bauweise von Torres. Andrés Segovia erklär-te die Hauser einmal zur „großartigsten Gi-tarre unserer Zeit". Als Hauser 1952 starb, übernahmen sein Sohn und sein Enkel das Geschäft: Hermann II baute Instrumente bis zu seinem Tod 1988; Hermann III betreibt das Geschäft noch heute, ebenso wie seine Tochter Kathrin.

ROMANILLOS LA BUHO

José Romanillos was born in Madrid in 1932 and moved to Britain in 1959. He set up a workshop near to Julian Bream's home in England in 1970. Bream played Romanillos guitars, among others, from 1973 and used the guitar shown until 1990. José based his guitars on the light, precise Hauser and Torres styles, and he became an authority on Torres, writing a well-received book in 1987 about the great Spanish maker. Romanillos's son Liam has made guitars since 1991.

José Romanillos wurde 1932 in Madrid geboren und zog 1959 nach Großbritan-nien. Nicht weit von Julian Breams Haus in England entfernt, errichtete er 1970 eine Werkstatt. Bream spielte unter anderem Romanillos-Gitarren von 1973; die hier abgebildete Gitarre nutzte er bis 1990. José konstruierte seine Gitarren auf Grund-lage der leichten, präzisen Hauser und Torres Bauweise. Als Torres-Experte schrieb er 1987 ein erfolgreiches Buch über den spanischen Gitarrenbauer. Romanillos Sohn Liam stellt seit 1991 Gitarren her.

If anyone can be said to have 'invented' modern classical guitar playing, it was **ANDRÉS SEGOVIA**. Born near Granada in Spain in 1893, Segovia played guitars by Manuel Ramírez (which were probably made in the Ramírez workshops by Santos Hernández), Hermann Hauser, Ignacio Fleta, and José Ramírez. He died in 1987.

Wenn man jemandem nachsagen kann, dass er das moderne Spiel der klassischen Gitarre ‚erfunden' hat, dann ANDRÉS SEGOVIA. Der 1893 in der Nähe von Granada geborene spanische Künstler spielte Gitarren von Manuel Ramírez (vermutlich von Santos Hernández in der Werkstatt von Ramírez gebaut), Hermann Hauser, Ignacio Fleta und José Ramírez. Andrés Segovia starb 1987.

JOSE RAMIREZ 1A

The Ramírez guitar established the standard form for the modern concert instrument, and the Ramírez dynasty began with brothers José I (1858–1923) and Manuel (1864–1916). The business passed to José II (1885–1923), José III (1922–1995), who headed the workshop that produced the guitar pictured here, José IV (1953–2000), and a team headed by Amalia Ramírez (she was born in 1955). The firm today produces guitars with on-board pre-amps, flamenco instruments, cutaway guitars, and models with built-in MIDI pickups, but at their heart is the great Ramírez design that has stood the test of time.

Die Ramírez-Gitarre gilt heute als Standard unter den modernen Konzertgitarren. Die Ramírez-Dynastie begann mit den Brüdern José I (1858–1923) und Manuel (1864–1916). Das Geschäft wurde an José II (1885–1923) und José III (1922–1995) vererbt, der die Werkstatt leitete, wo die hier abgebildete Gitarre gebaut wurde. Später übernahmen José IV (1953–2000) und schließlich ein Team unter der Leitung von Amalia Ramírez (geb. 1955). Heute produziert das Unternehmen Gitarren mit Onboard-Vorverstärkern, Flamenco-Gitarren, Gitarren mit Cutaway und Modelle mit eingebauten MIDI-Tonabnehmern. Den Kern bildet allerdings immer noch das großartige Ramírez-Design, das sich seit langem bewährt hat.

1990 – JOSE RAMIREZ 1A

Ramírez guitars have been seen in the hands of many famous and not-so-famous classical guitarists. Probably the widest audience for an associated instrument came when GEORGE HARRISON played his José Ramírez Estudio guitar for the performance of 'And I Love Her' in the 1964 Beatles movie A Hard Day's Night.

Ramírez-Gitarren wurden von vielen bekannten und weniger bekannten klassischen Gitarristen gespielt. Die vielleicht größte mediale Aufmerksamkeit erlangte der spanische Hersteller, als GEORGE HARRISON 1964 seine José Ramírez Estudio-Gitarre für das Stück ,And I Love Her' im Beatles-Film A Hard Day's Night spielte.

HUMPHREY MILLENIUM

Thomas Humphrey was born in Minnesota and began his guitar-making career in New York City in 1970 at the workshops of Michael Gurian. He decided to go his own way the following year, influenced at first by Hauser-like ideas for power and speed. The idea for the Millennium came to Humphrey in a dream, and he introduced the model in 1985. It had an unusual tapered top – wider at the bottom, narrower at the neck – and a negative neck angle, all of which provided good sound projection and improved access to the higher frets. Humphrey experimented with various strutting styles, later adopting a lattice pattern, and in the late 80s he developed a shortlived Millennium-style guitar for Martin. He died in 2008 at the age of just 59, and before his death he collaborated with an artist, Tamara Codor, on a proposed line of intricately-painted guitars.

Thomas Humphrey wurde in Minnesota geboren und startete seine Karriere als Gitarrenbauer 1970 in New York, in den Werkstätten von Michael Gurian. Als er ein Jahr später beschloss, sich selbstständig zu machen, war er zunächst von Hausers Ideen für mehr Kraft und Schnelligkeit beeinflusst. Das Konzept für die Millenium kam Humphrey im Traum, das fertige Modell stellte er 1985 vor. Es besaß eine ungewöhnlich spitz zulaufende Decke – unten breiter, schmaler am Hals – und einen negativen Halswinkel. Alles zusammen ergab eine gute Klangprojektion und einen verbesserten Zugang zu den höheren Bünden. Humphrey experimentierte zunächst mit unterschiedlichen Verstrebungsarten und entschied sich später für ein Gittermuster. Ende der 1980er-Jahre entwickelte er für Martin eine Millenium-Gitarre, die jedoch nicht lange produziert wurde. 2008 starb er mit nur 59 Jahren. Kurz vor seinem Tod arbeitete er mit der Künstlerin Tamara Codor an einer Serie kunstvoll bemalter Gitarren.

SMALLMAN

Australian guitar maker Greg Smallman developed some revolutionary designs, employing a thin top supported by a lattice of carbon-fibre and balsa. Smallman began making guitars in 1972, based on Fleta's designs, but by 1980 he was experimenting with his now famous lattice strutting system. The result was a loud guitar with strong sound projection, designed for the concert hall, and with an even balance across the frequency range. Guitarist John Williams began playing Smallman's guitars in 1981 and is the maker's highest-profile ambassador, having done much to popularise Smallman instruments around the world.

Der australische Gitarrenbauer Greg Smallman entwickelte revolutionäre Konstruktionen, wobei er eine von einem Gitter aus Kohlenstoff-Faser und Balsa gehaltene dünne Decke verwendete. Seine ersten Gitarren baute Smallman 1972, nach dem Vorbild von Ignacio Fletas Modellen. 1980 experimentierte er mit seinen mittlerweile legendären Gitterverstrebungen. Heraus kam eine für den Konzertsaal konzipierte laute Gitarre mit starker Klangprojektion und einem ausgeglichenen Frequenzspektrum. Smallmans berühmtester Werbeträger, der Gitarrist John Williams, spielt seine Gitarren seit 1981. Dank ihm wurden Smallmans Gitarren in der ganzen Welt bekannt.

Renowned as a leading classical guitarist, JOHN WILLIAMS was born in Melbourne, Australia, in 1941. He has used a number of instruments during his long career, most notably in his early years a guitar made by Ignacio Fleta in 1972. More recently, Williams has played and promoted guitars by the Australian maker Greg Smallman.

Der 1941 in Melbourne geborene JOHN WILLIAMS gilt als einer der führenden klassischen Gitarristen. Seit Beginn seiner Karriere verwendete er unterschiedlichste Instrumente, u. a. eine von Ignacio Fleta gebaute Gitarre aus dem Jahr 1972, die er in seinen frühen Jahren spielte. Seit einiger Zeit spielt Williams Gitarren des australischen Gitarrenbauers Greg Smallman.

CHET ATKINS CEC

In the 40s, CHET ATKINS secured a recording contract with RCA, and as a producer he made records with Elvis and the Everly Brothers, sometimes adding rhythm guitar. But it was his superb solo cuts, from 'Main Street Breakdown' to 'Yakety Axe', that impressed guitarists. Atkins died in 2001 aged 77.

In den 1940er-Jahren sicherte sich CHET ATKINS einen Plattenvertrag mit RCA. Als Produzent war er mit Elvis und den Everly Brothers im Studio, wo er für manche Songs auch die Rhythmusgitarre einspielte. Doch am meisten waren Gitarristen von seinen herausragenden Solocuts beeindruckt, von ‚Main Street Breakdown' bis hin zu ‚Yakety Axe'. Atkins starb 2001 im Alter von 77 Jahren.

MODEL 150SA

GIBSON CHET ATKINS CEC

This was the result of a collaboration between Gibson and Chet Atkins. Despite his reputation as an electric player, Atkins was by the 80s mostly playing nylon-string classical-style flattops, and he wanted a practical electric classical. He brought the idea to Gibson, using a semi-solid body and a piezo bridge pickup. Piezo pickups use crystals that produce an electric signal when moved. The idea was not a new one – makers such as Ovation had offered some solutions – but the Atkins guitar was a step toward a better amplified nylon-string instrument, and one that mostly looked and felt like a decent classical guitar.

Diese Gitarre war das Ergebnis einer Zusammenarbeit zwischen Gibson und Chet Atkins. Trotz seiner Reputation als E-Gitarrist spielte Atkins bis in die 1980er-Jahre vor allem klassische Flattops mit Nylonsaiten. Da er sich eine praktische, klassische E-Gitarre wünschte, stellte er Gibson seine Idee vor: eine Halbresonanzgitarre mit einem Steg mit Piezo-Tonabnehmer. Bei Piezo-Tonabnehmern produzieren Kristalle bei jeder Bewegung ein elektrisches Signal. Die Idee war nicht neu – Hersteller wie Ovation hatten bereits Lösungen im Angebot – doch die Atkins-Gitarre war die bessere verstärkte Gitarre mit Nylonsaiten, die überdies wie eine gute klassische Gitarre aussah und sich auch so spielte.

YAMAHA 150SA

Yamaha began when Torakusu Yamaha invented a pedal-driven reed organ in 1887, and ten years later he founded the Nippon Gakki Co Ltd, adding pianos in 1900 and guitars in 1946, with steel-string flattops appearing in the mid 60s. Yamaha also produced classical guitars, like the Japanese-made example shown here, a model with slightly squared shoulders that lasted into the 70s. It had a solid spruce top (a companion model, the 150C, had a cedar top), rosewood sides and back, a mahogany neck, and rosewood fingerboard.

Die Anfänge von Yamaha gehen zurück auf Torakusu Yamahas Erfindung eines Pedal betriebenen Harmoniums von 1887. Zehn Jahre später gründete er die Nippon Gakki Co. Ltd, die ab 1900 Klaviere und ab 1946 auch Gitarren anbot. Ab Mitte der 1960er-Jahre brachte das Unternehmen auch Flattops mit Stahlsaiten auf den Markt. Yamaha produzierte ebenfalls klassische Gitarren wie dieses eher geradschultrige Modell aus Japan, das bis in die 1970er-Jahre hergestellt wurde. Die Decke bestand aus massivem Fichtenholz (ein Schwestermodell, die 150C, hatte eine Decke aus Zedernholz), die Zargen, die Rückwand und das Griffbrett aus Palisander und der Hals aus Mahagoni.

MARTIN N-20

Most guitarists think of steel-string guitars when the name Martin is mentioned today, but the company made instruments for classical players since the 30s, with wide fingerboards, slotted headstocks, and loop bridges. However, none scored particularly well in what is largely a specialist area. This guitar and its sister model the N-10 were launched by the American firm in the 60s, with the better-appointed N-20 lasting into the 90s, with a slightly longer scale-length from 1970.

Heute denken die meisten Gitarristen bei Martin an Stahl-saiten-Gitarren, doch das Unternehmen produzierte seit den 1930er-Jahren auch klassische Gitarren, mit breitem Griffbrett, durchbrochener Kopfplatte und Loop-Steg. Keines der Modelle war sonderlich erfolgreich, da dieser Nischenbereich doch recht spezialisiert ist. Diese Gitarre und ihr Schwestermodell, die N-10, brachte Martin in den 1960er-Jahren auf den Markt. Die besser ausgestattete N-20 wurde bis in die 1990er-Jahre produziert, mit einer etwas größeren Mensur seit 1970.

The Mexican classical-guitar duo RODRIGO Y GABRIELA are Rodrigo Sanchez and Gabriela Quintero, and their fusion of several styles, from flamenco to rock, has earned them great success. They both play Yamaha nylon-string guitars with cutaway bodies, piezo pickup systems, and side-mounted controls.

Das mexikanische Gitarrenduo RODRIGO Y GABRIELA (alias Rodrigo Sanchez und Gabriela Quintero) hat mit seiner Verschmelzung verschiedener Stile von Flamenco bis Rock großen Erfolg. Die beiden spielen auf nylonbesaiteten Yamaha-Gitarren mit Cutaway-Korpus, Piezo-Tonabnehmersystemen und seitlich montierten Reglern.

Country superstar WILLIE NELSON is one of the few famous artists to play a Martin nylon-string guitar. He has played his N-20, which he calls "Trigger", for more than 40 years, and such long-term use has taken its toll. Nelson's picking has worn a hole right through the body – which he claims improves the sound.

Country-Superstar WILLIE NELSON ist einer der wenigen berühmten Künstler, der auf einer Martin mit Nylonbesaitung spielt. Seine N-20, die er „Trigger" nennt, spielt er seit über 40 Jahren – was man der Gitarre auch ansieht: Durch sein vehementes Picking-Spiel ist jetzt ein Loch im Gitarrenkorpus, was den Klang des Instruments laut Nelson verbessert hat.

WILLIE
NELSON

FLETA

Ignacio Fleta set up a workshop in Barcelona in 1927, and later he developed his typically wide-waisted guitars that had a diagonal strut under the treble side of the top, designed to increase the guitar's volume, and varnish under the top, to brighten the sound. His most famous player was Segovia, for whom he built the first of several instruments in 1957. By the time Fleta died in 1977, the waiting time for an instrument had stretched to 15 years. His sons Francisco and Gabriel were involved in the business since at least the 60s, and when Gabriel died in 2013 his son Gabriel Jr took over.

Ignacio Fleta eröffnete 1927 eine Werkstatt in Barcelona. Später entwickelte er seine typischen Gitarren mit breiter Taille, die unter der Diskantseite der Decke einen diagonalen Stab aufwiesen (um das Volumen der Gitarre zu vergrößern). Zugunsten eines helleren Klangs war die Unterseite der Decke lackiert. Sein berühmtester Kunde war Segovia, für den er 1957 die erste von mehreren Gitarren baute. Bis zu seinem Tod 1977 benötigte Fleta für die Fertigstellung einer Gitarre bis zu 15 Jahre. Seine Söhne Francisco und Gabriel stiegen vermutlich in den 1960er-Jahren in das Familienunternehmen ein. Als Gabriel 2013 starb, übernahm dessen Sohn Gabriel Junior die Geschäfte.

RUCK

Milwaukee-born Robert Ruck began as a student of classical and flamenco guitar and is today a celebrated instrument maker. His first guitars were championed by the Cuban guitarist Juan Mercadal, whose student Manuel Barrueco built his early career with a Ruck. Ruck has worked in Florida, Georgia, and Washington. In later years, Ruck added two "acoustic ports" either side of the neck heel, designed to give the player a more intimate involvement with the instrument's sound. He has built a wide range of stringed instruments, and until he stopped taking commissions – officially, at least – his speciality was the design and construction of custom orders.

Der aus Milwaukee stammende Robert Ruck studierte zunächst klassische und Flamenco-Gitarre und gilt heute als renommierter Gitarrenbauer. Seine ersten Gitarren wurden meisterhaft vom kubanischen Gitarristen Juan Mercadal gespielt, dessen Schüler Manuel Barrueco seine frühe Karriere mit einer Ruck begann. Robert Ruck arbeitete in Florida, Georgia und Washington. Später fügte er zwei weitere Schallöffnungen („acoustic ports") auf beiden Seiten des Halsansatzes hinzu, damit der Spieler in möglichst engem Kontakt mit dem Klang der Gitarre sein konnte. Von ihm stammen verschiedenste Saiteninstrumente, und bis er aufhörte, Aufträge anzunehmen – offiziell zumindest – designte und baute er vor allem Sonderanfertigungen.

MANUEL BARRUECO was born in Cuba in 1952, and has lived in the USA since the late 60s. His interest ranges wider than the expected Spanish "classical" guitar music, and he has also, for example, interpreted pieces by the jazz pianist Keith Jarrett and recorded works by modern American composers.

MANUEL BARRUECO wurde 1952 auf Kuba geboren, lebt jedoch seit Ende der 1960er-Jahre in den USA. Seine Interessen reichen weit über die spanische „klassische" Gitarrenmusik hinaus. So hat er zum Beispiel auch Stücke von Jazzpianist Keith Jarrett interpretiert und Stücke von modernen amerikanischen Komponisten aufgenommen.

STEEL-STRING GUITARS

DYER SYMPHONY HARP GUITAR STYLE 8

The Larson Brothers, Carl and August, were Swedish immigrants who arrived in Chicago during the 1880s. Their guitars had distinctively strong internal bracing so that they could be fitted with steel strings – a rarity at the time, but soon a welcome standard. Despite their innovations, the Larsons are less well known than they should be, mainly because they did not make Larson-brand guitars. Instead, they built for other firms, which sold instruments with brands such as Dyer (as here), Euphonon, Maurer, Prairie State, Stahl, and Stetson. This unusual harp guitar derives from the Larsons' dealings with Chris Knutsen, an obscure maker who patented his harp-guitar design. The Larsons made harp guitars for Dyer, an instrument dealer in St Paul, Minnesota, after Knutsen's patent expired. They have a long, hollow body extension that produces a remarkably reverberant sound, while the six sympathetic bass strings provide an increased bass response.

Die Gebrüder Larson, Carl und August, waren schwedische Auswanderer, die in den 1880er-Jahren nach Chicago kamen. Ihre Gitarren hatten eine besonders starke Innenverbalkung, so dass man sie auch mit Stahlsaiten bespannen konnte – damals eine Rarität, doch schon bald willkommener Standard. Trotz ihrer vielen neuen Ideen sind die Brüder Larson nicht so bekannt wie sie es sein sollten, denn was ihnen fehlte, war eine eigene Marke. Stattdessen bauten sie Gitarren für andere Firmen, die sie unter den Markennamen Dyer (wie hier), Euphonon, Maurer, Prairie State, Stahl und Stetson verkauften. Diese außergewöhnliche Harfengitarre stammt aus einer Zusammenarbeit mit dem Instrumentenbauer Chris Knutsen, der seine Harfengitarre patentieren ließ. Nachdem Knutsens Patent abgelaufen war, stellten die Brüder Larson Harfengitarren für Dyer, einen Instrumentenhändler aus St. Paul, Minnesota, her. Der Korpus ist lang ausladend und hohl und erzeugt einen erstaunlichen Hall, während die sechs Resonanzsaiten auf der Bassseite die Bassresonanz verstärkt.

SYMPHONY HARP GUITAR STYLE 8

MICHAEL HEDGES was a remarkable musician who pushed acoustic guitars to the limit in the creation of new sounds. He played a number of different instruments and was one of the few players to employ the extended range of the harp guitar. He died in a car crash in 1997 at the age of just 43.

MICHAEL HEDGES war ein begnadeter Musiker, der akustische Gitarren an die Grenzen neuer Sounds brachte. Er spielte auf vielen unterschiedlichen Instrumenten und war einer der wenigen Gitarristen, die den größeren Tonumfang der Harp-Gitarre einzusetzen wusste. Hedges starb 1997 bei einem Autounfall im Alter von 43 Jahren.

STELLA 12-STRING

The folk-music boom of the 60s brought a new popularity to the big sound of the 12-string, although 12-string guitars had been around for some years, from early US companies such as Washburn, Holzapfel & Beitel, Grunewald, and Bruno. The instrument achieved its sizeable sound by arranging the strings in six pairs tuned in octaves and unison doubling. Leadbelly was a big influence on the folk boom, and he played a Stella 12 similar to the one shown here. Stella was one of the in-house brands used by the Oscar Schmidt instrument company of Jersey City, New Jersey. Schmidt sold the name in 1935 to Fretted Instrument Manufacturers, who in turn sold it to Harmony five years later.

Der Folk-Boom der 1960er-Jahre verhalf der üppig klingenden, 12-saitigen Westerngitarre zu neuer Popularität, obwohl frühe amerikanische Firmen wie Washburn, Holzapfel & Beitel, Grunewald und Bruno bereits seit Jahren Zwölfsaiter herstellten. Seinen satten Klang erzielte das Instrument mittels sechs Saitenpaaren, von denen eines jeweils eine Oktave höher gestimmt wird, mit Ausnahme der H und E-Saite, die unisono gestimmt werden. Leadbelly war ein wesentlicher Einfluss auf die Vertreter des Folk-Booms. Er spielte eine Stella 12-String, die ähnlich aussah wie das hier abgebildete Modell. Stella war eine der hauseigenen Marken der Instrumentenfirma Oscar Schmidt aus Jersey City, New Jersey. 1935 verkaufte Schmidt den Namen an Fretted Instrument Manufacturers, die ihn fünf Jahre später wiederum an Harmony verkauften.

The country-blues singer and guitarist LEADBELLY was born Huddie Ledbetter in the 1880s in rural Louisiana. His earthy recordings made a sizeable impact during the skiffle, folk, and blues booms of the 50s and 60s, and in particular his regular use of the big sound of a 12-string flattop was widely influential.

Der Country-Blues-Sänger und Gitarrist LEADBELLY kam in den 1880er-Jahren als Huddie Ledbetter im ländlichen Louisiana zur Welt. Seine frühen Aufnahmen hatten großen Einfluss während des Skiffle-, Folk- und Blues-Booms der 1950er- und 1960er-Jahre. Der satte Klang seiner zwölfsaitigen Flattop war wegweisend.

MARTIN D-28

Players and collectors put a high value on D-28s made before 1947, identified by Martin's distinctive herringbone trim around the top of the guitar's body, because these are thought to be some of the best ever made. Martin reinstated the trim with the HD-28 model that appeared in 1976. The D-28 began life in 1931 as part of Martin's original Dreadnought series, at first stamped as model D-2. These first Dreadnoughts had a neck that joined the body at the 12th fret, but starting in 1934, following the success of Martin's OM models, the company provided the new D guitars with a neck-body join at the 14th fret, known as a 14-fret neck. This general shape and style would define the large-body flattop guitar for decades to come.

Spieler und Sammler legen viel Wert auf die Martin D-28, die vor 1947 gebaut wurde – leicht zu erkennen an dem charakteristischen Fischgrätmuster, das die Decke des Gitarrenkorpus umrandet – , da sie als eine der besten Gitarren aller Zeiten gilt. Martin setzte den Rand bei dem Modell HD-28 von 1976 erneut ein. Die erste D-28 wurde 1931 gebaut und gehörte zu Martins ursprünglicher Dreadnought-Serie. Zuerst trug sie die Bezeichnung D-2. Der Hals der ersten Dreadnoughts ging zunächst am 12. Bund in den Korpus über. Doch ab 1934, nach dem Erfolg der OM-Modelle, war der Hals-Korpus-Übergang bei den neuen D-Gitarren am 14. Bund. Diese allgemeine Form prägte die Flattops mit großem Korpus für die nachfolgenden Jahrzehnte.

JONI MITCHELL learned to play guitar from an instruction book by Pete Seeger and soon developed her own picking style and a fondness for alternative tunings. Her main guitar during her early career was a 50s Martin D-28; later she played Martin and Collings flattops as well as Ibanez George Benson electrics.

JONI MITCHELL lernte nach einem Buch von Pete Seeger Gitarre spielen und entwickelte schon bald ihren eigenen Picking-Style sowie eine Vorliebe für alternative Saitenstimmungen. Die Hauptgitarre zu Beginn ihrer Karriere war eine Martin D-28 aus den 1950er-Jahren. Später spielte sie auf Flattops von Martin und Collings sowie auf E-Gitarren von Ibanez George Benson.

MARTIN D-18

Martin first made its big dreadnought-style guitars in 1916 for the Ditson music stores, from a design suggested by Harry Hunt, manager of Ditson's store in New York City. Martin launched two models of its own to a similar design in 1931, the D-18 and the D-28. The restrained level of decoration of Style 18, as well as its easy playability, has made it popular with many musicians since. The model shown has a rare finish that Martin called shaded but most guitar people know as sunburst. D-series guitars are almost always seen with a plain natural finish, making this instrument a desirable collectable today. There have been a number of signature-edition D-18s, including the D-18DC for David Crosby in 2002.

Martin baute bereits 1916 die ersten großen Dreadnought-Gitarren für die Musikladen-Kette Ditson. Das Design war ein Vorschlag von Harry Hunt, dem Manager der New Yorker Ditson-Filiale. 1931 brachte Martin zwei eigene, ähnlich aussehende Modelle heraus, die D-18 und die D-28. Aufgrund ihrer dezente Verzierung und ihrer einfachen Spielbarkeit ist die D-18 noch heute bei vielen Musikern sehr beliebt. Das Finish des hier abgebildeten Modells nannte Martin „shaded", doch die meisten Gitarristen kennen es unter der Bezeichnung „Sunburst". Gitarren der D-Familie haben fast immer eine einfache, natürliche Oberfläche, weshalb dieses Instrument noch heute ein begehrtes Sammelobjekt ist. Es gab einige Signature-Modelle für diese Gitarre, eines davon besitzt David Crosby, die D-18DC von 2002.

ELVIS PRESLEY may not be remembered primarily as a guitar player, especially when he had guitarists like Scotty Moore and James Burton alongside him. But he loved playing and is often seen with guitars in photos and footage, including in the mid 50s a Martin D-18 with "ELVIS" letters stuck to the body.

ELVIS PRESLEY war sicher kein begnadeter Gitarrist – dafür hatte er Scotty Moore und James Burton – doch er liebte es Gitarre zu spielen und ist auf vielen Foto- und Filmaufnahmen mit einer Gitarre zu sehen. In den 1950er-Jahren spielte er eine Martin D-18, auf deren Korpus in großen Lettern ‚ELVIS' stand.

1940 — MARTIN
D-45

MARTIN D-45

The D-45 has long been a showy flagship of the Martin line, with the biggest body and the most lavish decorative style of any regular model. The body has fine "green heart" abalone inlay liberally applied around the edges and the soundhole, and the fancy hexagonal fingerboard inlays replaced the original snowflake types around 1939. Martin's D-45 was introduced as a custom item in 1933, at first with a neck-to-body join at the 12th-fret, moving to a 14-fret neck in 1936. Only 91 were made between 1933 and 1942, making these originals some of the most valuable and sought-after acoustic guitars on today's vintage market.

Die D-45 ist seit langem das Aushängeschild der Martin-Linie, mit dem größten Korpus und der aufwändigsten Verzierung unter den regulären Modellen. Die edlen Einlegearbeiten aus Abalone („ein grünes Herz") auf dem Korpus, rund um die Ränder und das Schallloch sowie die sechseckigen Inlays auf dem Griffbrett ersetzten die ursprünglichen Schneeflocken um 1939. Die Martin D-45 gab es ab 1933 nur als Sonderanfertigung, zunächst mit einem Hals-Korpus-Übergang am 12. Bund, ab 1936 dann am 14. Bund. Zwischen 1933 und 1942 wurden nur 91 Stück hergestellt. Daher gehören diese Originale zu den wertvollsten und meist gefragten Akustikgitarren auf dem heutigen Vintage-Markt.

NEIL YOUNG

DAVID CROSBY

GIBSON J-45

Gibson reacted to Martin's large Dreadnought D-series flattops by issuing in 1934 its biggest flattop, the Gibson Jumbo. The Jumbo name led to Gibson's J series of acoustics, and among the stars of the original line was the 16-inch-wide J-45, first sold in 1942. It turned out to be a popular guitar, with a relatively low price and an easy-playing style that suited many guitarists over the years. In its early days it found favour with everyone from the flatpicking ace Doc Watson to rock'n'roller Buddy Holly, who regularly used a J-45 for songwriting. The model still features in Gibson's catalogue today, including signature versions named for Donovan, John Hiatt, and Brad Paisley.

1934 reagierte Gibson auf Martins Dreadnought D-Flattops mit der Herausgabe seiner größten Flattop-Gitarre, der Gibson Jumbo. Aus „Jumbo" wurde die J-Familie, und zu den erfolgreichsten Akustikgitarren der Originalmodelle gehörte die 40 Zentimeter breite J-45, die erstmal 1942 verkauft wurde. Sie entpuppte sich zu einem Verkaufsschlager, weil sie recht günstig und leicht zu spielen war, was viele Gitarristen über die Jahre ansprach. In ihrer Anfangszeit wurde sie von allen gespielt, die Rang und Namen hatten, von Flatpicking-Virtuose Doc Watson bis hin zu Rock'n'Roll-Legende Buddy Holly, der auf seiner J-45 regelmäßig Songs schrieb. Gibson verkauft dieses Modell noch heute, darunter auch die J-45 Sondermodelle Donovan, John Hiatt und Brad Paisley.

With his dust-bowl ballads, WOODY GUTHRIE was the voice of the American blue-collar worker in the 30s Depression, singing 'This Land Is Your Land'. He famously adorned several of his guitars — mostly Gibson models such as a J-45, L-00, and SJ — with a sign that declared "This Machine Kills Fascists".

Mit seinen Dust Bowl Ballads und dem Song ‚This Land Is Your Land' verlieh WOODY GUTHRIE den amerikanischen Arbeitern während der Weltwirtschaftskrise in den 1930er-Jahren eine Stimme. Guthrie war bekannt dafür, seine Gitarren und insbesondere seine Gibson-Modelle J-45, L-00 und SJ mit einem Schild mit der Aufschrift „This Machine Kills Fascists" zu bekleben.

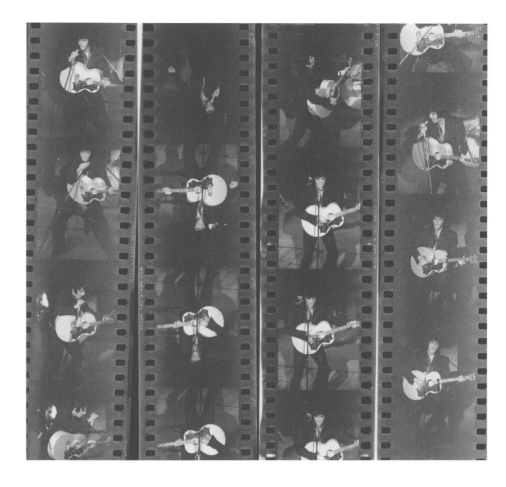

GIBSON J-200

Gibson's second big-flattop design, following the Jumbo of 1934, had a new narrow-waisted look, first seen in the Super Jumbo of 1938 – a model later and better known as the SJ-200 or J-200. The body was nearly 17 inches wide, and it was clearly an upscale model, with fancy pearl markers on the fingerboard, multiple binding on the neck and body, a flowering vine design on the pickguard, and an especially elaborate bridge, since nicknamed the "moustache" because of its ornate shape. It was no surprise when Gibson described the 200 for many years as the King of the Flattop Guitars. The instrument has attracted players from the Rev Gary Davis to Emmylou Harris, and it is still in the Gibson line today.

Gibsons zweites großes Flattop-Modell nach der Jumbo von 1934 hatte eine neue schmale Taille: die Super Jumbo von 1938 – eine Gitarre, die später besser unter der Bezeichnung Super Jumbo 200 (SJ-200 bzw. J-200) bekannt war. Mit einem 43 Zentimeter breiten Korpus war sie ein Luxusmodell – elegante Bundmarkierungen aus Perlmutt, mehrfache Randeinfassung an Hals und Korpus, ein rankendes Blumendesign auf dem Schlagbrett und ein besonders aufwändig konstruierter Steg, der aufgrund seiner Form auch „Schnurrbart" genannt wurde. Es war keine Überraschung, dass Gibson die J-200 über viele Jahre hinweg als Königin unter den Flattop-Gitarren bezeichnete. Sie wurde von Berühmtheiten wie Rev Gary Davis oder Emmylou Harris gespielt und wird noch heute hergestellt.

ELVIS PRESLEY had a few Gibson J-200 guitars, with their distinctive moustache bridges and flowery pickguards, and he used one for several songs on his 1968 TV comeback show. He can be seen with an earlier model of the big-bodied flattop in some of his movies, including King Creole and G.I. Blues.

ELVIS PRESLEY hatte einige Gibson J-200-Gitarren, mit charakteristischem Schnauzbart-Steg und einem Schlagbrett mit Blumenmuster. Bei seinem Comeback-Auftritt im Fernsehen im Jahre 1968 spielte er mehrere Songs auf einer seiner Gibsons. In einigen seiner Filme (u.a. in King Creole und G.I. Blues) spielte er ein älteres Modell der großen Flattop.

GIBSON J-160E

Guitarists have always found it difficult to successfully amplify an acoustic guitar. One of Gibson's attempts to solve the problem was the J-160E, with a single-coil pickup mounted at the end of the fingerboard. The company launched the 160 in 1954. Some years later, John Lennon and George Harrison each bought one, allowing them to perform live with dual-purpose acoustic/electric guitars for particular songs. They also used them widely in the studio. The guitar shown was owned by George Harrison, although Lennon and Harrison regularly swapped their 160s back and forth. It shows many battle scars from its Beatle days and later, including marks from an extra pickup once added between the bridge and soundhole, with plenty of pick-wear nearby.

Gitarristen hatten immer schon Schwierigkeiten damit, eine Akustikgitarre elektrisch zu verstärken. Einer von Gibsons Versuchen, das Problem zu lösen, war die J-160E, mit einem Single-Coil-Pickup, der am Ende des Griffbretts angebracht wurde. Das Unternehmen brachte das Modell 1954 auf den Markt. Einige Jahre später kauften sich auch John Lennon und George Harrison eine J-160E, um auf Konzerten einige Songs akustisch und elektrisch spielen zu können. Sie verwendeten sie allerdings auch häufiger bei Studioaufnahmen. Die hier abgebildete Gitarre gehörte George Harrison, wobei Lennon und Harrison ihre 160-E regelmäßig tauschten. Darauf zu erkennen sind so manche Kratzer aus Beatles-Tagen, Spuren von einem extra Pickup, der einmal zwischen den Steg und das Schallloch montiert worden war und jeder Menge Spuren drum herum.

1962 – GIBSON **J-160E**

JOHN LENNON and George Harrison acquired Gibson J-160Es in 1962 during the early days of The Beatles. They ordered the guitars from a shop in Liverpool, Rushworth's, and had to wait for them to be delivered from Gibson in the USA, because the model was not generally available then in the UK.

JOHN LENNON und George Harrison kauften sich 1962, in der Anfangsphase der Beatles, Gibson J-160Es. Sie bestellten die Gitarren bei Rushworth's, einem Laden in Liverpool, und mussten auf die Lieferung aus den USA warten, da das Gibson-Modell in Großbritannien nicht allgemein erhältlich war.

EVERLY BROTHERS

GIBSON EVERLY BROTHERS

Don and Phil Everly regularly played Gibson J-200 guitars. Gibson saw an opportunity for publicity and approached the hugely successful duo to create a new signature guitar. The result was the Everly Brothers model, launched in 1962, and it was even more flamboyant than the J-200. It's easily identifiable by the two large pickguards either side of the soundhole (later reduced in size) and star-shape inlays on the fingerboard, and a modified and enlarged bridge, designed by Don and Phil's father, guitarist Ike Everly. This fine example is owned by Pink Floyd guitarist David Gilmour.

Don und Phil Everly spielten regelmäßig eine Gibson J-200. Gibson witterte darin einen Marketing-Coup und bat das immens erfolgreiche Duo, ein neues Sondermodell für sie zu kreieren. Heraus kam das Modell Everly Brothers von 1962, das noch schillernder war als die J-200. Man kann es leicht am großen Schlagbrett auf beiden Seiten des Schalllochs erkennen (das später verkleinert wurde), an den sternförmigen Bundmarkierungen auf dem Griffbrett und dem modifizierten und vergrößerten Steg, der von Don und Phils Vater, dem Gitarristen Ike Everly entworfen wurde. Dieses wunderbare Exemplar gehört dem Pink Floyd-Gitarristen David Gilmour.

DON and PHIL EVERLY first came to the ears of most Americans with their 1957 hit single 'Bye Bye Love', and the close-harmony duo went on to international success with a run of chart singles and popular albums. From the early 60s to the early 70s, Gibson sold an Everly Brothers signature model, which has been reissued several times since.

Das Gitarren- und Gesangsduo DON und PHIL EVERLY landete 1957 mit seiner Single ,Bye Bye Love' in den USA einen Hit. Der internationale Durchbruch mit einer Reihe von Chart-Singles und erfolgreichen Alben ließ nicht lange auf sich warten. Von den frühen 1960ern bis Anfang der 1970er-Jahre verkaufte Gibson ein Everly Brothers Signature-Modell, das seitdem mehrfach aufgelegt wurde.

GUILD F-50R-NT

Guild was begun in 1952 by Alfred Dronge and George Mann, who employed a number of ex-Epiphone men at their factory in New York City. The company became known for electric archtop guitars and flattop acoustics. The factory was moved to New Jersey in 1956, and ten years later Avnet Inc bought Guild and moved production to Rhode Island. In 1995, Guild was sold to Fender, and in 2014, Fender sold Guild to Cordoba. Models such as this F50R, launched in 1965, established Guild's reputation, particularly among singer-songwriters and folk artists.

Guild wurde 1952 von Alfred Dronge und George Mann gegründet, die eine Reihe ehemaliger Epiphone Mitarbeiter in ihrer New Yorker Fabrik beschäftigten. Die Firma machte sich mit elektrischen Archtops und akustischen Flattops einen Namen. Die Fabrik siedelte 1956 nach New Jersey um. Zehn Jahre später wurde Guild von Avnet Inc. gekauft und die Produktion nach Rhode Island verlegt. 1995 wurde Guild an Fender verkauft, und 2014 verkaufte Fender die Marke Guild an Cordoba. Modelle wie diese F50R, die 1965 auf den Markt kam, haben Guild berühmt gemacht, besonders unter Singer-Songwritern und Folkmusikern.

JOHN RENBOURN mixes folk, jazz, ragtime, and blues for his solo work, sometimes called folk baroque because of his interest in medieval music. Renbourn was also a member of the 60s British folk group Pentangle, alongside guitarist Bert Jansch. Renbourn has played mainly Guild and Gibson flattops.

JOHN RENBOURN mischte in seinem Soloprogramm Folk, Jazz, Ragtime und Blues, was aufgrund seines Interesses an mittelalterlicher Musik manchmal auch als „Folk Baroque" bezeichnet wird. Renbourn spielte hauptsächlich auf Guild und Gibson Flattops und war in den 1960er-Jahren Mitglied der britischen Folk-Band Pentangle, in der auch der Gitarrist Bert Jansch spielte.

F-212CR-NT

GUILD F-212CR-NT

TIM BUCKLEY, who died at the age of 28 in 1975, was a pioneering American singer-songwriter. His remarkable voice and sometimes experimental arrangements were always the main story, but he relied on the strong accompaniment of a 12-string guitar, most often a Guild acoustic or a Fender electric.

TIM BUCKLEY, der 1975 im Alter von nur 28 Jahren starb, war ein einflussreicher US-amerikanischer Singer-Songwriter. Seine außergewöhnliche Stimme und die mitunter experimentellen Arrangements standen bei seinen Liedern zwar im Vordergrund, doch er vertraute immer auf die starke Begleitung einer zwölfsaitigen Westerngitarre. Meistens spielte er auf einer akustischen Guild oder einer elektrischen Fender.

The flattop acoustic 12-string guitar found new popularity in the folk and singer-songwriter boom of the 60s and 70s, and Guild's high-quality models were popular with affluent players. The 12-string has six pairs of strings in place of the usual six singles, providing a big sound, almost as if two guitars are playing at once, which makes it ideal as a guitar to accompany singing. This example of the Guild 212 model has a body cutaway, added as an option in 1976, and is owned by Yes guitarist Steve Howe.

Die akustische 12-saitige Flattop erlebte in den 1960er- und 1970er-Jahren einen neuen Boom durch Folk und Singer-Songwriter-Künstler, und die hochpreisigen Guild-Modelle waren vor allem bei zahlungskräftigen Gitarristen beliebt. Die 12-saitige Gitarre hat sechs Doppelsaiten statt der üblichen sechs Einzelsaiten und klingt somit sehr viel satter, so als würden zwei Gitarren gleichzeitig spielen. Daher ist sie zur Gesangsbegleitung geradezu ideal. Dieses Exemplar einer Guild 212 hat ein Cutaway, das 1976 als Option hinzugefügt wurde, und gehört Yes-Gitarrist Steve Howe.

TIM
BUCKLEY

OVATION ADAMAS 1687

Charles H. Kaman was an aeronautical engineer when he set up Ovation in Connecticut in 1966. The brand's revolutionary acoustic guitars had composite fibreglass Lyrachord bowl-shaped backs. They soon gained an even more important innovation: "piezo" pickups mounted under the bridge saddles to provide an amplified acoustic sound, with controls on the body's side. For years, guitarists had looked for an efficient and simple way to amplify acoustic guitars in live performance, with little success. The Ovation guitars, along with similar models from other makers that followed, enjoyed wide popularity, especially on the concert stage. Adamas models, like the one pictured, formed a separate, upscale Ovation line in the late 70s, featuring carbon graphite tops and multiple soundholes, with unusual finishes and decorations. Kaman sold Ovation to Fender in 2007, and Fender closed the Connecticut factory in 2014 with a plan to continue production outside the USA.

Charles H. Kaman war gelernter Luftfahrtingenieur als er 1966 die Marke Ovation in Connecticut gründete. Der charakteristische runde Rücken dieser revolutionären Akustikgitarren war aus dem Verbundwerkstoff Lyrachord gefertigt. Bald kam jedoch eine noch viel wichtigere Innovation hinzu: Ein Piezo-Tonabnehmer unterhalb der Stegeinlage für einen verstärkten Akustik-Sound, der seitlich am Korpus geregelt werden konnte. Jahrelang hatten Gitarristen nach einer effizienten und einfachen Methode gesucht, Akustikgitarren bei Auftritten zu verstärken, mit wenig Erfolg. Neben ähnlichen Modellen anderer Hersteller, die nachzogen, waren vor allem die Ovation-Modelle auf Konzertbühnen sehr beliebt. Adamas-Gitarren wie diese waren Ende der 1970er-Jahre eine eigenständige, hochpreisige Ovation-Produktreihe, mit Decken aus Kohlegraphit, mehreren Schalllöchern, ungewöhnlicher Verarbeitung und Verzierungen. 2007 verkaufte Kaman die Marke Ovation an Fender. Fender schloss das Werk in Connecticut 2014, plant aber, außerhalb der USA weiter zu produzieren.

JOAN ARMATRADING is a singer-songwriter best known for her impressive work of the 70s, although her biggest hit single was 'Drop The Pilot' in 1983. She accompanied herself with individually styled and sometimes aggressive guitar playing, almost always performed on one of her Ovation electric-acoustic guitars.

Singer-Songwriterin JOAN ARMATRADING ist vor allem für ihre beeindruckenden Lieder aus den 1970er-Jahren bekannt. Ihren größten Erfolg feierte sie jedoch 1983 mit ‚Drop The Pilot'. Ihr Gitarrenspiel war sehr individuell und bisweilen auch aggressiv, und sie spielte fast immer auf einer ihrer elektro-akustischen Ovation-Gitarren.

1969 — MARTIN
D12-45

2000 — MARTIN
000-42ECB

2000 — MARTIN
OM-42

PETE SEEGER was a star of the folk movement of the 60s. He wrote 'Where Have All The Flowers Gone' and as an activist popularised 'We Shall Overcome'. He played 12-string flattops custom-built by independent makers and with a triangular soundhole. Martin issued a tribute model in 2011 that copied those originals.

IN DEN 1960er-Jahren war Pete Seeger ein Star der Folk-Bewegung. Er schrieb ,Where Have All The Flowers Gone' und machte als Aktivist das Protestlied ,We Shall Overcome' weltbekannt. Seeger spielte auf zwölfsaitigen Flattops mit dreieckigem Schallloch, die von unabhängigen Gitarrenbauern für ihn angefertigt wurden. Martin brachte 2011 ein Tribute-Modell heraus, das diese Originale kopierte.

MARTIN D12-45

Other than a few rare early guitars, Martin did not start to make 12-string flattops until the folk boom of the 60s defined the demand for such instruments. The company's luxurious Style 45 appeared in 12-string form late in the decade: this first-year example was one of only three made in 1969. The 12-fret neck, as seen here, had been reintroduced as an unofficial option in 1954, and it became popular with many players on the burgeoning folk scene as part of the trend toward vintage-style features.

Abgesehen von ein paar seltenen frühen Gitarren begann Martin erst, 12-saitige Flattops zu bauen, als der Folk-Boom der 1960er-Jahre den Bedarf für derartige Modelle ansteigen ließ. Die luxuriöse 45er gab es erst Ende des Jahrzehnts als 12-saitige Variante: dieses Beispiel aus dem ersten Jahr war eine von nur drei Exemplaren, die 1969 hergestellt wurden. Der 12-bündige Hals, wie hier zu sehen, war 1954 als inoffizielle Option neu eingeführt worden und später bei vielen Folkmusikern beliebt, als der Trend wieder zu Vintage-Ausführungen ging.

MARTIN 000-42ECB

Martin's model numbers are split traditionally into a body size and a decorative style. With this guitar, for example, 000 is one of Martin's body sizes, with a relatively medium-sized (15 inches across) and waisted body, and style 42 has the distinctive pearl top border of Martin's most flamboyant styles. This all adds up to an attractive instrument, and for this Eric Clapton signature model Martin used some of its valued stocks of Brazilian rosewood, an increasingly rare wood now subject to tight international controls and certification.

Die Modellnummern bei Martin sind traditionell in Korpusgröße und Form der Verzierung aufgeteilt. Bei dieser Gitarre steht 000 für eine von Martins Korpusgrößen. Das Modell 42 ist mittelgroß (38 Zentimeter), tailliert und besitzt eine charakteristische Perlmuttumrandung – die schillerndste unter den Martin-Modellen. Das Ergebnis ist ein äußerst attraktives Instrument. Für dieses Eric Clapton-Modell griff man bei Martin sogar zum wertvollen brasilianischen Palisanderholz, eine immer seltenere Holzart, die heute strengsten internationalen Kontrollen und Zertifizierungen unterliegt.

MARTIN OM-42

Martin's OM (Orchestra Model) appeared back in the 30s and was the company's first with the neck joining the body at the 14th fret, effectively providing the player with easier access to more frets. They also had a slightly longer scale length – the distance from nut to bridge saddle – and many players found the OMs combined the volume of a D-style Martin with the balance of a smaller-body instrument. They were dropped in 1933 when Martin adapted other models to the 14-fret style, but decades later, Martin revived particular vintage-style OM models, including this OM-42, and invented new takes on the idea, such as the current OMC cutaway models.

Martins OM (Orchestra Model) gibt es schon seit den 1930er-Jahren. Es war die erste Martin mit einem Hals-Korpus-Übergang am 14. Bund, wodurch der Spieler leichter mehr Bünde erreichen konnte. Außerdem hatte sie eine etwas längere Mensur – der Abstand von Sattel zu Stegeinlage – und OM-Modelle besaßen die Lautstärke eines Martin D-Modells und die Balance eines kleineren Instruments. 1933 wurde die Produktion eingestellt, als Martin andere Modelle an den 14-Bund-Stil anpasste. Jahrzehnte später ließ Martin jedoch bestimmte alte OM-Modelle wieder aufleben – wie diese OM-42 – und erfand neue Varianten wie z. B. die aktuellen OMC Cutaway-Modelle.

ERIC CLAPTON played a vintage Martin 000-42 and a 000-28 on MTV's Unplugged TV show in 1992. The resulting album helped to popularise a new focus on acoustic music and acoustic guitars, and Martin issued several related Clapton models in the late 90s and early 2000s.

1992 spielte ERIC CLAPTON bei MTV Unplugged eine alte Martin 000-42 und eine 000-28. Das daraus entstandene Live-Album verhalf akustischer Musik und Akustikgitarren zu neuer Popularität. Um die Jahrtausendwende brachte Martin eine Reihe ähnlicher Clapton-Modelle auf den Markt.

PIERRE BENSUSAN was born in Algeria in 1957. He is a supreme finger-style player with roots in Celtic and World music, although he seems able to play anything he chooses with style, wit, and verve. With his three-CD set Encore, he celebrated 40 years as an enchanting live performer.

PIERRE BENSUSAN wurde 1957 in Algerien geboren. Sein Fingerpicking ist grandios und obwohl seine Musik inspiriert ist von keltischen Klängen und World Music, kann er im Grunde alles spielen. Seine Songauswahl trifft er schlau, stilsicher und schwungvoll. Mit seinem CD-Set Encore feierte er sein 40-jähriges Bühnenjubiläum.

1995 — LOWDEN 0-25

LOWDEN 0-25

George Lowden began making guitars in Bangor, Northern Ireland, in 1973, and after a period when he had some guitars built in Japan, production moved back entirely to Northern Ireland. In 2003, George left the company, which became Avalon, and he set up George Lowden Guitars in Downpatrick, south of Belfast. The O of the Lowden guitar shown stands for Original Series, the design that George developed in the mid 70s. Other sizes include the medium F and concert S. The O here has Lowden's split two-piece saddle, intended to provide better intonation, and, for this model, a cedar top and rosewood back and sides. Other Original models included the 22 (cedar top, mahogany back and sides), 23 (cedar and walnut), and 32 (sitka spruce and rosewood).

George Lowden baute seine ersten Gitarren 1973 im nordirischen Bangor. Nachdem er einige Gitarren in Japan hatte herstellen lassen, wanderte die Produktion wieder komplett zurück nach Nordirland. 2003 verließ George das Unternehmen, das mittlerweile Avalon hieß und gründete George Lowden Guitars in Downpatrick, südlich von Belfast. Das O der hier gezeigten Lowden Gitarre steht für „Original Series" – das Design, das George Mitte der 1970er-Jahre entwickelt hatte. Andere Größen sind Medium F und Concert S. Die hier gezeigte O besitzt Lowdens zwei geteilten Steg, der für bessere Intonation sorgt. Die Decke besteht aus Zedernholz, der Rücken und die Zargen aus Palisander. Andere Original-Modelle sind u. a. die 22 (Decke aus Zedernholz, Rücken und Zargen aus Mahagoni), die 23 (Zedernholz und Walnuss), und die 32 (Sitka-Fichte und Palisander).

PAT METHENY has never been limited by the label "jazz guitarist": his scope and interests range much wider, as do his tastes in instruments. At first he played a jazz classic, the Gibson ES-175, but he's employed everything from a 42-string Manzer to a "robot orchestra" guitar-to-MIDI Orchestrion.

Der Stempel „Jazzgitarrist" reicht für jemanden wie PAT METHENY nicht aus: Sein Können und seine Interessen sind sehr viel weiter gefasst. Gleiches gilt auch für seinen Gitarrengeschmack. Er spielte zunächst eine klassische Jazzgitarre, die Gibson ES-175, setzt aber von einer 42-saitigen Manzer bis hin zum Orchestrion („Roboterorchester") alle möglichen Instrumente ein.

1995 – MANZER PIKASSO II

MANZER PIKASSO II

Linda Manzer is that rarity, a female guitar maker. Not all the Canadian maker's guitars are as unusual as this example, custom made for collector Scott Chinery in the 90s. In 1986, Pat Metheny asked Manzer to make him a guitar with as many strings as possible. The result was the original 42-string Pikasso, with built-in piezo pickup system. Chinery saw a picture of that guitar and had to have one. The fully-acoustic Pikasso II even came with a stand, to leave a guitarist's hands free when playing the thing. It has echoes of the early harp guitars pictured elsewhere in this book, and although it centres on a conventional 6-string guitar, it has an additional short fretless 12-string neck and three further sets of sympathetic strings on a short, angled 12-string neck and on 4-string and 8-string body extensions.

Linda Manzer ist eine wahre Seltenheit: eine Gitarrenbauerin. Nicht alle Gitarren der Kanadierin sind so ungewöhnlich wie dieses Beispiel aus den 1990er-Jahren, eine Sonderanfertigung für den Sammler Scott Chinery. 1986 bat Pat Metheny Manzer, ihm eine Gitarre mit möglichst vielen Saiten zu bauen. Heraus kam die 42-saitige Pikasso, mit eingebautem Piezo-Pick-up-System. Chinery hatte ein Bild von dieser Gitarre gesehen und wollte unbedingt eine haben. Die voll akustische Pikasso II hatte sogar einen Stän-der, damit der Gitarrist beim Spielen die Hände frei hatte. Sie erinnert ein wenig an die ersten Harfengitarren, die ebenfalls in diesem Buch auftau-chen. Und obwohl sie im Grunde eine gewöhnliche Gitarre mit sechs Saiten ist, hat sie einen zusätzlichen kurzen 12-saitigen Hals ohne Bünde und drei weitere Resonanzsaitenpaare an einem kurzen, abgewinkelten 12-saitigen Hals sowie an 4- und 8-saitigen Korpusverlängerungen.

SAMUEL BEAM plays a range of guitars for his recordings and live shows as Iron & Wine, but the acoustics are nearly always by Taylor. The first Iron & Wine album, The Creek Drank The Candle, appeared in 2002, and Beam has since built a dedicated following for his atmospheric songs and artful productions.

SAMUEL BEAM spielt alle möglichen Gitarren bei Aufnahmen und Konzerten als Iron & Wine. Seine Akustikgitarren sind jedoch fast alle von Taylor. Das erste Iron & Wine-Album The Creek Drank The Candle wurde 2002 veröffentlicht. Seitdem haben seine atmosphärischen Songs und künstlerischen Produktionen eine eingeschworene Fangemeinde.

TAYLOR 712CE

The first digit of a Taylor model numbers identifies the series, in this case a 7, indicating the 700 series. Generally, the higher the series number, the better appointed and more expensive the instrument. The cheaper series are made in Taylor's Mexican plant and usually have laminated backs and sides, while the higher series are US-made and use all-solid woods. The middle number of this guitar is 1, meaning a six-string (while a 5 would indicate a 12-string). The third number indicates the body shape, here a 2, for what Taylor calls its Grand Concert shape. The "c" means the guitar has a cutaway; the "e" means it has onboard electronics.

Die erste Zahl bei Taylor Modellnummern steht für die Serie. In diesem Fall ist es eine 7 und bezeichnet die 700er-Serie. Allgemein kann man sagen, je höher die Seriennummer, desto besser ausgestattet und hochpreisiger das Instrument. Die günstigeren Serien werden in Taylors Fertigungsstätte in Mexiko produziert und haben meist laminierte Rückteile und Zargen, während die hochpreisigeren komplett aus Massivholz gefertigt sind und in den USA hergestellt werden. Die zweite Zahl dieser Gitarre ist eine 1 und bezeichnet ein sechssaitiges Modell (eine 5 steht für 12 Saiten). Die dritte Zahl, hier eine 2, steht für die Form des Korpus, die Taylor als „Grand Concert"-Form bezeichnet. Das „c" bedeutet, die Gitarre hat ein Cutaway; das „e" steht für integrierte Elektronik.

Singer-songwriter SUZANNE VEGA regularly uses Taylor flattops for her concert and studio work, most often opting for a 514ce model, with cutaway and on-board piezo pickup and controls. On-stage she adds a soundhole cover, a sort of rubber dish that fills the soundhole and improves fidelity.

Singer-Songwriterin SUZANNE VEGA spielt auf Konzerten und im Studio häufig Taylor-Flattops. Meistens greift sie auf ein 514ce-Modell zurück, mit Cutaway, eingebautem Piezo-Tonabnehmer und Reglern. Auf der Bühne verwendet sie einen Schalllochstöpsel aus Gummi, um die Klangtreue zu verbessern.

TAYLOR 514CE

Bob Taylor, Kurt Listug, and Steve Schemmer set up in the guitar business in California in 1974. At the close of the 80s, Taylor had invested in computer-controlled production techniques. At that time, most flattop makers were too small or too conservative to use these modern methods, but they proved to be important factors in Taylor's subsequent growth, along with some sleek neck profiles that many electric players find familiar and easily playable. Today, with factories in El Cajon, California (since 1992), and in Tecate, Mexico (since 2000), Taylor is a big mainstream success, rivalling Martin, with Taylor and Listug still at the helm – although in 2014 Bob Taylor announced that Andy Powers would take over from him.

Bob Taylor, Kurt Listug und Steve Schemmer stiegen 1974 in Kalifornien ins Gitarrengeschäft ein. Ende der 1980er-Jahre hatte Taylor in computergesteuerte Fertigungstechniken investiert. Damals waren die meisten Flattop-Hersteller zu klein oder zu konservativ für derart moderne Methoden. Doch gerade diese erwiesen sich als entscheidender Grund für Taylors Erfolg, neben einigen schlanken Halsprofilen, die viele E-Gitarristen als besonders handlich und gut spielbar empfinden. Heute besitzt Taylor Fabriken in El Cajon, Kalifornien (seit 1992) und in Tecate, Mexiko (seit 2000) und macht Martin ernsthaft Konkurrenz. Taylor und Listug führen das Unternehmen noch immer – wenngleich Bob Taylor 2014 ankündigte, dass Andy Powers bald für ihn übernehmen würde.

Country star LYLE LOVETT has used a variety of flattop guitars to accompany his songs, and they have included several models by Collings. Bill Collings first built a guitar for Lovett in the late 70s, at a time when the guitar-maker was still working out of a small apartment in Houston, Texas.

Country-Star LYLE LOVETT begleitet seinen Gesang mit unterschiedlichen Flattops, darunter auch einige Collings-Modelle. In den 1970er-Jahren baute Bill Collings die erste Gitarre für Lovett. Damals betrieb der Gitarrenbauer seine Werkstatt noch in einer kleinen Wohnung in Houston, Texas.

COLLINGS CJ SB

Bill Collings began to make flattops in 1973, at first in Houston and then a few years later in Austin, Texas, where his company is still based today. He gained a glowing reputation for his guitars, at first as a one-man shop and strongly influenced by 30s Martins, although he also built some fine archtops. In later years he added electrics, but it's still his handmade flattops that attract many discerning players. The CJ series is Collings's take on Martin's slope-shouldered 12-fret early Dreadnoughts, and this one has the optional sunburst finish.

Bill Collings baute seine ersten Flattops 1973, zuerst in Houston, Texas, dann wenige Jahre später in Austin, wo seine Firma noch heute ihren Sitz hat. Seinen Ruf als exzellenter Gitarrenbauer (stark beeinflusst von 30er Martins) verdiente er zunächst mit seiner Ein-Mann-Werkstatt. Seine Archtops waren von feinster Qualität. Später kamen auch E-Gitarren hinzu, doch viele anspruchsvolle Gitarristen bevorzugen weiterhin seine handgefertigten Flattops. Die CJ-Serie ist Collings' Version einer frühen Martin Dreadnought mit abfallenden Schultern (slope shoulders) und 12 Bünden. Diese hat die optionale „Sunburst"-Oberfläche.

YAMAHA LL11E

Yamaha has made popular and playable steel-string flattops since the late 60s. Its upscale L-series dreadnoughts first appeared in the 70s, with a new heel block design that Yamaha called the L-block: it had an L-shape extension under the fingerboard that was claimed to increase the responsiveness of the guitar's top. Starting in the 80s, the company revived the design for the refined Japanese-made LL models, including this 11E – the "E" indicates the guitar is fitted with Yamaha's electronics system, consisting of a piezo saddle pickup, an internal mic, and an external pre-amp controller.

Seit Ende der 1960er-Jahre baut Yamaha beliebte und spielbare Stahlsaiten-Flattops. Die höherpreisige Dreadnought L-Serie kam in den 1970er-Jahren auf den Markt, mit Yahamas neuem L-Block, der Hals und Korpus perfekt verbindet: Unter dem Griffbrett befand sich eine L-förmige Erweiterung, die angeblich die Sensibilität der Gitarrendecke verstärken sollte. In den 1980er-Jahren begann das Unternehmen, das Design für die exklusiven, in Japan gefertigten LL-Modelle wieder aufzugreifen, darunter auch diese 11E – das „E" zeigt an, dass die Gitarre mit Yamahas Elektroniksystem ausgestattet ist, bestehend aus einem Piezzo-Stegtonabnehmer, einem internen Mikrofon und einem externen Vorverstärkerregler.

BERT JANSCH was a Scottish fingerstylist who in his later career became a role model for many younger players. In the 60s, he was a member of the British folk group Pentangle, alongside guitarist John Renbourn. His solo work continued to intrigue and inspire musicians and fans until his death in 2011, aged 67.

Der Schotte BERT JANSCH war vor allem für sein Fingerpicking bekannt. Während seiner späteren Karriere wurde er zum Vorbild für viele jüngere Gitarristen. In den 1960er-Jahren spielte er neben Gitarrist John Renbourn in der britischen Folkgruppe Pentangle. Seine Soloarbeiten inspirierten und faszinierten Musiker und Fans, bis er 2011 im Alter von 67 Jahren starb.

JANIS IAN was born in New York City in 1951 and became a child prodigy on the city's folk scene, famously scoring a teenage hit with 'Society's Child' in 1967. During the fruitful career that followed, she has played flattop acoustics by makers such as Martin and Santa Cruz.

JANIS IAN wurde 1951 in New York geboren und galt in der Folk-Szene der Metropole als Wunderkind. Als Teenager landete sie 1967 mit dem Song 'Society's Child' einen Hit. Während ihrer erfolgreichen Karriere, die auf diesen Hit folgte, spielte sie Flattop-Akustikgitarren von Gitarrenbauern wie Martin und Santa Cruz.

SANTA CRUZ OM/E

Richard Hoover began his career as an instrument maker in 1972, building guitars and mandolins, but a few years later he discovered his true calling, making fine steel-string flattop acoustics. The brand name comes from the company's location in Santa Cruz, California. Many models have followed those beginnings, and like many flattop makers, Santa Cruz is strongly influenced by Martin's classic designs, primarily the Dreadnought "D" models, the OM guitars, such as the one shown here, and the 000 style.

Richard Hoover startete seine Karriere 1972 mit dem Bau von Mandolinen und Gitarren. Einige Jahre später fand er jedoch zu seiner wahren Berufung: dem Bau von hochwertigen Flattop-Akustikgitarren mit Stahlsaiten. Der Name der Marke ist angelehnt an den Standort der Firma im kalifornischen Santa Cruz. Viele Modelle sind diesen Anfängen gefolgt, und wie viele Flattop-Bauer, ist auch Santa Cruz stark von Martins klassischen Designs geprägt. Das gilt insbesondere für die Dreadnought „D"-Modelle, die OM-Gitarren, wie hier auf diesem Bild, sowie für den 000-Stil.

455CE

LEO KOTTKE is a fingerpicking virtuoso whose equal admiration for both major types of flattop acoustic was underlined when he titled a 1969 album as 6- & 12-String Guitar. Kottke has used instruments from several brands during his long and varied career, including a Taylor signature model.

LEO KOTTKE beherrscht die Fingerpicking-Technik auf virtuose Art. Seine Verehrung der beiden wichtigsten akustischen Flattop-Gitarrenarten spiegelt ein Albumtitel von 1969 wider: 6- & 12-String Guitar. Kottke hat während seiner langen und abwechslungsreichen Karriere bereits Instrumente verschiedener Marken gespielt, unter anderem ein Taylor Signature-Modell.

TAYLOR 455CE

Twelve-string models have come and gone in Taylor's line through the years, tracking the popularity of this big-sounding flattop variety. The model shown, later renamed as the 456, has Taylor's Venetian cutaway, a flattened shape used originally for the signature 12-string that the company developed with Leo Kottke, the LKSM, launched in the early 90s. The cutaway was based on the style of the famous Selmer acoustics of the 30s, associated with Django Reinhardt. Taylor's 12-strings, including this 455ce, have heavier non-scalloped internal bracing designed to handle the increased tension of extra strings and support the top, while the LKSM 12 had scalloped bracing designed to suit Kottke's favoured low tuning.

Taylor nimmt die 12-saitige Westerngitarre immer wieder ins Programm, was mitunter die Popularität dieser satt klingenden Flattop-Variante beweist. Das hier gezeigte Modell, das später in 456 umbenannt wurde, besitzt Taylors Venezianisches Cutaway und eine flachere Form, die ursprünglich bei der charakteristischen 12-saitigen Westerngitarre zum Einsatz kam, die das Unternehmen Anfang der 1990er-Jahre zusammen mit Leo Kottke entwickelte. Das Cutaway basierte auf dem Stil der berühmten Selmer-Akustikgitarren der 1930er-Jahre, wie Jean „Django" Reinhardt sie spielte. Taylors 12-saitige Gitarren, darunter diese 455ce, haben eine schwerere innere, nicht ausgehöhlte Beleistung, um die erhöhte Spannung der zusätzlichen Saiten auszuhalten und die Decke zu stützen, während die LKSM 12 eine ausgehöhlte Beleistung besaß, passend für Kottkes bevorzugt tiefe Stimmung.

CHAPTER 02
HOLLOW
BODIES

In this part of the book we examine the other type of acoustic construction and in particular the way the electric version of this style of hollowbody guitar has developed through the years. The archtop guitar is named for its curved top, in contrast to the flat top of the other kind of acoustic. At first, guitar makers would carve the solid wooden tops by hand to create the distinctive arch, but later they also used machines to make this feature, and then laminated constructions were offered, primarily because they were easier to make than the original solid types.

Gibson, the American firm, did much to popularise this form of guitar in the early 20th century. Early designs by the company's founder, Orville Gibson, were for archtop instruments, and in later decades Gibson would lead the way for this type of hollowbody acoustic guitar, with strong competition from makers such as Epiphone.

A demand for louder instruments grew in the 20s and 30s, and some guitarists tried to modify their guitars for electric playing. The first production electric guitars were mostly hollowbody archtop guitars with a magnetic pickup or pickups and associated controls fitted to the top, from brands such as Rickenbacker, National, Gibson, and Epiphone. A number of players felt this interference with the integrity of the guitar's sounding board was detrimental to its acoustic qualities, while others welcomed the louder guitar's ability to compete with other instruments in big-bands and other sizeable ensembles of the period.

Gibson's first electric Spanish hollowbody guitar was the ES-150 model, launched in the mid 30s, and the company went on to make a series of electric archtop instruments, including the ES-175 (highly regarded by jazz guitarists) and the Byrdland (with its new skinnier thinline body). Some makers used idiosyncratic methods to make their electric hollowbody models: Rickenbacker, for example, used what is known as a through-neck, which travels the whole length of the guitar, while Gretsch sometimes used sound posts inside the body to connect the front to the back, in an attempt to enhance sustain and minimise feedback.

Gibson popularised the semi-solid electric guitar when it launched its ES-335 model in 1958, a double-cutaway guitar that is still considered today to be one of the greatest electric instruments. The idea here was to combine the qualities of an old-style hollowbody guitar and the new kind of solidbody electric guitar (and we will examine the solidbody in the next section of this book). The 335 had a solid central block inside its otherwise thinline hollow body, which meant it could provide a combination of the airy jazziness of a hollowbody with the volume and power of a solidbody.

Today, hollowbody archtop guitars are something of a speciality, both in terms of their makers and their players. But the electric hollowbody guitar, in one of several constructional forms, is a mainstay of modern music and a must-have tool for many of today's guitarists.

Dieses Kapitel beschäftigt sich mit einer anderen akustischen Gitarrenbauart – der Archtop. Dabei geht es insbesondere darum, wie sich die elektrische Version der Hohlkörpergitarre (bzw. Hollowbody) über die Jahre entwickelt hat. Wie die Flattop ist auch die Archtop nach der Form ihrer Decke benannt, die hier im Gegensatz zur Flattop gewölbt ist. Zunächst schnitzten Gitarrenbauer die charakteristische Wölbung von Hand aus massiven Holzbrettern; später wurden Maschinen zum Fräsen der Wölbung eingesetzt. Schließlich wurden Hollowbodies aus Schichthölzern angeboten, vor allem weil sie einfacher herzustellen waren als die ursprünglichen Instrumente aus Massivholz.

Zu Beginn des 20. Jahrhunderts machte vor allem der amerikanische Hersteller Gibson diese Art von Gitarre bekannt. Die ersten Designs für Archtop-Gitarren stammten vom Firmengründer Orville Gibson, der den weiteren Entwicklungen für diese Art von akustischer Hohlkörpergitarre den Weg ebnete. Andere Hersteller wie Epiphone standen in starker Konkurrenz zu Gibson.

In den 1920er- und 1930er-Jahren wuchs die Nachfrage nach lauteren Instrumenten. Einige Gitarristen versuchten, ihre Instrumente in E-Gitarren umzubauen. Die ersten elektrisch verstärkten Gitarren waren hauptsächlich Archtops mit einem oder mehreren magnetischen Tonabnehmern und entsprechenden Reglern, die auf der Decke montiert waren. Bekannte Hersteller waren u.a. Rickenbacker, National, Gibson und Epiphone. Viele Gitarristen waren der Meinung, dass sich diese Beeinflussung des Resonanzbodens negativ auf die akustischen Eigenschaften auswirkte. Andere hingegen begrüßten die so gewonnene Lautstärke, die nun dafür sorgte, dass die Gitarre mit anderen Instrumenten in den Bigbands und großen Ensembles dieser Zeit mithalten konnte.

Mitte der 1930er-Jahre brachte Gibson mit der ES-150 die erste elektrische spanische Holowbody auf den Markt. Infolge produzierte das Unternehmen dann eine ganze Serie elektrischer Archtop-Gitarren, u.a. die ES-175 (unter Jazzgitarristen hoch geschätzt) und die Byrdland (mit dünnerem Korpus). Einige Hersteller hatten ihre ganz eigenen Methoden für den Bau ihrer elektrischen Hollowbodies: Rickenbacker beispielsweise verwendete einen durchgehenden Hals, der durch den Korpus über die gesamte Länge der Gitarre verlief. Gretsch hingegen setzte bisweilen Stimmstöcke ein, um das Sustain zu verbessern und die Rückkopplung auf ein Minimum zu reduzieren.

Als Gibson 1958 schließlich die ES-335 auf den Markt brachte, wurden E-Gitarren in halbmassiver Bauweise sehr populär. Das Modell ES-335 verfügt über ein Double-Cutaway und gilt noch heute als eine der besten E-Gitarren überhaupt. Die zugrundeliegende Idee war, die Eigenschaften einer traditionellen Hollowbody mit denen der modernen, massiv gebauten E-Gitarre (darüber mehr im nächsten Teil des Buches) zu kombinieren. Die 335

besaß einen massiven Mittelblock in ihrem vergleichsweise flachen Hohlkorpus und vereinte den lässigen Jazzklang einer Hollowbody mit der Kraft und Lautstärke einer massiv gebauten E-Gitarre.

Klassische Hollwbody-Archtops sind heutzutage eher eine Besonderheit, sowohl was die Hersteller als auch die Gitarristen angeht. Die elektrischen Hollowbodies in ihren zahlreichen Varianten haben jedoch einen festen Platz in der modernen Musik und in der Sammlung vieler Gitarristen.

DAN AUERBACH formed The Black Keys with drummer Patrick Carney in Ohio in 2001. The blues-rock duo does much more than that limiting label implies, and Auerbach's guitar textures are thoughtfully applied. He usually favours retro guitars, which have included a Guild Thunderbird and a Harmony H-77.

DAN AUERBACH gründete 2001 zusammen mit Schlagzeuger Patrick Carney die Band The Black Keys. Das Bluesrock-Duo aus Ohio geht weit über dieses Genre hinaus, und Auerbach setzt seine Gitarrenläufe mit Bedacht ein. Er bevorzugt Retrogitarren und spielt u.a. eine Guild Thunderbird und eine Harmony H-77.

GIBSON ES-150

This was Gibson's first Spanish electric guitar – where Spanish means a guitar played in what we now think of as the conventional manner, and not on the lap like a Hawaiian guitar. The ES-150 was launched in 1936, in effect one of Gibson's f-hole archtop guitars with a magnetic pickup bolted into the top along with a couple of controls. It marked the start of Gibson's long-running ES series of hollowbody electrics, the ES standing for Electric Spanish. Guitar production at Gibson more or less stopped when America entered World War II in 1941, but afterward Gibson concluded that the electric guitar was set to become an important part of its reactivated business. The ES-150 was an important first step in that direction.

Dies war Gibsons erste spanische E-Gitarre – mit „spanisch" ist hier jedoch gemeint, dass der Gitarrist sie auf konventionelle Weise spielte und nicht etwa auf dem Schoß wie eine hawaiianische Gitarre. Die ES-150 kam 1936 auf den Markt und war eine von Gibsons Archtops mit F-Loch und einem magnetischen Pickup, der zusammen mit einigen Reglern in die Decke eingeschraubt wurde. Die ES (kurz für Electric Spanish) war der Beginn von Gibsons langjähriger ES-Serie von E-Gitarren mit Hohlkörper. 1941, mit dem Eintritt der USA in den Zweiten Weltkrieg, stellte Gibson seine Produktion von Gitarren fast komplett ein, kam danach jedoch zu dem Schluss, dass die E-Gitarre maßgeblich zur Reaktivierung der Geschäfte beitragen würde. Die ES-150 war ein wichtiger erster Schritt in diese Richtung.

CHARLIE CHRISTIAN was a pioneering electric guitarist. Using early Gibson electric models in Benny Goodman's bands, he showed that the amplified instrument could work as a soloing instrument in jazz and, by implication, in other music. Christian was born in Texas and died, just 25 years old, in 1942.

CHARLIE CHRISTIAN war ein atemberaubender E-Gitarrist. Während seiner Zeit in Benny Goodmans Band spielte er erste E-Modelle von Gibson und bewies, dass ein verstärktes Instrument auch als Soloinstrument im Jazz, und folglich auch für andere Musik, taugte. Christian wurde in Texas geboren und starb 1942 im Alter von nur 25 Jahren.

GIBSON L-5

Lloyd Loar joined Gibson in 1919, primarily as a designer, and his greatest contribution was the Master Series of guitar, mandolin, mandola, and mandocello, introduced between 1922 and 1924. Innovations included violin-style f-holes rather than round or oval soundholes, as well as a number of constructional, developments and adjustments. At the time, when the American scene was dominated by the tenor banjo, these qualities were not immediately obvious. By the 30s, however, the L-5 and other f-hole guitars that followed had become the staple of a new breed of jazz guitarist. This L-5 is one of a small number that Loar signed inside, and dates from the same year that he left Gibson, later setting up his own ultimately unsuccessful firm, Vivi Tone.

Lloyd Loar kam 1919 als Designer zu Gibson. Sein wichtigster Beitrag war die Master-Serie mit Gitarre, Mandoline, Mandola und Mandocello, die zwischen 1922 und 1924 eingeführt wurden. Zu den Neuerungen gehörten das F-Loch (sonst typisch für Streichinstrumente) statt den runden oder ovalen Schalllöchern sowie eine Reihe baulicher Veränderungen, Entwicklungen und Anpassungen. Damals, als die amerikanische Gitarrenszene noch vom Tenor-Banjo beherrscht war, stießen diese Qualitäten nicht sofort positiv hervor. Doch in den 1930er-Jahren avancierten die L-5 und andere nachfolgende Gitarren mit F-Loch bei einer neuen Generation von Jazz-Gitarristen zur ersten Wahl. Diese L-5 ist eine von wenigen, die Loar im Inneren signiert hat, und die aus dem gleichen Jahr stammt, in dem er Gibson verließ. Später baute er seine eigene Firma Vivi Tone auf, mit der er jedoch letztlich keinen Erfolg hatte.

1916 – GIBSON
STYLE O

GIBSON STYLE O

Orville Gibson moved from New York state to Kalamazoo, Michigan, around 1880, and he started to make archtop mandolins and guitars there during the 1890s. The now famous Gibson company was formed in 1902 when Orville teamed up with a group of businessmen, but he soon left the firm. Among the products of the early Gibson Mandolin-Guitar Manufacturing Company was this Style O, introduced in 1902, Gibson's leading archtop guitar until the arrival of the L-5. The O went through many changes during its more than 20-year life, with the elaborate scroll and flat cutaway seen here first appearing around 1907. A Gibson logo was added to the headstock toward the end of the 1910s.

Orville Gibson zog um 1880 von New York State nach Kalamazoo, Michigan, wo er in den 1890er-Jahren begann, Archtop-Mandolinen und Gitarren zu bauen. Die heute weltberühmte Gitarrenfirma Gibson wurde 1902 gegründet, als sich Orville mit mehreren Geschäftsleuten zusammenschloss. Kurz darauf verließ er das Unternehmen jedoch wieder. Zu den ersten Produkten der frühen Gibson Mandolin-Guitar Manufacturing Company gehörte auch dieses O-Modell von 1902, Gibsons beste Archtop-Gitarre bis zur Einführung der L-5. Das O-Modell wurde während des 20-jährigen Produktionszeitraums immer wieder verändert, z. B. mit der aufwändigen Schnecke und dem flachen Cutaway (s. Gitarre von ca. 1907). Gegen Ende des ersten Jahrzehnts des 20. Jahrhunderts wurde auf der Kopfplatte ein Gibson-Logo angebracht.

DJANGO REINHARDT was by far the best known player of Selmer guitars. The legendary gypsy guitarist at first played a Selmer Orchestre, with its distinctive D-shape soundhole, and later he moved to an oval-soundhole Modèle Jazz. Django died in his Belgian homeland at the age of 43 in 1953.

DJANGO REINHARDT war bei weitem der bekannteste Spieler von Selmer-Gitarren. Der legendäre Gypsy-Gitarrist spielte zunächst auf einer Selmer Orchestre, die ein charakteristisches D-förmiges Schallloch hat, und wechselte später zu einer Modèle Jazz mit ovalem Schallloch. Django starb 1953 in seinem Heimatland Belgien im Alter von 43 Jahren.

SELMER MODELE JAZZ

Mario Maccaferri was an Italian guitarist and guitar-maker, and in the 30s he teamed up with Selmer, the French saxophone maker, to produce some innovative guitars. Maccaferri moved to London in 1928 and met Ben Davis, who ran the Selmer music store there. Davis was always looking for new lines, and he arranged for Selmer in Paris to build guitars to Maccaferri's designs. The first ones appeared in 1932, and they had large D-shaped soundholes, internal resonators, and flat cutaways, with the main steel-string model called the Orchestre. Following a dispute in 1933, Maccaferri left the firm and returned to performing. Selmer revised the line and renamed the Orchestre as the Modèle Jazz, changing the soundhole to a round and then a small oval one, like the example here, which was made a year before Selmer closed its guitar business.

Mario Maccaferri war ein italienischer Gitarrist und Gitarrenbauer. In den 1930er-Jahren tat er sich mit dem französischen Saxophonbauer Selmer zusammen und entwarf mehrere innovative Gitarrenmodelle. Maccaferri zog 1928 nach London und traf Ben Davis, den Geschäftsführer der dortigen Selmer-Filiale. Da Davis stets auf der Suche nach neuen Produktlinien war, ließ er Selmer in Paris Gitarren nach Maccaferris Entwürfen bauen. Die ersten Modelle erschienen 1932 mit großen D-förmigen Schalllöchern, internen Resonatoren und flachen Cutaways. Das Hauptmodell mit Stahlsaiten hieß „Orchestre". Als es 1933 zum Streit kam, verließ Maccaferri die Firma und kehrte auf die Bühne zurück. Selmer überarbeitete die Linie und benannte die Orchestre in Modèle Jazz um. Das Schallloch wurde erst rund, dann klein und oval, wie hier bei dieser Gitarre, die im letzten Jahr entstand, bevor Selmer seine Gitarrenproduktion einstellte.

EPIPHONE ZEPHYR EMPEROR REGENT

Before Epiphone was bought by Gibson in 1957, the company had moved four years earlier from its old base in New York City to a new home in Philadelphia, but it took few of its valued workers with it. This luxurious model was known at first as the Zephyr Emperor Vari Tone, and it was the flagship electric Epiphone of the time, complete with three single-coil pickups – these are known as New York types – and an impressive six-button "color tone" system to help the player switch between them.

Vier Jahre bevor Epiphone 1957 von Gibson gekauft wurde, war das Unternehmen von seinem alten Sitz in New York nach Philadelphia umgezogen, hatte aber nur einen kleinen Teil seiner geschätzten Belegschaft mitgenommen. Dieses Luxusmodell war die sogenannte „Zephyr Emperor Vari Tone", das damalige Aushängeschild unter den Epiphone E-Gitarren, mit drei Single-Coil-Pickups (vom Typ New York) und sechs (!) Knöpfen, mit denen Gitarristen zwischen den einzelnen Pickups wechseln konnten.

FREDDIE GREEN became a mainstay of the Count Basie sound until the bandleader's death in 1984. Green himself, a native of South Carolina, died three years later, aged 85. He hardly ever played with amplification, despite the boisterous surroundings, and his acoustic archtops included Epiphone Emperors and Stromberg Master 400s.

FREDDIE GREEN war einer der größten Vertreter des Count Basie-Sounds, bis der Bandleader 1984 starb. Green, der aus South Carolina stammte, starb drei Jahre später im Alter von 85 Jahren. Er spielte trotz der Lautstärke in den Bigbands fast immer ohne Verstärker. Seine akustischen Archtop-Gitarren waren u.a. Epiphone Emperors und Stromberg Master 400s.

KENNY BURRELL was a Detroit-born jazzman of great skill and wide-ranging tastes, playing as a sideman and on his own refined solo projects. He started, like many, on a Gibson ES-175, but later he used a Gibson L-5, a D'Angelico New Yorker, and a number of Gibson's Super 400CES models.

KENNY BURRELL aus Detroit spielte hervorragend Jazz und hatte einen weitreichenden Musikgeschmack. Er spielte als Sideman in Bands und hatte eigene Soloprojekte. Wie viele andere Gitarristen begann er auf einer Gibson ES-175. Später spielte er auf einer Gibson L-5, einer D'Angelico New Yorker und auf verschiedenen Super 400CES Modellen von Gibson.

1960 — D'ANGELICO
NEW YORKER

D'ANGELICO NEW YORKER

John D'Angelico was a guitar maker who revealed the potential of an archtop hollowbody guitar to the musicians who came to his workshop in New York City from the 30s through to the 60s. At first he made guitars in the style of Gibson's L-5, but soon he developed his own ideas, custom-making big, powerful instruments for keen individuals and professional players alike. His records revealed that before his death in 1964 he made 1,164 numbered guitars, and a short obituary in The New York Times said "the making of fine guitars was his obsession". His instruments are today highly valued by collectors and musicians. This New Yorker model has D'Angelico's stairstep headstock decoration and tailpiece design, inspired by his home city's art deco architecture.

John D'Angelico war ein Gitarrenbauer aus New York, der Musikern, die zwischen den 1930er- und 1960er-Jahren in seine Werkstatt kamen, das Potential einer Archtop Hollowbody verdeutlichte. Zuerst baute er Gitarren im Stil einer Gibson L-5, entwickelte jedoch bald eigene Ideen: Er wollte große, leistungsstarke Instrumente für Einzelpersonen und Profigitarristen anfertigen. Seinen Aufzeichnungen zufolge hatte er bis zu seinem Tod im Jahr 1964 1.164 nummerierte Gitarren gebaut. In einem kurzen Nachruf in der New York Times stand „der Bau feinster Gitarren war seine Leidenschaft". Seine Instrumente sind heute bei Sammlern und Musikern heiß begehrt. Dieses New Yorker Modell besitzt D'Angelicos Kopfplattenverzierung und Saitenhalter-Design, inspiriert von der Art Déco Architektur seiner Heimatstadt.

1953 — GIBSON
ES-175D

1952 — GIBSON
ES-5N

1952 — GIBSON
SUPER 400CESN

GIBSON ES-175D

Launched in 1949, the 175 was the first Gibson hollowbody electric with a pointed cutaway and a pressed, laminated top of three-ply maple and basswood rather than the regular type of carved solid top. This construction added an individual tone colour that was more bright and cutting, and this attracted a number of jazz guitarists of the period to the instrument, including Jim Hall, Herb Ellis, and Kenny Burrell. The original 175 was a one-pickup model, but in 1953 a two-pickup version was added, like this example (the D in the model name here stands for double pickup).

Die 175, die 1949 auf den Markt kam, war die erste Gibson Hollowbody E-Gitarre mit spitz zulaufendem Cutaway. Anstelle der sonst massiven, geschnitzten Decke hatte sie eine gepresste, laminierte Decke aus 3-lagigem Ahorn- und Lindenholz. Bei dieser Konstruktion kam eine individuelle, hellere und schärfere Klangfarbe hinzu, die einigen Jazz-Gitarristen dieser Zeit interessant erschien, darunter Jim Hall, Herb Ellis und Kenny Burrell. Die Original 175 verfügte über nur einen Pickup, 1953 kam eine Version mit zwei (wie hier gezeigt) dazu – das D in der Modellbezeichnung steht für Doppel-Pickup.

JIM HALL's wonderfully understated playing on a Gibson ES-175 was heard on his own well-crafted solo albums, but like most jazzmen he also worked as a sideman, notably with pianist Bill Evans and saxophonist Paul Desmond. Hall died in 2013 in New York City, aged 73.

JIM HALLS wundervoll subtiles Spiel auf einer Gibson ES-175 ist auf seinen meisterhaften Soloalben zu hören. Wie viele andere Jazz-Gitarristen spielte er aber auch als Sideman, zum Beispiel für den Pianisten Bill Evans und den Saxophonisten Paul Desmond. Hall starb 2013 im Alter von 73 Jahren in New York.

GIBSON ES-5N

Gibson's first electric guitar with a body cutaway had been the ES-350, launched in 1947, and a couple of years later came the cutaway ES-5, which was distinguished by three P-90 pickups where almost every other electric of the day had one or two pickups. A 1950 catalogue described the new model in glowing terms – "The supreme electronic version of the famed Gibson L-5, the ES-5 combines the acclaimed features of the L-5 with the finest method of electronic guitar amplification" – and thanks to the three pickups called it the "instrument of a thousand voices". The N in Gibson's model-number scheme indicates a natural-finish example: about a third of the ES-5s made between 1949 and 1956 had this finish; the rest were in the more popular sunburst.

Gibsons erste E-Gitarre mit Cutaway war die ES-350 von 1947. Einige Jahre später folgte die ES-5 mit Cutaway, die sich durch drei P-90 Tonabnehmer unterschied, denn die meisten anderen E-Gitarren dieser Zeit besaßen nur einen oder zwei Pickups. Ein Katalog von 1950 pries das neue Modell in höchsten Tönen an: „Die ES-5 ist eine herausragende elektrische Version der berühmten Gibson L-5. Sie kombiniert die besten Eigenschaften der L-5 mit der modernsten Methode zur elektrischen Gitarrenverstärkung". Aufgrund der drei Pickups wurde es auch das „Instrument der tausend Stimmen" genannt. Das N in Gibsons Modellnummern steht für naturbelassen, was für rund ein Drittel aller ES-5-Modelle, die zwischen 1949 und 1956 gebaut wurden, galt. Die anderen hatten die noch populärere „Sunburst"-Oberfläche.

GIBSON SUPER 400CESN

Gibson launched its finest two hollowbody electrics in 1951, the L-5CES and the Super 400CES. For the 400, the company took its existing Super 400C acoustic and provided it with two P-90 pickups and associated controls, adding stronger internal bracing so that it would be less prone to feedback when amplified. Feedback is caused by guitar pickups picking up their own sound from the amplifier's loudspeakers, and then feeding that back into the system. Players at the time considered it a technical nuisance to be avoided – until the mid 60s, when its musical possibilities began to be exploited. The 400CES borrowed some impressive features from its acoustic forebear, including a big 18-inch-wide body, split-block fingerboard inlays, a

T-BONE WALKER was one of the first to see the potential of the electric guitar, as much for showmanship as musicianship, and he had a widespread reputation and influence among many early players. The Texan most often played a flashy three-pickup Gibson ES-5. He died in 1975 at the age of 64.

T-BONE WALKER war einer der Ersten, die das Potenzial der E-Gitarre erkannten, sowohl für die geschickte Zurschaustellung als auch für das musikalische Können. Mit seinem ausgezeichneten Ruf beeinflusste er viele Gitarristen. Der Texaner spielte meist eine schillernde Gibson ES-5 mit drei Tonabnehmern. Er starb 1975 im Alter von 64 Jahren.

"marbleized" tortoiseshell pickguard, and a split-diamond headstock inlay. The rounded cutaway shown here lasted until 1960, when Gibson introduced its pointed cutaway style.

Gibson brachte 1951 seine beiden besten Hollowbody E-Gitarren auf den Markt, die L-5CES und die Super 400CES. Für letzteres Modell nahm Gibson seine Super 400C Akustikgitarre und stattete sie mit zwei regelbaren P-90 Tonabnehmern aus. Außerdem wurde eine stärkere innere Beleistung hinzugefügt, damit es zu weniger Rückkopplung kam, wenn die Gitarre verstärkt wurde. Rückkopplung entsteht, wenn Gitarren-Pickups ihren eigenen Ton erfassen, der über die Lautsprecher des Verstärkers kommt und dann ins System rückgekoppelt wird. Spieler empfanden dies damals als technisches Ärgernis, das es zu vermeiden galt. Doch das war Ende der 1960er-Jahre vorbei, als man begann, die damit verbundenen musikalischen Möglichkeiten auszuschöpfen. Die 400CES übernahm einige eindrucksvolle Eigenschaften ihres akustischen Vorgängers, darunter einen großen 18-Zoll Korpus, Split-Block-Inlays auf dem Griffbrett, ein „marmorisiertes" Schlagbrett und Split-Diamond Intarsien aus Schildpatt an der Kopfplatte. Das abgerundete Cutaway, wie hier gezeigt, wurde 1960 von einem spitz zulaufenden Cutaway abgelöst.

SCOTTY MOORE was Elvis Presley's guitarist during the singer's golden period and played on all Elvis's great early cuts for Sun and RCA. Moore, who liked Gibson's big-body archtop electrics and was most often seen and heard with a Super 400CES, was born in Tennessee in 1931.

SCOTTY MOORE war der Gitarrist von Elvis Presley, als dieser auf dem Höhepunkt seiner Gesangskarriere war. Moore spielte auf allen frühen Tracks von Elvis für Sun und RCA. Der 1931 in Tennessee geborene Gitarrist hatte eine Vorliebe für große Archtop-E-Gitarren von Gibson und spielte meistens auf einer Super 400CES.

CHUCK BERRY invented so many things about rock'n'roll electric guitar playing, including the signature licks that almost every budding guitarist wanted to copy in the 50s and early 60s. Born in Missouri in 1926, Berry's axe of choice in those early days was a stylish thinline Gibson ES-350T.

CHUCK BERRY gehört zu den Wegbereitern in Sachen Rock´n´Roll auf der E-Gitarre und erfand markante Licks, die fast alle aufstrebenden Gitarristen der 1950er- und frühen 1960er-Jahre nachahmten. Das Instrument seiner Wahl war eine schnittige Thinline Gibson ES-350T.

GIBSON ES-350T

Along with the Byrdland and the ES-225T, this was the third of the thinline models that joined Gibson's electric hollowbody line in 1955. The new bodies were just over two inches deep, where most of Gibson's other hollowbody electrics were about three and a half inches deep. The idea was to make them more comfortable to play than the existing deep-body guitars. They also had a shorter scale length and a shorter, narrower neck, which made them feel easier to play. It was a successful combination, and it set the style for many of the electric hollowbody guitars to come, from Gibson as well as from other firms.

Neben der Byrdland und der ES-225T war diese Gitarre die dritte der Thinline-Reihe, die Gibson 1955 in seine elektrische Hollowbody Produktpalette mit aufnahm. Die neuen Korpusse waren nur knapp über 2 Zoll tief, während die meisten anderen Hollowbody E-Gitarren eine Korpustiefe von 3,5 Zoll besaßen. Die Idee war, dass sie bequemer zu spielen sein sollten als die bisherigen Gitarren mit größerer Korpustiefe. Außerdem hatten sie eine kürzere Mensur sowie einen kürzeren und schmaleren Hals, wodurch sie leichter zu spielen waren. Die Kombination war erfolgreich, und das Modell definierte den Stil für viele weitere Hollowbody E-Gitarren – sowohl von Gibson als auch von anderen Firmen.

1957 – GIBSON
ES-350T

John Lennon got his electric Hofner Club 40 in 1959, and GEORGE HARRISON acquired one around the same time. Lennon's came through a credit deal at a local Liverpool store, while Harrison swapped his Hofner President for one with another Liverpudlian guitarist. Neither guitar lasted into the classic Beatles period, but they provided useful early training.

1959 kaufte sich John Lennon in einem Musikgeschäft in Liverpool seine elektrische Höfner Club 40 auf Kredit. Bandkollege GEORGE HARRISON tauschte zu dieser Zeit seine Höfner President mit einem anderen Gitarristen aus Liverpool gegen eine elektrische Höfner. Beide Gitarren haben es nicht in die klassische Beatles-Zeit geschafft, boten den Musikern jedoch ein gutes Training.

HOFNER CLUB 40

The German company started by Karl Höfner began making guitars in the 20s, with electrics following in the 50s. A special line was made from 1953 for sale in Britain by Selmer. Among those models were the large-body Committee, President, and Senator, and from 1956 the smaller-body Club models, like this Club 40, which provided many a budding electric guitarist with his first taste of the magic of six silver strings. The Club 40 was a single-pickup guitar, the equivalent of Hofner's 125 model, and the matching Club 50, like the Hofner 126, had two pickups. Early examples have a circular control panel, and from about 1958 this changed to a rectangular panel, like the one on this example.

Das deutsche, von Karl Höfner gegründete, Unternehmen baute erstmals in den 1920er-Jahren Gitarren, ab den 1950er-Jahren stellte es auch E-Gitarren her. Ab 1953 wurde eine Sonderreihe produziert, die in Großbritannien über Selmer verkauft wurde. Darunter befanden sich die große Committee, President und Senator, ab 1956 dann die kleineren Club-Modelle wie z. B. diese Club 40, mit der viele aufstrebende E-Gitarristen die Magie der sechs Stahlsaiten kennenlernten. Die Club 40 verfügte über nur einen Pickup, vergleichbar mit der 125 von Höfner. Die dazu passende Club 50 hatte wie die Höfner 126 zwei Pickups. Bei den frühen Modellen war das Bedienfeld noch rund, ab ca. 1958 wurde es, wie in diesem Beispiel zu sehen, rechteckig.

GIBSON BYRDLAND

Guitarists Billy Byrd and Hank Garland inspired the design for the Byrdland model, which when it appeared in 1955 was among Gibson's first hollowbody electrics with a new thinline body style. It was in effect a short-scale thin-body L-5CES, and it had Gibson's new Alnico pickups, with rectangular polepieces, designed to be louder than Gibson's existing P-90 pickups. Hank Garland was a talented session player and a solo artist in his own right. Byrd was best known for his time as guitarist with country bandleader Ernest Tubb, an evangelist for the electric guitar at a time when many in the Nashville establishment were unconvinced of the new instrument's worth.

Die Gitarristen Billy Byrd und Hank Garland waren Inspiration für das Design der Byrdland-Gitarre, die bei ihrer Einführung 1955 zu Gibsons ersten Hollowbody E-Gitarren mit Thinline-Korpus zählte. Es handelte sich im Grunde um eine kurze L-5CES mit dünnerem Korpus und Gibsons neuen Alnico-Pickups mit rechteckigen Magnetstücken, die lauter waren als die bisher verwendeten P-90 Pickups. Hank Garland war ein begnadeter Studio-Gitarrist und Solokünstler, Byrd berühmt für seine Zeit als Gitarrist des Countrysängers Ernest Tubb, dem damals größten Befürworter der E-Gitarre als viele im Nashville Establishment den Wert dieses neuen Instruments noch nicht erkannt hatten.

ES-5 SWITCHMASTER

CARL PERKINS was a great Sun-label rockabilly guitarist, singer, and songwriter – he wrote 'Blue Suede Shoes' – and would have become more famous had he not been out of action for a long stretch following a car crash in 1956. His guitars included Strats, Les Pauls, and Gibson Switchmasters. He died in 1998 aged 65.

Rockabilly-Gitarrist und Singer-Songwriter CARL PERKINS war bei Sun Records unter Vertrag. Er schrieb den Song ‚Blue Suede Shoes' und wäre sicher noch berühmter geworden, wäre er nicht durch einen Autounfall im Jahr 1956 für lange Zeit außer Gefecht gewesen. Er besaß einige Strats, Les Pauls und Gibson Switchmasters. Perkins starb 1998 im Alter von 65 Jahren.

GIBSON ES-5 SWITCHMASTER

This model replaced the ES-5 that we saw earlier. It retained the three pickups, but it had become clear that it was hard to control them on the ES-5, which had no pickup switching. The only way to achieve a balance between the three pickups on that guitar was to set the three individual volume knobs at the player's favoured positions. The Switchmaster, new for 1956, had redesigned electronics. Three individual tone knobs were added to the three volumes, and a four-way pickup switch was added near the cutaway. Gibson's catalogue explained that the switch "activates each of the three pickups separately, a combination of any two, or all three simultaneously". To have that "combination of any two", the guitarist would have to select the all-three position on the switch and then use the volume controls to choose which pickups were in play.

Dieses Modell ersetzte die eben abgebildete ES-5. Beibehalten wurden die drei Pickups, wobei diese sich bei der ES-5 als schwer regelbar erwiesen hatten, da man nicht zwischen ihnen wechseln konnte. Der einzige Weg, eine Balance zwischen den drei Tonabnehmern zu schaffen, war die drei Lautstärkeknöpfe individuell zu regeln. Die 1956 eingeführte Switchmaster hatte eine neu designte Elektronik. Zu den drei Lautstärkereglern kamen drei einzelne Tonregler hinzu, und in der Nähe des Cutaways wurde ein 4-fach-Pickupschalter installiert. In Gibsons Katalog hieß es, der Schalter „könne jeden der drei Tonabnehmer einzeln aktivieren, sowie eine Kombination aus zweien oder alle drei gleichzeitig". Für diese „Kombination aus zweien" müsse der Gitarrist die „all-three" Position des Schalters auswählen und anschließend über die Lautstärkeregler entscheiden, mit welchen Pickups er spielen will.

EDDIE COCHRAN was a great and underrated guitarist. Best known for hits such as 'Summertime Blues', he could play anything, including rockabilly and blues, with dexterity and taste. He played a Gretsch 6120, modified with a Gibson P-90 pickup at the neck. Cochran died aged just 21 in a car crash in 1960.

EDDIE COCHRAN war ein großartiger und unterschätzter Gitarrist, der neben Rockabilly und Blues so ziemlich alles mit hoher Fingerfertigkeit spielen konnte. ,Summertime Blues' gehörte zu seinen bekanntesten Hits. Er spielte eine Gretsch 6120 mit Gibson P-90 Tonabnehmer am Gitarrenhals. Cochran starb 1960 im Alter von nur 21 Jahren bei einem Autounfall.

1955 – GRETSCH
CHET ATKINS HOLLOW BODY 6120

GRETSCH CHET ATKINS HOLLOW BODY 6120

Jimmie Webster from Gretsch persuaded Chet Atkins to put his name to the company's first signature guitar, following Gibson's success with its Les Paul models. Atkins was becoming well known in the 50s for easy-on-the-ear solo records served up with a relaxed delivery that disguised a considerable talent. He was also a busy Nashville session man who played rhythm guitar on recordings by Elvis Presley, The Everly Brothers, and others. This is a launch-year example – the model's long name is commonly reduced to, simply, 6120 – and it was owned by Atkins. It has all the classic 6120 features: Western-theme fingerboard inlays and a steer's-head headstock logo; a "G" brand on an orange body; Atkins's signature on the gold pickguard; Gretsch DeArmond pickups; and a Bigsby vibrato bridge and tailpiece.

Nach Gibsons Erfolg mit den Les Paul Modellen überredete Jimmie Webster von Gretsch Chet Atkins, seine Unterschrift auf die erste Signature-Gitarre des Unternehmens zu setzen. Atkins wurde in den 1950er-Jahren bekannt für seine eingängigen Solostücke, die eine solche Leichtigkeit besaßen, dass sein außergewöhnliches Talent dahinter verborgen blieb. Er war zudem ein viel beschäftigter Studiomusiker in Nashville und spielte Rhythmusgitarre auf den Platten von Elvis Presley, den Everly Brothers und vielen anderen. Dieses Beispiel stammt aus dem Einführungsjahr 1955 – die lange Modellbezeichnung wird oft in 6120 abgekürzt – und gehörte Chet Atkins. Sie besitzt alle klassischen 6120-Eigenschaften: Bundmarkierungen im Western-Stil und ein Rinderkopf-Logo auf der Kopfplatte; das „G" auf dem orangefarbenen Korpus; Atkins Unterschrift auf dem goldenen Schlagbrett; Gretsch DeArmond Pickups; einen Bigsby Vibratosteg und Saitenhalter.

In the 50s, CLIFF GALLUP used his Gretsch Duo Jet (probably a '55 or '56 model) for a remarkable series of cameo solos with Gene Vincent's band, The Blue Caps, beginning in summer 1956 with the hit 'Be Bop A Lula'. Gallup died in 1988 at the age of 58.

In den 1950er-Jahren verwendete CLIFF GALLUP seine Gretsch Duo Jet (vermutlich ein 55er- oder 56er-Modell) für eine bemerkenswerte Reihe von Cameo-Auftritten mit Gene Vincents Band, den Blue Caps, die im Sommer 1956 mit der Hit-Single 'Be Bop A Lula' begannen. Gallup starb 1988 im Alter von 58 Jahren.

1956 – GRETSCH
DUO JET

GRETSCH DUO JET

Gretsch was established in New York City in 1883. Fred Gretsch Jr became president in 1948, overseeing a period in the 50s and 60s when Gretsch's guitars became as well known as the company's fine drum kits. The Duo Jet debuted in 1953, and while it may have the appearance of a solidbody electric guitar, it drew on Gretsch's knowledge of hollowbody instruments and was constructed as a semi-solidbody guitar. Gretsch added further Jet models to the line, including the Silver Jet (1954), which had sparkling silver plastic drum covering fixed to the body, and the Jet Fire Bird (1955), which had a red body front. This Duo Jet is owned by Jeff Beck, who acquired it for his 1993 Gene Vincent-influenced album Crazy Legs.

Gretsch wurde 1883 in New York gegründet. Fred Gretsch Jr. wurde 1948 Präsident der Firma. Unter seiner Führung wurden Gretsch-Gitarren in den 1950er- und 1960er-Jahren so bekannt wie die exzellenten Schlagzeuge des Unternehmens. Die Duo Jet wurde 1953 eingeführt. Während sie äußerlich eher einer Solidbody E-Gitarre ähnelt, profitierte sie von Gretschs Expertenwissen über Hollowbodys und war daher wie eine Halb-Solidbody konstruiert. Gretsch brachte noch weitere Jet-Modelle heraus, darunter die Silver Jet (1954), deren Korpus mit einem silber-glitzernden Schlagzeugbelag aus Plastik überzogen war, sowie die Jet Fire Bird (1955) mit einer roten Vorderseite. Diese Duo Jet ist im Besitz von Jeff Beck, der sie 1993 für sein von Gene Vincent beeinflusstes Album Crazy Legs kaufte.

Oasis were the stars of Britpop, the 90s trend for UK guitar groups who clearly loved the music of the 60s. Beyond the bombast and headlines, NOEL GALLAGHER – born in Manchester in 1967– was an adept, influential, and sometimes inspired guitarist. His main axes included Gibson Les Pauls and Epiphone Rivieras and Sheratons.

Oasis waren in den 1990er-Jahren die Stars der Britpop-Bewegung – Gitarrenbands aus England mit einem eindeutigen Faible für die Musik der 1960er-Jahre. Neben der Bombastik und den Schlagzeilen war NOEL GALLAGHER, der 1967 in Manchester geboren wurde, auch ein versierter, einflussreicher und bisweilen genialer Gitarrist. Meistens griff er zu Gibson Les Pauls, Epiphone Rivieras und Sheratons.

EPIPHONE SHERATON E212T

After Gibson bought Epiphone in 1957, some of the new Epiphone models were made in a similar style to new or existing Gibson guitars. This Sheraton, for example, was like the new Gibson ES-335 semi-solid-body model, using the same "centre block" body construction, but it had more lavish appointments than the Gibson – and this one was fitted with Epiphone's new Tremotone vibrato tailpiece. The Sheraton joined four more new hollowbody electric Epiphone models, from the budget Century, through the Zephyr and Broadway, and on to the top-of-the-line Emperor.

Nachdem Gibson Epiphone 1957 gekauft hatte, wurden einige der neuen Epiphone-Modelle ähnlich gebaut wie neue oder bereits existierende Gibson-Gitarren. Diese Sheraton war beispielsweise genau wie die neue Gibson ES-335 Halbresonanzgitarre mit einem Holzblock in der Korpusmitte ausgestattet, hatte dafür aber aufwändigere Verzierungen als die Gibson. Außerdem wurde dieses Modell zusätzlich mit Epiphones Tremotone Vibrato Saitenhalter ausgestattet. Zur Sheraton kamen noch vier weitere neue Hollowbody Epiphone E-Gitarren dazu: von der günstigeren Century, über die Zephyr und Broadway, bis hin zur hochwertigen Emperor.

GIBSON ES-335TN

The now-classic 335 was one of Gibson's most important new models of the 50s. It was a development of the thinline style, but the 335 had two radical new body features: double cutaways and a semi-solid structure. The two cutaways made it easier to reach the upper frets, while a solid maple block inside the body, effectively extending the neck to the end of the body, tamed feedback and combined solidbody-like sustain with the woody warmth of a hollowbody. The result was a comfortable electric guitar for the modern player who wanted to explore traditional tones at elevated volume levels. The example here has a factory-fitted Bigsby vibrato, which meant that the two holes already drilled in the body for the regular bridge were disguised by filling them with pearl dots.

Die mittlerweile legendäre 335 war eine von Gibsons wichtigsten neuen Modellen der 1950er-Jahre. Sie war eine Weiterführung des Thinline-Styles, allerdings mit zwei radikal neuen Korpus-Eigenschaften: doppelten Cutaways und halb hohlem Korpus. Durch die beiden Cutaways war es leichter, die oberen Bünde zu erreichen. Der solide Block aus Ahornholz im Inneren des Korpus, der den Hals bis zum Korpusende verlänger-

ALVIN LEE led his band Ten Years After, which combined blues and rock, often at some length. Formed in London in 1966, the trio lasted until 1974, famously playing Woodstock where they performed the marathon 'I'm Going Home'. Lee played a Gibson 335 complete with ban-the-bomb stickers. He died in 2013 aged 68.

Bandleader ALVIN LEE wurde mit seinem 1966 in London gegründeten Bluesrock-Trio Ten Years After berühmt. Legendär ist ihr Auftritt beim Woodstock-Festival, wo sie ,I'm Going Home' spielten. Im Jahr 1974 löste sich die Band auf. Lee spielte eine Gibson 335, die mit Ban-the-bomb Stickern beklebt war. Er starb 2013 im Alter von 68 Jahren.

te, reduzierte die Rückkopplung und kombinierte die Ausschwingdauer eines massiven Korpus mit der hölzernen Wärme einer Hollowbody. Das Ergebnis: eine handliche E-Gitarre für den modernen Gitarristen, der traditionelle Töne mit höherer Lautstärke austesten wollte. Dieses Exemplar besitzt ein werkseitig gefertigtes Bigsby-Vibrato. Die beiden Löcher im Korpus, die bereits für den regulären Steg gebohrt worden waren, wurden mit Perlmutt-Pins verdeckt.

1960 – GIBSON
ES-330TDN

GRANT GREEN's agile style and fat sound met somewhere on the border between jazz and funk. He played a Gibson 330 for his classic early-60s Blue Note albums, and the title of a later compilation, Street Funk & Jazz Grooves, perfectly summarises his potent fusion. He died in 1979 aged 43.

Die schnelle Spielweise und der fette Sound von GRANT GREEN trafen sich irgendwo zwischen Jazz und Funk. Für seine klassischen Blue Note-Alben Anfang der 1960er-Jahre verwendete er eine Gibson 330. Der Titel einer späteren Compilation, Street Funk & Jazz Grooves, fasst seine wirksame Fusion perfekt zusammen. Green starb 1979 im Alter von 43 Jahren.

GIBSON ES-330TDN

At first glance the 330, which appeared in 1959, seemed similar to Gibson's new semi-solid models such as the 335. However, although it had the advantage of the new double-cutaway thinline design, the 330 was a true hollowbody, without the maple centre block of the 335, and during this period its neck was set further into the body, joining at the 17th rather than the 335's 19th-fret join. It was a cheaper model, continuing with single-coil P-90 pickups when many of its contemporaries had Gibson's new humbuckers, and it had a simple "trapeze" tailpiece as well as a plain headstock with no ornamentation.

Auf den ersten Blick wirkte die 330 von 1959 ganz ähnlich wie die neuen Halbresonanzgitarren von Gibson, z. B. die 335. Doch die 330 war trotz des praktischen Doppel-Cutaway Thinline-Designs ein echtes Hollowbody-Modell, ohne den mittigen Ahornblock der 335. Während dieser Zeit wurde der Hals weiter in den Korpus versetzt, so dass der Übergang am 17. Bund war anstatt am 19. Bund wie bei der 335. Im Gegensatz zu dieser war sie ein günstigeres Modell und sie besaß weiterhin Single-Coil-Pickups vom Typ P-90, als viele ihrer Zeitgenossen bereits mit Gibsons neuen Humbuckern ausgestattet waren. Außerdem kam sie mit einem einfachen Trapez-Saitenhalter sowie einer simple Kopfplatte ohne Verzierung aus.

GIBSON ES-345TDN

JOHN MCLAUGHLIN has moved through many jazz-flavoured styles in his career. He played with Miles Davis on the important jazz-rock albums In A Silent Way and Bitches Brew, and he formed his own Mahavishnu Orchestra in 1971. He's played various guitars, including a 1972 ES-345 with custom scalloped fingerboard.

JOHN MCLAUGHLIN hat in seiner Musikerkarriere schon viele Jazz-Stile ausprobiert. Er spielte mit Miles Davies auf den wichtigen Jazzrock-Alben In A Silent Way und Bitches Brew und gründete 1971 sein eigenes Mahavishnu Orchestra. Er spielte zahlreiche Gitarren, u.a. eine 1972 ES-345 mit gewelltem Griffbrett.

Stereo was a buzzword in the late 50s, when stereo records first appeared. Gibson's first attempt at a stereo guitar was the 345 of 1959. The circuitry simply directed the output of each pickup to a separate amplifier, and while this could create a wide sound picture, it owed little to a true stereo effect. Another new feature of the 345 was its big round Varitone control, a six-way switch to select between preset tone options. But the 345's stereo and Varitone features failed to appeal to guitarists, who often disconnected the Varitone and played the guitar in regular mono mode. The 345 came with Gibson's new two-coil humbucking pickups, fitted to many models from 1958 and designed to "buck" or stop the hum that plagued single-coil pickups. Many players soon came to value the tonal power and musical potential of humbuckers.

Als Ende der 1950er-Jahre die ersten Stereoplatten veröffentlicht wurden, war das Wort „stereo" in aller Munde. Gibsons erster Versuch einer Stereogitarre war die 345 von 1959. Der Schaltkreis leitete den Output jedes Pickups einfach an einen separaten Verstärker weiter. Doch obwohl dadurch ein breites Klangbild entstand, hatte dies nur wenig mit einem echten Stereoeffekt zu tun. Ein weiteres Feature der 345 war der große runde Varitone-Schalter, mit dem man zwischen sechs verschiedenen, voreingestellten Tonoptionen wählen konnte. Doch die Stereo- und Varitone-Features der 345 kamen bei Gitarristen nicht an, die den Varitone oft gar nicht erst benutzten, sondern ihre Gitarren in regulärem Mono-Modus spielten. Die 345 war, wie viele Modelle aus dem Jahr 1958, mit Gibsons neuen Two-Coil Humbucker-Tonabnehmern ausgestattet. Humbucker sollten das lästige Brummen (wie es bei Single-Coil-Pickups auftritt) unterdrücken – daher der Name „Brummunterdrücker". Viele Gitarristen wussten die tonale Power und das musikalische Potential von Humbucker-Tonabnehmern bald zu schätzen.

GIBSON ES-335TDC

Gibson's 335 continued its successful run into the 60s following its introduction in 1958. Its internal centre-block meant the guitar provided players with a useful mix of solidbody and hollowbody qualities in one instrument. This one, bought new by Eric Clapton in the 60s, shows the small changes made by Gibson to the model. Compared to 335s of the 50s, it has a shorter pickguard that does not extend beyond the bridge, and the fingerboard inlays are now small pearl blocks rather than the dot inlays of the original. Clapton changed the tuners to Grover models, for extra stability, and the knobs to black top-hat types, which he preferred. The guitar is finished in Gibson's classic cherry colour of the period, indicated by the C in the model number's suffix (the T means thinline and the D, double cutaway).

Die Gibson 335 blieb nach ihrer Einführung 1958 bis spät in die 1960er-Jahre erfolgreich. Durch den innen einge-bauten Block in der Mitte des Korpus profitierten Spieler von einem praktischen Mix aus Solidbody- und Hollowbo-dy-Qualitäten in einem Instrument. Diese Gitarre kaufte Eric Clapton in den 1960er-Jahren neu. Sie weist die kleinen Veränderungen auf, die Gibson an dem Modell vornahm. Anders als die 335 der 1950er-Jahre reicht das Schlagbrett nicht über den Steg hinaus und die Bundmarkierungen auf dem Griffbrett bilden nun kleine Perlmuttblöcke statt der Punkte wie beim Original. Clapton tauschte die Mechanik gegen Grover-Modelle (für mehr Stabilität) und die Knöpfe gegen schwarze Knöpfe von Top Hat aus, die er bevorzugte. Die Oberfläche der Gitarre ist klassisch kirschfarben, wie in damaliger Zeit für Gibson typisch – das C in der Modell-nummer steht dementsprechend für „Cherry" (das T für „Thinline" und das D für „Double Cutaway").

GIBSON ES-355TDSV

The 355 was Gibson's top-of-the-line semi electric, intro-duced in 1958 and with the 335's double-cutaway semi-solid body, but with upscale appointments such as block fingerboard makers, gold-plated hardware, split-diamond headstock motif, and multiple body binding. This one has Gibson's popular cherry finish and the 345's stereo wiring and Varitone six-way selector. Gibson's model-numbering scheme emphasises some of its design features: as usual, the ES prefix means Electric Spanish; the suffix here has T for thinline, D for double-cutaway, S for stereo, and V for Varitone.

Die 355 war Gibsons beste Halbresonanzgitarre. Sie wurde 1958 eingeführt, hatte einen doppelten Cutaway und den halb hohlen Korpus der 335, verfügte dafür aber über luxu-riösere Ausstattung wie vergoldete Hardware, Blockmarkie-rungen auf dem Griffbrett, ein Split-Diamond Motiv auf der Kopfplatte und mehrfache Einfassungen (Bindings). Hier besteht die Oberfläche aus Gibsons beliebtem Kirschbaum-holz. Außerdem besitzt sie die Stereoverkabelung der 345 und einen 6-fachen Varitone-Schalter. Gibsons Nummerie-rungssystem repräsentiert die einzelnen Designmerkmale. Wie immer steht ES für „Electric Spanish", T für „Thinline", D für „Double Cutaway", S für „stereo" und V für „Varitone".

1964 — GIBSON ES-335TDC

1960 — GIBSON ES-355TDSV

For many guitar players, B.B. KING is the blues. Born Riley B. King in Mississippi in 1925, he adopted the nickname Blues Boy, soon shortened to B.B. His taut blues licks, classic performances, and his longevity are legendary, and for most of his career he has relied on Gibson ES-355 guitars that he calls Lucille.

Für viele Gitarristen verkörperte B.B. KING den Blues. Er wurde 1925 als Riley B. King in Missis-sippi geboren, nannte sich zunächst Blues Boy, und bald darauf nur noch B.B.. Seine straffen Blues Licks, klassischen Auftritte und seine Ausdauer auf der Gitarre sind legendär. Er spielte meist auf Gibson ES-355 Gitarren, die er Lucille nannte.

ERIC CLAPTON said his '64 ES-335TDC was his first serious guitar, and it was the one he kept the longest. He got it while in The Yardbirds and famously played it at Cream's farewell concert in London in 1968. Clapton sold it at auction in 2004 for $847,500, a record at the time.

ERIC CLAPTON sagte einmal, die ES-335TDC von 1964 war seine erste richtige Gitarre, und es war das Instrument, das er auch am längsten behielt. Er bekam sie während seiner Zeit mit den Yardbirds und spielte sie 1968 beim legendären Abschiedskonzert von Cream. Clapton verkaufte die Gitarre 2004 für die damalige Rekordsumme von 847.500 US-Dollar.

WES MONTGOMERY L-5CES

GIBSON WES MONTGOMERY L-5CES

The L-5CES was one of two big hollowbody electrics that Gibson launched at the start of the 50s, along with the Super 400CES, based on its most prestigious acoustic archtops, the L-5C and Super 400C. The L-5CES went through a number of changes over the years, gaining Gibson's humbucking pickups in the late 50s, moving from a rounded to a pointed cutaway around 1960, and reverting to the rounded cutaway at the end of the 60s. The guitar shown is a tribute model from Gibson's Custom Shop based on the guitar that the great jazz guitarist Wes Montgomery ordered from Gibson in the early 60s and used on most of his best-known recordings and performances. It reproduces Montgomery's specific requests for a single humbucker, two knobs, and rounded cutaway.

Die L-5CES war neben der Super 400CES eine von zwei großen Hollowbody E-Gitarren, die Gibson zu Beginn der 1950er-Jahre auf den Markt brachte, basierend auf den namhaftesten Akustik-Archtops, der L-5C und der Super 400C. Die L-5CES wurde über die Jahre einige Male verändert: Ende der 1950er-Jahre wurde sie mit Gibsons Humbucker-Pickups ausgestattet. Um 1960 ersetzte zunächst ein spitz zulaufendes Cutaway das bis dahin abgerundete, bis diese Entscheidung Ende der 1960er-Jahre wieder rückgängig gemacht wurde. Die hier gezeigte Gitarre ist ein Tribute-Modell aus dem Gibson Custom Shop und basiert auf der Gitarre, die der große Jazz-Gitarrist Wes Montgomery Anfang der 1960er-Jahre bei Gibson als Sonderanfertigung in Auftrag gab. Montgomery spielte sie auf seinen bekanntesten Aufnahmen und Konzerten. Bei diesem Exemplar wurden Montgomerys besondere Wünsche – ein einzelner Humbucker-Pickup, zwei Knöpfe und ein abgerundetes Cutaway – wieder aufgegriffen.

GUILD ARTIST AWARD

Guild introduced this acoustic model in 1956 as the Johnny Smith Award, designed to equal or surpass the D'Angelico that Smith played at the time. However, Smith switched allegiance to Gibson, in 1961 endorsing a Johnny Smith model for Guild's rival, and that same year Guild had little choice but to change the name of its instrument, calling it the Artist Award. This example has a "floating" pickup attached. The pickup is fixed to the side of the fingerboard and has a fingerboard mounted volume control and jack, for connection to an amplifier. Many jazz players opted for this system, because it did not interfere with the guitar's body and (in theory) its tonal qualities, like a fully electric model might, but it allowed some gentle amplification that was useful for live performance.

Diese Akustikgitarre führte Guild im Jahr 1956 unter der Modell-Bezeichnung Johnny Smith Award ein. Sie sollte mit der D'Angelico, die Smith damals spielte, gleichziehen oder sie sogar noch übertrumpfen. Doch Smith wechselte 1961 zu Gibson und warb für ein Johnny Smith Modell von Guilds Konkurrenten. Und so blieb Guild nichts anderes übrig, als den Namen der Gitarre noch im gleichen Jahr in Artist Award umzuändern. Dieses Modell besitzt einen „Floating"-Pickup, und der Tonabnehmer ist seitlich am Griffbrett befestigt. Am Griffbrett sind ein Lautstärkeregler und ein Verstärkeranschluss angebracht. Viele Jazzgitarristen entschieden sich für dieses System, weil es den Korpus des Instruments und (in der Theorie) die Tonqualität nicht störte wie bei voll elektrischen Gitarren. Somit war auch eine leichtere Verstärkung möglich, was bei Konzerten günstig war.

ARTIST AWARD

WES MONTGOMERY was the greatest jazz guitarist of the 60s. Born in Indiana in 1923, he had an instantly recognisable sound thanks to his picking technique, using his thumb instead of a pick, and the way he used octave runs, usually on his custom Gibson L-5CES. He died in 1968.

WES MONTGOMERY wurde 1923 in Indiana geboren und gilt als der beste Jazzgitarrist der 1960er-Jahre. Sein Sound war aufgrund seiner Picking-Technik, bei der er den Daumen statt eines Plektrums benutzte, unverkennbar. Auch seine Oktavläufe sind legendär. Er spielte meistens auf der für ihn angefertigten Gibson L-5CES. Montgomery starb im Jahr 1968.

GEORGE BENSON is a bluesy jazzman who can sing well, too, and from his debut album in 1966 it was clear he was special. By the mid 70s he was a star, thanks to his 1976 album Breezin' and the hit single from it, 'This Masquerade'. He has continued to perform ever since.

Jazzgitarrist GEORGE BENSON lebt für den Jazz und ist zudem kein schlechter Sänger. Schon das Debütalbum von 1966 machte deutlich, dass Benson ein Ausnahmetalent ist. 1976 wurde er mit seinem Album 'Breezin'' und der Hit-Single 'This Masquerade' weltberühmt. George Benson steht bis heute auf der Bühne.

1978 – IBANEZ
GB10 GEORGE BENSON

IBANEZ GB10 GEORGE BENSON

Ibanez is the main brand of the Japanese Hoshino company, and it has grown from its early associations in the 70s with copies of American guitars to become one of the most successful brands of more recent years. Ibanez is probably best known today for its guitars aimed at metal and extreme rock guitarists, but it has a long history of wider musical interests. George Benson teamed up with Ibanez in the late 70s for a lasting partnership that has produced a number of electric hollowbody signature guitars, including this example of one of the first two Benson models, the GB10 (the GB20 had a larger body). This is a small, comfortable guitar that fulfilled Benson's idea to make a jazz-leaning guitar that lived somewhere between a big Gibson Johnny Smith and a smaller Gibson Les Paul. Benson remains as one of Ibanez's longest-standing endorsers.

Ibanez ist die Hauptmarke des japanischen Herstellers Hoshino, der noch in den 1970er-Jahren für seine Kopien amerikanischer Gitarren verschrien war, sich in jüngerer Zeit jedoch zu einer der erfolgreichsten Marken gemausert hat. Ibanez ist heute vermutlich vor allem unter Heavy Metal und Extreme Rock Gitarristen bekannt, wobei das Unternehmen schon immer breitere musikalische Interessen hegte. Ende der 1970er-Jahre gingen George Benson und Ibanez eine langjährige Partnerschaft ein, aus der eine Reihe elektrischer Hollowbody Signature-Gitarren hervorgingen, darunter auch dieses Exemplar. Das erste der beiden Benson-Modelle, die GB10 (die GB20 hatte einen größeren Korpus), ist eine kleine, handliche Gitarre, die Bensons Vorstellungen von einer Jazzgitarre entsprach, irgendwo zwischen einer großen Gibson Johnny Smith und einer kleineren Gibson Les Paul. Benson ist noch heute einer der treuesten Werbeträger von Ibanez.

1964 – HARMONY
H-77

1962 – GRETSCH
WHITE FALCON STEREO

1962 – GRETSCH
CHET ATKINS COUNTRY GENTLEMAN

GRETSCH WHITE FALCON STEREO

Designed by Jimmie Webster, the White Falcon was a gleaming, spectacular object that appeared in 1955. It was made at first simply to dazzle visitors to a trade show exhibit, but the demand caused by that viewing forced Gretsch to make production versions. The double-cutaway example shown here is from the middle phase of Gretsch's largely unpopular experiments with stereo guitars. Even for Gretsch, this guitar has a baffling multitude of switches: four pickup tone switches; a pickup selector switch; master volume and tone; and two controls for the mute pads by the bridge. Gretsch continued to offer a stereo version of the White Falcon through the 70s and finally called a halt in 1981.

NEIL YOUNG began his long career as guitarist in Buffalo Springfield alongside Stephen Stills, and the two later joined up in Crosby, Stills, Nash & Young. Young has a refined taste in guitars, and in CSNY he was often seen with a magnificent and unmistakeable Gretsch White Falcon.

NEIL YOUNG begann seine lange Karriere als Gitarrist in der Band Buffalo Springfield, in der auch Stephen Stills spielte. Später gründeten die beiden Gitarristen Crosby, Stills, Nash & Young. Young hat einen erlesenen Gitarrengeschmack. Bei den Auftritten von CSNY spielte er häufig eine großartige und unverkennbare Gretsch White Falcon.

Die White Falcon, gebaut nach den Entwürfen von Jimmie Webster, war eine schillernde Vorzeigegitarre und kam erstmals 1955 auf den Markt. Zunächst existierte nur ein Exemplar, das Besucher auf Messen in Erstaunen versetzen sollte. Doch weil infolge die Nachfrage so groß war, sah sich Gretsch gezwungen, die Gitarre produzieren zu lassen. Dieses Exemplar mit Double Cutaway stammt aus der Zeit, als Gretsch zum Missfallen aller mit Stereogitarren experimentierte. Selbst für eine Gretsch besitzt diese Gitarre eine beeindruckende Anzahl von Schaltern: Vier Pickup-Tonregler, ein Pickup-Wahlschalter, ein Hauptlautstärke- und Tonregler sowie zwei Regler für die Mute Pads am Steg. Noch in den 1970er Jahren hatte Gretsch eine Stereoversion der White Falcon im Angebot, bis die Produktion 1981 schließlich eingestellt wurde.

GEORGE HARRISON was a fan of Gretsch guitars from the start. His first was a Duo Jet, but his best known Gretsch was the Country Gentleman, which he began to use on stage in 1963. He had two, acquiring a second when the first needed serious repairs after constant touring and recording.

GEORGE HARRISON war von Anfang an ein Fan von Gretsch-Gitarren. Seine erste Gitarre war eine Duo Jet, doch seine bekannteste Gretsch war die Country Gentleman, die er ab 1963 auf Konzerten spielte. Als diese nach ständigen Tourneen und Aufnahmen grundsaniert werden musste, kaufte er ein zweites Exemplar.

HARMONY H-77

Harmony was a big, successful manufacturer based in Chicago, where it was founded by a German immigrant, Wilhelm Schultz, in 1892. By the 60s, it claimed to be the world's biggest guitar maker, and it did a good job producing mid-price, playable instruments that appealed to budding guitarists as well as working musicians. This impressive model is typical of the higher end of the Harmony line of the period, with three DeArmond-made pickups controlled by a bank of three on/off switches and a volume and tone knob for each. It was available in red (like this H-77) or sunburst (H-75) and was Harmony's best hollowbody electric throughout the 60s.

Harmony war ein erfolgreicher Gitarrenhersteller aus Chicago, der 1892 vom deutschen Auswanderer Wilhelm Schultz gegründet wurde. In den 1960er-Jahren pries sich das Unternehmen als weltgrößter Gitarrenbauer an, und tatsächlich leistete es ganze Arbeit bei der Produktion von mittelpreisigen, gut spielbaren Instrumenten, die aufstrebende Gitarristen und Berufsmusiker gleichermaßen ansprachen. Dieses eindrucksvolle Modell ist typisch für die luxuriösere Ausführung der Harmony-Serie aus dieser Zeit, mit drei Pickups von DeArmond, gesteuert von drei Ein/Aus-Schaltern und je einem Lautstärke/Ton-Knopf. Sie war in Rot (wie diese H-77) oder in der Farbe "Sunburst" (H-75) erhältlich und galt als Harmonys beste Hollowbody E-Gitarre der 1960er-Jahre.

GRETSCH CHET ATKINS COUNTRY GENTLEMAN

Following the success of Gretsch's first Chet Atkins signature guitar, the 6120, in 1957 the company issued a new Atkins model, the Country Gentleman. It was the first Gretsch with a thinline body, about two inches deep where most other Gretsch hollowbody guitars were around three inches, and also was wider than the 6120. Until the 70s, the Gent had painted fake f-holes, with the visual impression of the f-shape but no actual holes. Atkins believed this helped the sound of the guitar and helped to prevent feedback. The example shown is in the later double-cutaway style, introduced in 1961, complete with a pair of Gretsch's Filter'Tron pickups, thumbnail fingerboard markers, dial-up mute controls, and a Bigsby vibrato.

Nach dem Erfolg der ersten Chet Atkins Signature Gitarre, der 6120, brachte Gretsch 1957 ein neues Atkins-Modell heraus: die Country Gentleman. Es war die erste Gretsch mit Thinline-Korpus und einer Tiefe von rund 2 Zoll (bei den meisten anderen Hollowbody-Gitarren von Gretsch waren es etwa 3 Zoll). Außerdem war sie breiter als die 6120. Bis in die 1970er-Jahre hatte die Gentleman aufgemalte F-Loch-Attrappen. Atkins dachte, dies könnte den Klang der Gitarre verbessern und Rückkopplungen vermeiden. Das hier gezeigte Exemplar wurde 1961 eingeführt und besitzt die für spätere Zeit typischen Double Cutaways. Sie verfügt über zwei Filter'Tron Pickups von Gretsch, Thumbnail Griffbrett-Inlays, Dial-Up Mute-Schalter und ein Bigsby-Vibrato.

ROGER MCGUINN of The Byrds is one of the best-known players of the Rickenbacker electric 12-string guitar. He got his first in 1964 after seeing George Harrison with one in the Hard Day's Night movie, and he used its jingle-jangling sound on almost every Byrds cut that followed.

ROGER MCGUINN von The Byrds ist einer der bekanntesten Gitarristen der zwölfsaitigen Rickenbacker E-Gitarre. Seine erste Rickenbacker kaufte er 1964, nachdem er George Harrison im Film Hard Day's Night gesehen hatte. Er setzte den Klimper-Sound der Gitarre für fast alle darauffolgenden Byrds-Tracks ein.

1964 – RICKENBACKER 360/12

RICKENBACKER 360/12

Rickenbacker began life as the Ro-Pat-In company in Los Angeles in the 30s, founded by Adolph Rickenbacker, a Swiss immigrant. Adolph sold out to Francis Hall in 1953, and Hall employed a German maker, Roger Rossmeisl, to design new models. Rickenbacker introduced an electric 12-string in 1964, and it proved to be the company's masterstroke. It was not the first electric 12, but it turned into the most popular, helped considerably when it was chosen by Roger McGuinn in The Byrds and George Harrison in The Beatles. The example shown was the first one that Harrison owned, actually an early prototype and given to him by Rickenbacker during the group's first tour of the United States early in 1964. Harrison used its big chiming sound on many Beatle live shows and recordings, including 'A Hard Day's Night', 'I Should Have Known Better', and 'Ticket To Ride'. Rickenbacker wurde in den 1930er-Jahren von einem

Schweizer Einwanderer namens Adolph Rickenbacker unter dem Namen Ro-Pat-In Corporation in Los Angeles gegründet. 1953 verkaufte Rickenbacker an Francis Hall, der wiederum den deutschen Gitarrenbauer Roger Rossmeisl zum Entwurf neuer Modelle einstellte. 1964 brachte Rickenbacker eine zwölfsaitige E-Gitarre heraus, die sich als Glanzstück des Unternehmens herausstellen sollte. Es war zwar nicht die erste elektrische Zwölfsaiter, avancierte dafür aber zum beliebtesten Modell, insbesondere als Roger McGuinn von The Byrds und George Harrison von den Beatles sie für sich entdeckten. Das hier gezeigte Exemplar war Harrisons erste eigene Gitarre (ein Prototyp), die er von Rickenbacker während der ersten US-Tour der Beatles 1964 geschenkt bekam. Harrison verwendete den satten Klang der Gitarre bei vielen Konzerten und Aufnahmen der Beatles, u. a. für ‚A Hard Day's Night', ‚I Should Have Known Better' und ‚Ticket To Ride'.

After Paul McCartney bought an Epiphone Casino in 1964, George Harrison and JOHN LENNON soon followed, acquiring one each in 1966 and using them immediately on the sessions for Revolver. They also used them on the final Beatles live dates, and Lennon later stripped the sunburst finish from his to reveal the natural wood.

Nachdem sich Paul McCartney 1964 eine Epiphone Casino gekauft hatte, legten sich 1966 auch George Harrison und JOHN LENNON diese Gitarre zu und spielten sie in den Sessions für Revolver. Sie kam auch bei den letzten Live-Auftritten der Beatles zum Einsatz. Lennon entfernte die Sunburst-Oberfläche, um das Naturholz freizulegen.

EPIPHONE CASINO E230TD

Here was another new Epiphone model introduced soon after Gibson bought the company and based on an existing Gibson. The Casino was launched in 1961 and based on Gibson's ES-330, with that model's double-cutaway fully-hollow 16-inch body and single-coil P-90 pickups. This example was factory-fitted with a Bigsby vibrato, an option to the regular tailpiece, and it is still owned by Paul McCartney, who bought the guitar in London new in late 1964. McCartney strung the right-handed guitar to suit his left-handedness and managed to overcome the awkward position of the controls when he played the instrument upside-down.

Dies ist ein weiteres neues Epiphone-Modell, das kurz nach der Übernahme durch Gibson eingeführt wurde und auf einem bereits bestehenden Gibson-Modell basiert, der ES-330. Die Casino kam 1961 auf den Markt, und wie die ES-330 war sie eine 16-Zoll Hollowbody mit Double Cutaway und Single-Coil-Pickups vom Typ P-90. Dieses Exemplar besitzt ein werkseitig gefertigtes Bigsby-Vibrato als Variante zum regulären Saitenhalter und ist noch immer im Besitz von Paul McCartney, der die Gitarre 1964 in London neu kaufte. Der Linkshänder ließ die Rechtshänder-Gitarre umbespannen und schaffte es, die für ihn störenden Bedienelemente an der Gitarre zu umgehen, ob wohl er sie einfach andersherum spielte.

BENEDETTO LA VENEZIA

Robert Benedetto began making guitars in New Jersey in 1968. At first, he researched the way that violins are made to help him develop his working methods and ideas about hollowbody guitars. Benedetto relocated to Florida in the mid 70s and to Pennsylvania at the start of the 90s, and following a return to Florida is today based in Savannah, Georgia. His La Venezia model, launched in the 90s, did much to underline his growing reputation for handmade archtop guitars. It was based on a guitar he'd designed in the 80s with jazz guitarist Chuck Wayne. Today, he offers four more 17-inch models alongside the Venezia – the Americana, Cremona, Fratello, and Manhattan – among a small line of other models.

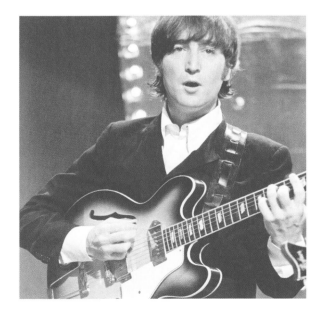

1962 – EPIPHONE CASINO E230TD

2003 – BENEDETTO LA VENEZIA

Robert Benedetto baute 1968 seine ersten Gitarren in New Jersey. Zuerst wollte er herausfinden, wie Geigen hergestellt werden, damit er seine eigenen Arbeitsmethoden und Ideen über Hollowbody-Gitarren entwickeln konnte. Benedetto zog in den 1970er-Jahren nach Florida und Anfang der 1990er-Jahre nach Pennsylvania. Nach einem weiteren Aufenthalt in Florida lebt er heute in Savannah, Georgia. Seine La Venezia, die in den 1990er-Jahren herauskam, trug viel dazu bei, seine wachsende Reputation für handgefertigte Archtops zu untermauern. Vorbild für das Modell war eine Gitarre, die er in den 1980er-Jahren gemeinsam mit Jazzgitarrist Chuck Wayne entworfen hatte. Heute hat er neben der Venezia noch vier weitere 17-Inch-Modelle im Angebot – die Americana, Cremona, Fratello und die Manhattan – sowie eine kleine Produktreihe anderer Modelle.

CHAPTER 03
SOLID BODIES

In the 30s in America, the little lap-steel guitar was the first type of guitar to go electric. Rickenbacker in California led the way with a new electro-magnetic pickup, designed to feed sound from the strings to an amplifier. The electric steel appealed to professional musicians, especially in Hawaiian music and among country-and-western bands. However, guitar-makers and musicians didn't understand or appreciate the potential for electric guitars, which were still in their infancy.

We've seen how many early electrics were converted hollowbody archtops – but few guitarists made a mark with these new instruments. Some makers, musicians, and amateur inventors wondered about the possibility of a solidbody instrument. The attraction to players was that a solid guitar would cut the feedback that amplified hollowbody guitars sometimes produced, and also it would reduce the body's interference with the guitar's tone and so more accurately reproduce and sustain the sound of the strings.

Rickenbacker had introduced a relatively solid Bakelite-body electric guitar in the mid 30s, but it was small and awkward. Around 1940, in New York City, guitarist Les Paul built what he called his log and his clunkers, testbed electrics that he cobbled together from various bits and pieces. In California, Paul Bigsby hand-built a small number of distinctive instruments, including in 1948 the historic Merle Travis guitar, a solidbody that had through-neck construction and a headstock with the tuners all on one side.

It was the Fender company in California that made the solidbody electric guitar into a world-beater. Leo Fender started making lap-steel guitars and small amplifiers in the 40s, and he founded Fender Electric Instruments in 1947. At first, in 1950, Fender called its revolutionary new solidbody guitar the Esquire, then the Broadcaster, and finally, the following year, after a complaint from Gretsch about prior use of that name, the Telecaster. That model is still in production today, along with the equally popular Stratocaster, which Fender launched in 1954.

Don Randall, the original sales head at Fender, devised the early Fender catalogues, and in 1950 he wrote a succinct description of the attractions of the new instrument. "Because the body is solid, there is no acoustic cavity to resonate and cause feedback as in all other box type Spanish guitars. The guitar can be played at extreme volume without the danger of feedback."

As we show in this section, the solidbody electric guitar has thrived since Fender's early breakthroughs. Many more makers have joined in: some have made important contributions; others copied the instruments still considered as classics: Fender's Tele and Strat, and Gibson's Les Paul. There have been attempts to merge the abilities of a solidbody with synthesizer sounds and, more recently, to make available digitally stored sounds through guitar modelling. But it's the driving sound of a relatively simple solidbody electric guitar that still serves at the heart of much modern music, and it's a sound that seems unlikely to die any time soon.

In den 1930er-Jahren kam in den USA mit der Lap-Steel-Gitarre das erste Instrument auf den Markt, das sich elektrisch verstärken ließ. Die Firma Rickenbacker aus Kalifornien ebnete den Weg mit einem modernen, elektromagnetischen Tonabnehmer, der den Sound von den Saiten zu einem Verstärker transportierte. Unter professionellen Musikern war die E-Gitarre beliebt – vor allem in hawaiianischer Musik sowie bei Country- und Westernbands. Allerdings wussten sowohl Hersteller als auch Gitarristen das Potenzial von E-Gitarren, die damals noch in den Kinderschuhen steckten, kaum zu würdigen.

Bei vielen frühen E-Gitarren handelte es sich um modifizierte Hollowbody-Archtops, aber nur wenige Gitarristen setzten mit diesen neuen Instrumenten ein deutliches Zeichen. Einige Hersteller, Musiker und Amateurerfinder machten sich über die Möglichkeiten eines massiv gebauten Instruments ihre Gedanken. Gitarristen gefiel vor allem die Tatsache, dass die massive Bauweise die Rückkopplung reduzierte, die verstärkte Hollowbodies manchmal verursachten. Außerdem wurde so der Klang durch den Gitarrenkorpus weniger gestört, was eine genauere Klangwiedergabe und besseres Sustain der Saiten zur Folge hatte.

Mitte der 1930er-Jahre brachte Rickenbacker eine relativ massive elektrische Bakelit-Gitarre auf den Markt, die jedoch recht klein war und etwas seltsam anmutete. Um 1940 baute der Gitarrist Les Paul in New York testweise E-Gitarren, die er aus zahlreichen Einzelteilen zusammenschusterte. In Kalifornien fertigte Paul Bigsby von Hand eine Reihe charakteristischer Instrumente, beispielsweise die historische Merle Travis-Gitarre von 1948, eine massiv gebaute Gitarre mit durchgehendem Hals und Kopfplatte, an der die Mechaniken auf einer Seite in Reihe angebracht waren.

Das kalifornische Unternehmen Fender verhalf der Solidbody-E-Gitarre schließlich zu Weltruhm. Bereits seit den 1940er-Jahren baute Leo Fender Lap-Steel-Gitarren und kleine Verstärker, bevor er 1947 das Unternehmen Fender Electric Instruments gründete. Drei Jahre später führte Fender die revolutionäre neue Solidbody-Gitarre Esquire ein. Die Nachfolgeversion namens Broadcaster wurde nach einer Beschwerde von Gretsch, die diesen Namen bereits vorher verwendet hatten, in Telecaster umbenannt. Das Modell wird auch heute noch hergestellt, ebenso wie die beliebte Stratocaster, die Fender erstmals 1954 präsentierte.

Don Randall, der ursprüngliche Verkaufsleiter bei Fender, gestaltete die frühen Fender-Kataloge. 1950 schrieb er eine prägnante Beschreibung über die Anziehungskraft des neues Instruments: „Da der Korpus massiv ist, gibt es keinen akustischen Hohlraum, der mitschwingen und eine Rückkopplung erzeugen kann, wie es bei allen anderen spanischen Hohlkörpergitarren der Fall ist. Die Gitarre kann extrem laut gespielt werden, ohne dass eine Rückkopplung entsteht."

Seit Fenders frühem Durchbruch behauptet sich die Solidbody-E-Gitarre erfolgreich auf dem Markt. Viele Hersteller sind auf den Zug aufgesprungen: Manche haben wichtige Beiträge geleistet, andere haben die Instrumente kopiert, die weithin als Klassiker gelten: Fenders Tele und Strat sowie Gibsons Les Paul. Zwar gab es Versuche, die Fähigkeiten einer Solidbody-Gitarre mit Synthesizer-Sounds zu kombinieren. Seit einiger Zeit wird sogar damit experimentiert, digital gespeicherte Klänge über Gitarrensimulation verfügbar zu machen. Aber es ist der eindringliche Klang einer relativ einfachen Solidboy-E-Gitarre, der noch immer den Nerv der modernen Musik trifft. Ihr Klang wird auch in Zukunft nicht wegzudenken sein.

MUDDY WATERS was a great Telecaster-playing bluesman. He bought his famous red Tele in the late 50s, adding a rosewood fingerboard, that new finish, and amplifier-style black knobs. He used it on countless classic blues cuts and live dates until his death in 1983, and Fender issued a repro in 2001.

MUDDY WATERS war ein begnadeter Bluesmusiker. Er erwarb seine berühmte Telecaster in den späten 1950er-Jahren. Seine Tele hatte ein Griffbrett aus Palisander, schwarze Knöpfe und ein neues rotes Finish. Waters spielte darauf zahllose klassische Bluesstücke ein und benutzte sie bis zu seinem Tod 1983 bei Live-Auftritten. Fender brachte 2001 eine Nachbildung seiner Gitarre heraus.

1948 – BIGSBY
MERLE TRAVIS

1951 – FENDER
NOCASTER

1957 – FENDER
TELECASTER

DANNY GATTON was the Telecaster player's Tele player, and the title of his 1978 album Redneck Jazz hinted at just two components of his wide-ranging skills. Gatton's position among his peers and honours such as a Fender signature model were not enough to prevent the troubled guitarist's suicide in 1994 at the age of 49.

DANNY GATTON spielte überwiegend Telecaster-Gitarren, und der Titel seines Albums Redneck Jazz aus dem Jahr 1978 deutete lediglich auf zwei Komponenten seines weitreichenden Könnens hin. Gattons Stellung unter seinen Kollegen und ein eigenes Fender Signature-Modell konnten seinen tragischen Selbstmord 1994 im Alter von 49 Jahren nicht verhindern.

BIGSBY MERLE TRAVIS

This guitar is of great historical importance, because it looks closer to our idea of a modern solid electric guitar than anything that had been made before it. Merle Travis was a successful country guitarist, and Paul Bigsby was a proficient mechanic and skilled woodworker who raced and fixed motorcycles and built custom pedal-steel guitars. The Bigsby-Travis guitar the two came up with in California in the late 40s pre-dates Fender's first solidbody by some years, although Bigsby – better known for his subsequent vibrato bridge – went on to produce similar guitars only in small numbers. In line with its historical status, the guitar is kept today at the Country Music Hall Of Fame museum in Nashville, Tennessee.

Diese Gitarre ist von großer geschichtlicher Bedeutung, weil sie einer modernen E-Gitarre ähnlicher sieht als alle anderen zuvor. Merle Travis war ein erfolgreicher Country-Gitarrist und Paul Bigsby ein geschickter Mechaniker und erfahrener Holzarbeiter, der Motorräder reparierte, Rennen auf ihnen bestritt und darüber hinaus Pedal-Steel-Gitarren anfertigte. Die Bigsby Travis, die die beiden Ende der 1940er-Jahre in Kalifornien entwarfen, ist einige Jahre älter als die erste Solidbody von Fender, obwohl Bigsby – der für seinen Vibrato-Steg eigentlich noch besser bekannt ist – später ähnliche Gitarren baute, nur in kleinerer Zahl. Gemäß ihres historischen Status' ist die Gitarre heute im Country Music Hall Of Fame Museum in Nashville, Tennessee ausgestellt.

FENDER NOCASTER

Fender's Telecaster – known in its early years as the Broadcaster – was the instrument that established the idea of the modern mass-produced solidbody electric guitar. Leo Fender set up his company in California in the 40s and introduced the new Spanish solidbody model in 1950. Still in production today, the original had a utilitarian design geared for mass production. It had a maple neck bolted to a blonde-finish ash body, two single-coil pickups, a strings-through-body bridge, and a straight-string-pull headstock. Gretsch complained about the use of the name Broadcaster, which it used (spelled Broadkaster) for drums, and during 1951 Fender changed it to Telecaster. In the interim, Fender snipped off the Broadcaster name from the decal it used on the headstock, and these rare transitional guitars, like the one shown here, have since been nicknamed Nocaster models.

Die Telecaster von Fender – die in ihren Anfangsjahren noch Broadcaster hieß – war das Instrument, das den Grundstein für die moderne, massenproduzierte Solidbody E-Gitarre legte. Leo Fender gründete das Unternehmen Ende der 1940er-Jahre und führte das neue spanische Solidbody-Modell im Jahr 1950 ein. Das Original, das noch heute produziert wird, hatte ein praktisches, für die Massenproduktion ausgerichtetes Design. Der Hals aus Ahornholz ging über in einen hellen Korpus aus Esche mit zwei Single-Coil-Pickups, die Saiten waren durch den Korpus und nicht durch den Steg gezogen und sie besaß eine „Straight String Pull"-Kopfplatte. Gretsch beschwerte sich über die Verwendung des Namens Broadcaster, weil das Unternehmen bereits ein Schlagzeug mit der gleichen Bezeichnung (Broadkaster geschrieben) im Programm hatte. 1951 änderte Fender den Namen in Telecaster und kürzte in der Zwischenzeit den Aufkleber auf der Kopfplatte um das Wort Broadcaster. Die seltenen Übergangsmodelle, wie hier abgebildet, tragen seither den Spitznamen Nocaster.

FENDER TELECASTER

Fender made some changes to the Telecaster after its launch at the start of the 50s. In 1954, the Tele and its single-pickup brother, the Esquire, gained a new white pickguard to replace the original black one. Those earlier versions are known today as blackguard Teles and are highly regarded among players and collectors. The finish was modified, too, around 1955, sometimes with a less yellow blonde finish, as seen on this example, while the serial number, originally stamped into the bridge plate, was moved to the rear neck plate. A year or so later, the Fender logo was shifted further up the headstock, and at the end of the 50s, the fretted maple neck would be changed to a two-piece style with a dark rosewood fingerboard.

Fender nahm an der Telecaster nach ihrer Einführung Anfang der 1950er Jahre einige Änderungen vor. 1954 wurde das ursprünglich schwarze Schlagbrett der Tele und das ihres Schwestermodells, der Esquire (mit Single-Pickup), durch ein neues weißes ersetzt. Die früheren Versionen heißen heute Blackguard Teles und sind bei Sammlern und Gitarristen heiß begehrt. Auch die Oberfläche wurde um 1955 verändert, manchmal mit einem weniger hellen Finish als hier. Das Schild mit der Seriennummer wanderte vom Steg hinten an den Hals. Etwa ein Jahr später wurde das Fender-Logo auf der Kopfplatte ein Stück weiter nach oben versetzt, und Ende der 1950er-Jahre wurde der einteilige Ahornhals durch einen Ahornhals mit aufgeleimtem Griffbrett aus dunklem Palisander ersetzt.

LES PAUL was the most famous guitarist in America in the 50s, thanks to big hits with singer Mary Ford, notably their number one smash of 1951, 'How High The Moon'. Gibson signed him to endorse their new solidbody electric guitar, the Les Paul model, which was launched in 1952.

Dank der Erfolgshits mit Sängerin Mary Ford war LES PAUL in den 1950er-Jahren der populärste Gitarrist in den USA. Der berühmteste Hit des Duos war ‚How High The Moon' aus dem Jahr 1951. Gibson verpflichtete ihn, die neue Solidbody-E-Gitarre zu bewerben, die 1952 auf den Markt kam: das Les Paul-Modell.

GIBSON LES PAUL GOLDTOP

It was hard to ignore Fender's activities over in California, and even a conservative company like Gibson didn't wait too long to react. Soon it had a team busy designing Gibson's own new solidbody electric, launched in 1952 and endorsed by the most famous guitarist in America, Les Paul. Known ever since as the Goldtop – although Gibson's official name was the Les Paul Model – this first Les Paul solidbody reflected Gibson's craft heritage, in contrast to Fender's simplicity and utility. The Goldtop had a carved maple cap on a mahogany body, a glued-in mahogany neck, ornate fingerboard inlays, and an impressive gold finish. This first-year example has the P-90 pickups and the long trapeze bridge and tailpiece of the period. The Goldtop and its Les Paul companions still define the solidbody Gibson guitar today.

Fenders Aktivitäten in Kalifornien ließen sich nur schwer ignorieren, und selbst eine konservative Firma wie Gibson wollte nicht allzu lange untätig zusehen. Schon bald war ein ganzes Team mit dem Entwurf einer neuen Gibson Solidbody E-Gitarre beschäftigt, die 1952 erschien, unterstützt vom berühmtesten Gitarristen Amerikas als Markenbotschafter: Les Paul. Eigentlich hieß das Modell offiziell Les Paul, doch es ist seit jeher unter der Bezeichnung Goldtop bekannt. Bei dieser ersten Les Paul Solidbody wird das handwerkliche Erbe deutlich, im Gegensatz zu Fenders praktisch-einfachem Ansatz. Die Goldtop hatte eine gewölbte Decke aus Ahorn auf einem Mahagoni-Korpus, einen eingeleimten Hals aus Mahagoni, aufwändig verzierte Bundmarkierungen und eine eindrucksvoll goldfarbene Oberfläche. Dieses Exemplar aus dem Anfangsjahr hat Pickups vom Typ P-90 und einen langen Trapez-Saitenhalter aus dieser Zeit. Die Goldtop und ihre Les Paul Schwestermodelle sind noch heute der Inbegriff einer Gibson Solidbody.

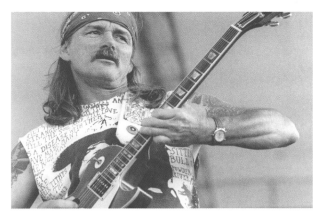

In their golden years, The Allman Brothers became a distinguished showcase for the Gibson Les Paul. Duane Allman played a Goldtop and, notably, a sunburst Standard before his untimely death in 1971, and DICKEY BETTS had several 50s Les Pauls, preferring a Standard for slide and a Goldtop for regular lead work.

Während ihrer größten Erfolgsjahre waren die Allman Brothers wahre Markenbotschafter für die Gibson Les Paul. Duane Allman spielte eine Goldtop und insbesondere eine Sunburst Standard vor seinem frühzeitigen Tod im Jahr 1971. DICKEY BETTS besaß mehrere Les Pauls aus den Fünfzigern. Für Leadparts bevorzugte er eine Goldtop, für Glissandi eine Standard.

FREDDIE KING used a Les Paul Goldtop to record many of his bluesy instrumentals, including 'Hide Away', a hit in 1961. It soon reached the ears of a young British musician named Eric Clapton, who would cover it to great effect a few years later playing his own Les Paul with John Mayall.

FREDDIE KING benutzte eine Les Paul Goldtop zum Einspielen vieler seiner bluesigen Instrumentalstücke, u.a. für seinen Hit 'Hide Away' aus dem Jahr 1961. Schon bald wurde ein junger britischer Musiker namens Eric Clapton auf das Stück aufmerksam und schrieb einige Jahre später zusammen mit John Mayall eine erfolgreiche Coverversion – auf seiner eigenen Les Paul.

GIBSON LES PAUL GOLDTOP

The Goldtop was adapted and improved during its first years of production. It soon became clear that the original guitar's neck pitch, or angle, was too shallow and had forced the use of the trapeze combined bridge-and-tailpiece, and that the combination added up to poor sustain and intonation. During 1953, Gibson adjusted the neck angle and dropped the original trapeze unit, replacing it with a specially designed single bar-shaped bridge and tailpiece, known now as the stopbar, which mounted on the body with two height-adjustable studs. The result, as seen on this mid 50s example – which also by now has the classic Rhythm/Treble disc under the pickup selector switch – was a much more player-friendly guitar.

Die Goldtop wurde in den ersten Produktionsjahren angepasst und verbessert. Bald war klar, dass der Halswinkel der ursprünglichen Gitarre zu flach war, was eine neue Trapez und Brücken-Saitenhalter-Kombination notwendig machte, die allerdings das Sustain und die Intonation verschlechterte. 1953 passte Gibson den Halswinkel an und ersetzte das ursprüngliche Trapezstück durch eine speziell designte, stabförmige Brücke, auch „Stopbar" genannt, die mit zwei höhenverstellbaren Bolzen am Korpus angebracht wurde. Das Ergebnis, wie man bei diesem Exemplar von Mitte der 1950er-Jahre sehen kann, besitzt mittlerweile auch die klassische Rhythmus/Treble-Platte unter dem Pickup-Wahlschalter und war für Gitarristen sehr viel besser zu spielen.

GIBSON LES PAUL GOLDTOP

The final change that Gibson made to the Les Paul Goldtop came in 1957, when the two single-coil P-90 pickups were dropped and the guitar was fitted with a pair of the company's new humbucking pickups. Gibson had also fitted the Goldtop with its new adjustable Tune-o-matic bridge since 1955. The humbuckers were designed to defeat the hum that often troubled single-coil pickups, using two coils wired together electrically out of phase and with opposite magnetic polarity. The result was less prone to noise, and incidentally provided a tone that some players have come to love. At first, a decal with "Patent Applied For" was stuck to the base of each pickup, and these PAF pickups are now considered some of the best-sounding examples.

Die letzte Änderung nahm Gibson 1957 an der Les Paul Goldtop vor, als die beiden Single-Coil Pickups vom Typ P-90 durch zwei der neuen Gibson Humbucker Pickups ersetzt wurden. 1955 hatte Gibson außerdem begonnen, die Goldtop mit der neuen, verstellbaren Tune-o-matic Brücke auszustatten. Die Humbucker-Pickups sollten das Brummen unterdrücken, das bei Single-Coil-Pickups sehr laut war. Hierfür wurden zwei gegenläufig gewickelte Single-Coil-Pickups mit entgegengesetzter magnetischer Polarität miteinander verdrahtet. Das Ergebnis: Die Gitarre war weniger anfällig für Brummen und erzeugte zufällig genau den Sound, den Gitarristen heute lieben. Auf der Pickup-Unterseite wurde zunächst ein Aufkleber mit der Aufschrift „Patent Applied For" angebracht; heute gelten diese „PAF"-Pickups als die mit dem besten Klang.

LES PAUL CUSTOM

GIBSON LES PAUL CUSTOM

Gibson's next move following the success of its first solidbody electric, the Les Paul Gold-top, was to devise further models to create a series. The upscale Custom appeared in 1954, with a classy black finish and gold-plated hardware, ornate block marker in an ebony fingerboard, multiple binding, and an all-mahogany body in place of the Goldtop's maple and mahogany sandwich. Gibson promoted the Custom as the Fretless Wonder thanks to its use of very low and flat fretwire, and at first used its new but shortlived Alnico pickup in the neck position. The Custom was the first Les Paul with the new Tune-o-matic bridge, which was used in combination with a separate bar-shaped tailpiece and was the first Gibson bridge to offer adjustment of individual string-length, designed to improve intonation and tuning accuracy.

Nach dem Erfolg seiner ersten Solidbody E-Gitarre, der Les Paul Goldtop, wollte Gibson mit Nachfolgemodellen eine ganze Serie kreieren. Die hochwertigere Les Paul Custom von 1954 war klassisch schwarz mit vergoldeter Hardware, verzierter Bundmarkierung auf einem Griffbrett aus Ebenholz, mehrfacher Einfassung und einem Korpus komplett aus Mahagoni statt der Ahorn-Magahoni-Kombination der Goldtop. Gibson bewarb das Custom-Modell als „Fretless Wonder ", (bundloses Wunder) dank des sehr tiefen und flachen Bunddrahts. Zuerst hatte die Custom am Hals einen Alnico-Pickup, den Gibson damals neu, allerdings nicht sehr lange herstellte. Das Modell war die erste Les Paul mit neuer Tune-o-matic Brücke, die mit einem separaten Stop-Tailpiece (Saitenhalter) verwendet wurde. Es war die erste Gibson-Brücke, deren Saitenlänge man individuell anpassen konnte, um die Intonation und die Stimmgenauigkeit zu verbessern.

STEVE JONES of The Sex Pistols was not the typical three-chord thrasher of punk mythology. He had a refined taste for Gibson guitars, too, and as well as his Les Paul Special and a few Customs, he found room for a Firebird and a SG Standard, and in his early years he played a Flying V.

STEVE JONES von den Sex Pistols spielte nicht nur die für den Punk typischen drei Akkorde. Er hatte eine Vorliebe für Gibson-Gitarren, besaß eine Les Paul Special, einige Customs, hatte Platz für eine Firebird und eine SG Standard. In seinen frühen Jahren spielte er außerdem auf einer Flying V.

LES PAUL CUSTOM

GIBSON LES PAUL CUSTOM

The Les Paul Custom appeared in revised form in 1957, when Gibson replaced the original layout of two single-coil pickups with one that had three of the company's new humbucking pickups. It was probably a reaction to Fender's three-pickup Stratocaster, launched three years earlier, which was gaining steadily in popularity. The Custom in its new guise kept a three-way pickup selector, providing neck or bridge pickup as before, but in the centre position it gave middle and bridge pickups together for a different tone. The three-pickup models are less popular today among collectors and players compared to the original-style two-pickup Customs.

Die Les Paul Custom kam 1957 in überarbeiteter Form auf den Markt, als Gibson die ursprüngliche Ausführung mit zwei Single-Coil-Pickups durch eine mit den neuen Humbucker-Pickups ersetzte. Vermutlich reagierte das Unternehmen damit auf die immer populärer werdene Stratocaster mit drei Pickups, die Fender drei Jahre zuvor herausgebracht hatte. Die neue Custom behielt ihren alten, dreifachen Pickup-Wahlschalter und den Hals- bzw. Brücken-Pickup, hatte in der Mitte jedoch mittlere und Brücken-Pickups für einen unterschiedlichen Klang. Die Customs mit drei Pickups sind bei Sammlern und Gitarristen heute weniger populär verglichen mit dem Original.

ROBERT FRIPP has guided various incarnations of King Crimson through some of the most demanding music ever played by a band of rock musicians. Fripp's guitar of choice for some time was his beloved 50s Les Paul Custom, which he bought secondhand in London in 1968 after signing Crimson's first record deal.

ROBERT FRIPP ist einer der Gründer und Vordenker der Rockband King Crimson, die mit wechselnden Formationen sehr anspruchsvolle Rockmusik spielt. Fripps Lieblingsgitarre war lange Zeit seine 50s Les Paul Custom, die er nach Unterzeichnung seines ersten Plattenvertrags 1968 in London gebraucht kaufte.

DAVID GILMOUR has often relied on a Fender Stratocaster for his electric guitar work with Pink Floyd, notably on albums such as Wish You Were Here from 1975. Fender honoured Gilmour with a signature model in 2008, based on his famous black-finished Strat.

Bei Pink Floyd vertraute DAVID GILMOUR meist auf eine Fender Stratocaster, insbesondere auf Alben wie Wish You Were Here von 1975. Fender ehrte ihn 2008 mit einem Signature-Modell, das seiner berühmten „Black Strat" nachempfunden ist.

FENDER STRATOCASTER

Fender wanted to build on the success of its two solidbody guitars, the Telecaster and the Precision Bass, and the result was the Stratocaster, which appeared in 1954. It was a beautiful design, drawing on the simplicity that had been at the heart of Fender's guitars so far and adding some pleasing flourishes of its own. Its sleek lines and contoured body must have been a shock to guitarists of the 50s, it was the first solidbody with three pickups, and it had a clever new take on the vibrato, integrating adjustable bridge, tailpiece, and vibrato system into one self-contained unit. Strats from the 50s, like this fine example, have a solid fretted maple neck bolted to an ash body, a volume and two tone controls, and a three-way switch to select the pickups. The Stratocaster is, quite simply, one of the most famous guitars of all time.

Fender wollte an den Erfolg seiner zwei Solidbody-Gitarren, der Telecaster und dem Precision Bass, anknüpfen, was mit der Stratocaster von 1954 auch gelang. Das einfache, schöne Design der Fender-Gtiarre blieb, hinzu kamen einige hübsch anzusehende Verzierungen. Die schlanken Linien und der geschwungene Korpus müssen für die Gitarristen der 1950er-Jahre ein Schock gewesen sein. Es war die erste Solidbody mit drei Pickups, und sie besaß eine intelligente neue Variante des Vibratos, bei der eine verstellbare Brücke, Saitenhalter und ein Vibratosystem zu einer eigenständigen Einheit verbunden wurden. Strats aus den 1950er-Jahren, wie dieses wunderbare Beispiel zeigt, hatten einen massiven Ahornhals, der an einen Korpus aus Eschenholz geschraubt wurde, einen Lautstärke- und zwei Tonregler und einen Dreiwegschalter zum Auswählen der Pickups. Die Stratocaster ist unumstritten eine der berühmtesten Gitarren der Welt.

Television provided a boost for the three-year-old Fender Stratocaster in late 1957 when BUDDY HOLLY appeared on the Ed Sullivan Show and picked a Strat. The guitar also featured prominently on the cover of Holly's '57 album The Chirping Crickets. Suddenly, thousands of aspiring guitarists knew the guitar they must aim for.

Das Fernsehen hatte der drei Jahre alten Fender Stratocaster Ende 1957 zu einem Durchbruch verholfen, als BUDDY HOLLY in der Ed Sullivan Show zu einer Strat griff. Die Gitarre war auch auf dem Cover von Hollys Album The Chirping Crickets, das ebenfalls 1957 erschien. Plötzlich erlangte die Strat einen hohen Bekanntheitsgrad und stand schnell auf der Wunschliste vieler Gitarristen.

STRATOSPHERE TWIN

Russ and Claude Deaver founded the small Stratosphere firm in Springfield, Missouri, in the early 50s. This rare Twin model is the one for which the brothers will go down in guitar history, because it was the first production double-neck electric guitar. Stratosphere's 12-string electrics – made in single-neck form as well as part of the double-neck – were another first from this innovative if shortlived brand. The Stratosphere 12 used a bizarre tuning system, unique to this model, that required the player to consider his playing techniques afresh. Chet Atkins used a Twin for both sides of a 1955 single, 'Shine On Harvest Moon', and west coast session man Jimmy Bryant played his Twin on a 1954 single, 'Stratosphere Boogie', duetting with steel player Speedy West. However, Stratosphere's instruments soon faded from the scene.

Russ und Claude Deaver gründeten Anfang der 1950er-Jahre in Springfield, Missouri ihr kleines Unternehmen Stratosphere. Mit diesem seltenen Twin-Modell haben die beiden Brüder Gitarrengeschichte geschrieben, denn es war die erste produzierte E-Gitarre mit zwei Hälsen. Die 12-saitige E-Gitarre von Stratosphere – die es mit einem Hals und als Teil der Doppelhalsgitarre gab – war eine weitere Premiere dieser innovativen Marke, die allerdings nicht lange überlebte. Die Stratosphere 12 hatte ein merkwürdiges Stimmsystem, einmalig bei diesem Modell, bei der Gitarrist seine Spieltechnik komplett überdenken musste. Chet Atkins spielte eine Twin auf der A- und B-Seite der Single ,Shine On Harvest Moon' von 1955 und Jimmy Bryand, ein Studiomusiker von der Westküste, spielte auf der Single ,Stratosphere Boogie' von 1954 seine Twin im Duett mit Steel-Gitarrist Speedy West. Doch die Instrumente von Stratosphere waren bald nicht mehr gefragt.

LES PAUL JUNIOR

MICK JONES of The Clash was inspired by his hero Johnny Thunders of The New York Dolls to play a Gibson Les Paul Junior. He also used Les Paul Standards and Customs, but he remembered his original double-cutaway Junior fondly as his first proper guitar and said that Juniors in general are his favourites.

MICK JONES von The Clash ließ sich von seinem Helden Johnny Thunders von den New York Dolls inspirieren, eine Gibson Les Paul Junior zu spielen. Er spielte auch Les Paul Standards und Customs, nennt aber seine Double-Cutaway Junior liebevoll seine erste richtige Gitarre und sagt, dass Juniors allgemein seine Lieblingsgitarren sind.

GIBSON LES PAUL JUNIOR

At the same time that Gibson introduced the upscale Les Paul Custom, it added the Les Paul Junior, launched in 1954. This was clearly a budget model, listing at $99.50, when the Goldtop was $225 and the Custom $325. The Junior did not pretend to be anything but a cheaper guitar. It had a flat-topped solid mahogany body, without the carving of the Goldtop and Custom, one P-90 pickup, at the bridge, with single volume and tone controls, and simple dot position-markers on the unbound fingerboard. It was finished in Gibson's traditional two-tone brown-to-yellow sunburst and had the stopbar bridge-tailpiece like the one on the latest Goldtop. It lasted like this until a new double-cutaway version replaced it in 1958.

Zur selben Zeit, als Gibson die hochwertigere Les Paul Custom einführte, legte das Unternehmen 1954 mit der Les Paul Junior nach – mit einem Preis von 99,50 Dollar ein eindeutig billigeres Modell, als die Goldtop noch 225 Dollar und die Custom 325 Dollar kosteten. Die Junior sollte einfach nur günstig sein. Sie war eine dünne Solidbody aus Mahagoni ohne das Carving der Goldtop und der Custom, mit nur einem P-90 Pickup an der Brücke, je einem Regler für Ton und Lautstärke und einem einfachen Griffbrett mit Punkteinlage. Für die Oberfläche wählte Gibson sein traditionelles braun-gelbes „Sunburst" und verwendete wie bei der neuesten Goldtop eine Stopbar-Brücke. 1958 wurde sie durch eine neue Version mit Double-Cutaway ersetzt.

LES PAUL SPECIAL

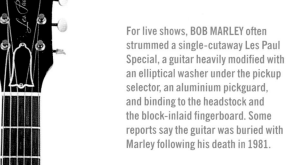

For live shows, BOB MARLEY often strummed a single-cutaway Les Paul Special, a guitar heavily modified with an elliptical washer under the pickup selector, an aluminium pickguard, and binding to the headstock and the block-inlaid fingerboard. Some reports say the guitar was buried with Marley following his death in 1981.

Bei Live-Auftritten spielte BOB MARLEY häufig eine Single-Cutaway Les Paul Special, die stark modifiziert war und mit einer ellipsenförmigen Unterlegscheibe unter dem Tonabnehmerschalter, einem Schlagbrett aus Aluminium, einer Randeinfassung an der Kopfplatte und dem Griffbrett mit Blockintarsien ergänzt wurde. Laut Gerüchten soll der 1981 verstorbene Marley mit der Gitarre beerdigt worden sein.

GIBSON LES PAUL SPECIAL

When Gibson expanded its Les Paul line earlier in the 50s, it added the upscale Custom and the budget Junior, as well as a yellow-finished Junior known as the TV. In 1955, along came the Special, in effect a Junior with two P-90s and the necessary four controls and pickup selector. A few years later, Gibson redesigned the budget models, giving them a new double-cutaway body during 1958 and 1959. The Special shown is from early 1959, before Gibson realised that the neck pickup was too near the neck joint; later versions avoided this potential structural weakness by shifting the neck pickup a little further back, and at the same time Gibson moved the pickup selector switch behind the tailpiece. This Special was finished in cherry, and the model was also available in yellow (but, unlike the Junior, it was not called a TV in that colour).

Als Gibson seine Les Paul Reihe Anfang der 1950er-Jahre ausweitete, kamen die hochwertigere Custom, die preisgünstigere Junior sowie eine gelbe Junior hinzu, die TV genannt wurde. 1955 erschien die Special, eine Junior mit zwei P-90 Pickups und den erforderlichen vier Reglern und Pickup-Wahlschalter. Einige Jahre später veränderte Gibson das Design der günstigen Modelle und verpasste ihnen 1958 und 1959 einen neuen Korpus mit Double Cutaway. Die hier gezeigte Special ist von Anfang 1959, bevor Gibson klar wurde, dass der Hals-Pickup zu nah am Übergang zum Korpus war. Bei späteren Versionen wurde diese potentielle Konstruktionsschwäche umgangen, indem der Hals-Pickup etwas weiter zurück versetzt wurde. Gleichzeitig verschob Gibson den Pickup-Wahlschalter hinter den Saitenhalter. Das Finish bei dieser Special ist Kirsche, das Modell gibt es aber auch in gelb (wobei es anders als die Junior in dieser Farbe nicht TV hieß).

1958 — GIBSON **FLYING V**

1958 — GIBSON **EXPLORER**

1967 — GIBSON **FLYING V**

GIBSON FLYING V

Partnering the Explorer was the equally angular Flying V, launched in 1958 to almost universal disapproval. Like the Explorer, the V used an unusual wood for the body and neck: korina, a tradename for a West African hardwood usually known as limba. Gibson had already used the timber for an earlier lap-steel guitar, the Skylark. Only about 100 Flying Vs were made before production ceased the following year, and despite some appearances at the time, notably with Albert King and Lonnie Mack, it wasn't until later that players began to appreciate the Flying V for the great guitar that it was. From the 70s, the V (along with the Explorer) became a blueprint for the modern pointy guitar aimed at metal players, and at last it seemed that a 50s design had found its place, decades after its original release.

Das Schwestermodell der Explorer, die pfeilförmige Flying V, kam 1958 auf den Markt und stieß einstimmig auf Ableh-nung. Wie bei der Explorer, sind Hals und Korpus der Flying V aus ungewöhnlichem Holz: Korina, ein westafrikanisches Hartholz, auch Limbaholz genannt. Gibson hatte dieses bereits einmal für die Skylark, eine frühere Lapsteel-Gitar-re, verwendet. Bevor die Produktion im Folgejahr eingestellt wurde, wurden nur rund 100 Flying Vs hergestellt. Obwohl das Modell in dieser Zeit einige Male öffentlich gespielt wurde, insbesondere von Albert King und Lonnie Mack, erkannten Gitarristen erst später, was für eine großartige Gitarre die Flying V ist. Seit den 1970er-Jahren gilt die "V" (neben der Explorer) als Vorlage für die moderne, spitz zulaufende Gitarre, zu deren Abnehmern vorwiegend Me-tal-Gitarristen gehören. Und so kam es, dass ein Design aus den 1950er-Jahren am Ende doch noch seine Nische fand, Jahrzehnte nach seiner ersten Einführung.

EDGE of U2 bought a new 1976 Gibson Explorer while on holiday with his parents in New York City, attracted by the guitar's variety of sounds and angular looks. He used it on nearly all the band's early records and live shows, and it's remained one of his favourite instruments ever since.

EDGE von U2 kaufte sich 1976 eine neue Gibson Explorer, als er mit seinen Eltern Urlaub in New York machte. Die Klangvielfalt und der kantige Look der Gitarre hatten es ihm angetan. Er nahm mit ihr die meisten Stücke der frühen U2-Alben auf und spielte sie auf Konzerten. Die Gibson Explorer ist nach wie vor eine seiner Lieblingsgitarren.

GIBSON EXPLORER

Until the late 50s, Gibson's solidbody designs had been traditional. That changed dramatically with the Modern-istic guitars: the Flying V, the Explorer, and the unissued Moderne. Before these designs, solid electric guitars had reflected established acoustic styling: a waisted body with a smaller top bout balancing a larger bottom. But Gibson's latest arrivals featured original and adventurous styling. The Explorer and Flying V reflected design trends in 50s furniture, with modern straight lines instead of traditional curves. It was such a radical departure that the response from retailers and players was negative. The Explorer was even less popular than the Flying V, and only a handful were made – making for a much sought-after collectable today. Eric Clapton sold the example shown at auction in 1999 for $134,500, benefitting his Crossroads charity.

Bis Ende der 1950er-Jahre waren die Designs der Solidbo-dies von Gibson eher traditionell. Das änderte sich drama-tisch mit Einführung der Modernistic-Reihe: die Flying V, die Explorer und die nicht mehr hergestellte Moderne. Davor waren massive E-Gitarren ähnlich gebaut wie Akustik-gitarren: ein taillierter Korpus mit einem kleineren Oberbug und einem größeren Unterbug als Ausgleich. Doch der Stil der neusten Gibson-Modelle war originell und abenteuer-lich. Die Explorer und die Flying V spiegelten das aktuelle Möbel-Design der 1950er-Jahre wieder, mit modernen ge-raden Linien statt traditionell geschwungenen Kurven. Das Abwenden vom Alten war derart radikal, dass die Reaktion von Kunden und Händlern eher schlecht ausfiel. Die Explo-rer, die noch unbeliebter war als die Flying V, wurde nur in sehr kleiner Zahl hergestellt – was sie heute zu einem be-gehrten Sammlerobjekt macht. Eric Clapton verkaufte das hier gezeigte Exemplar 1999 bei einer Auktion für 134.500 Dollar zugunsten seiner Crossroads-Stiftung.

GIBSON FLYING V

After the buzz created in the mid 60s when Dave Davies of The Kinks played a 50s Flying V, in 1967 Gibson decided to relaunch the model, and this time it proved popular and was more widely played. Gibson used different materials and a revised design compared to the original: it had a solid mahogany body and neck, lost the 50s model's through-body stringing, and gained a large white pickguard, a Tune-o-matic bridge, and a new control layout, with the three knobs – two volumes and a tone – arranged in a triangular group. The guitar pictured was once owned by Jimi Hendrix, who used it for a couple of years from 1967 as his main onstage guitar for blues numbers, and it has been restored to re-create the psychedelic body decorations that Hendrix added to the guitar.

Nach dem Hype Mitte der 1960er-Jahre, als Dave Davies von den Kinks eine Flying V aus den 1950er-Jahren spielte, beschloss Gibson im Jahr 1967 eine Neuauflage des Mo-dells. Diesmal war der Erfolg größer, und die Gitarre stieß auf deutlich mehr Anklang. Gibson verwendete unterschied-liche Materialien und ein verändertes Design als beim Original: Korpus und Hals waren aus massivem Mahagoni; die Saiten verliefen nicht mehr durch den Korpus wie bei dem Modell aus den 1950er-Jahren; sie erhielt ein großes, weißes Schlagbrett, eine Tune-o-matic-Brücke und eine neue Steuerung mit drei Knöpfen (zwei Lautstärke-, ein Ton-Regler), als Dreieck angeordnet. Die hier abgebildete Gitarre gehörte einmal Jimi Hendrix, der sie ab 1967 für ein paar Jahre als eine seiner Haupt-Gitarren bei Blues-Stücken auf der Bühne spielte. Die psychedelischen Verzierungen auf dem Korpus wurden nachträglich restauriert.

Although best known as a Stratocaster player, JIMI HENDRIX used a '67 Flying V in the late 60s as his main guitar for blues, and he decorated it with painted patterns. Hendrix used a couple more Vs: a sunburst model, and then a black left-handed V, custom-made for him by Gibson.

JIMI HENDRIX ist vor allem als Stratocaster-Spieler bekannt. In den späten 60ern spielte er jedoch hauptsächlich auf einer Flying V aus dem Jahr 1967, die er mit Mustern verzierte. Hendrix hatte noch andere Vs: ein Sunburst-Modell und eine schwarze Linkshänder-V, die Gibson speziell für ihn anfertigte.

One of the first famous guitarists seen with an original 50s Flying V was DAVE DAVIES of The Kinks. He adopted an odd playing style, hooking his right arm through the "legs" of the V, and the popularity of The Kinks was one of the factors that forced Gibson to reissue the Flying V in 1967.

Einer der ersten berühmten Gitarristen, der mit einer originalen 50s Flying V gesehen wurde, war DAVE DAVIES von The Kinks. Er entwickelte einen eigensinnigen Stil und hakte seinen rechten Arm durch die ‚Beine' des V. Der Bekanntheitsgrad der Band war ein Grund, warum Gibson die Flying V 1967 neu auflegte.

PETER GREEN was the best white British blues-rock guitarists of the late 60s and early 70s. He bought his Les Paul Standard in 1965 and used it for classic work with John Mayall and Fleetwood Mac. Green sold it to Gary Moore in the 70s, who sold the guitar to a collector in 2006.

PETER GREEN war der beste weiße Bluesrock-Gitarrist der späten 1960er- und frühen 1970er-Jahre in Großbritannien. 1965 kaufte er seine Les Paul Standard, die er während seiner Zeit mit John Mayall und Fleetwood Mac spielte. Green verkaufte die Gitarre in den 1970er-Jahren an Gary Moore, der sie 2006 an einen Sammler veräußerte.

GIBSON LES PAUL STANDARD

Sales of the Les Paul Goldtop had declined, and Gibson searched for a way to improve matters. The company's solution implies they thought that players found the gold finish too radical, because in 1958, Gibson gave the model a traditional sunburst finish, with a red edge and yellow centre. This variant was shortlived – it was made in 1958, 1959, and 1960 – but has become one of the most revered and valued solidbody electrics of all time. All the elements came together: the twin humbucking pickups, the maple/mahogany body construction, the mahogany neck with rosewood fingerboard, the Tune-o-matic bridge, and that sunburst finish on the maple cap. The legend of these guitars is also due to the players who have used them, and this famous beaten and faded example, minus its pickguard, was owned at various times by Peter Green and Gary Moore.

Als die Verkäufe der Les Paul Goldtop zurückgingen, suchte Gibson nach einem Weg, die Lage zu verbessern. Das Unternehmen muss den Rückgang wohl darauf zurückgeführt haben, dass sich Gitarristen an der goldenen Farbe störten, denn 1958 brachte Gibson das Modell mit traditionellem „Sunburst"-Finish neu heraus, rot am Rand und gelb in der Mitte. Diese Variante wurde lediglich von 1958 bis 1960 produziert doch heute ist sie die am meisten verehrte und geschätzte Solidbody E-Gitarre aller Zeiten. Alle Elemente kommen hier zusammen: Twin-Humbucker-Pickups, Ahorn/Mahagoni-Korpus, Hals aus Mahagoni mit Palisander-Griffbrett, Tune-o-matic-Brücke, und „Sunburst"-Finish auf einer Decke aus Ahorn. Legendär wurden diese Modelle auch aufgrund der Gitarristen, die sie gespielt haben. Dieses berühmte, in die Jahre gekommene Beispiel (ohne Schlagbrett), war bereits mehrfach im Besitz von Peter Green und Gary Moore.

GIBSON LES PAUL STANDARD

The sunburst Les Paul Standard, produced originally in 1958, 1959, and 1960, is one of the greatest electric guitars ever made. This one is owned by Jimmy Page, and it is arguably the most famous Les Paul in the world. Page used it for almost every Led Zeppelin album and tour, and his affectionate name for it was Number 1. It has a few modifications that Page made to suit his requirements, including one that is commonly seen: the original (somewhat flimsy) tuners have been replaced, here with gold-plated Grover Rotomatics. The bridge pickup is not original, and work done to the neck has erased the serial number, which is usually the easiest clue to a Gibson's year of manufacture. Experts have suggested Page's Number 1 was made probably in late 1959 or early 1960.

Die „Sunburst" farbene Les Paul Standard von 1958, 1959 und 1960 gilt als eine der besten E-Gitarren aller Zeiten. Diese gehört Jimmy Page, und sie ist die wohl berühmteste Les Paul der Welt. Page spielte sie auf fast allen Led Zeppelin Alben und Tourneen und nannte sie liebevoll seine „Number 1". Er ließ sie nach seinen Wünschen leicht verändern, u. a. ersetzte er – wie viele andere – die (etwas schwache) Mechanik durch vergoldete Rotomatics-Mechaniken von Grover. Der Steg-Pickup ist nicht original, und durch Arbeiten am Hals gibt es nun keine Seriennummer mehr, woran das Herstellungsjahr einer Gibson normalerweise am schnellsten zu erkennen ist. Experten zufolge wurde die „Number 1" von Jimmy Page Ende 1959 oder Anfang 1960 hergestellt.

JIMMY PAGE started as a session player in the 60s. When he joined The Yardbirds in 1966 he played a Telecaster, which he continued to use in Led Zeppelin. In 1969, he acquired a Gibson Les Paul Standard from Joe Walsh and used it on almost all the subsequent Zeppelin studio sessions and live dates.

JIMMY PAGE begann seine Karriere in den 60ern als Sessionmusiker. Als er 1966 Mitglied der Yardbirds wurde, spielte er eine Telecaster, die er später auch bei Led Zeppelin einsetzte. 1969 erwarb er eine Gibson Les Paul Standard von Joe Walsh und absolvierte damit seitdem fast alle Zeppelin Studiosessions und Live-Auftritte.

1959/60 – GIBSON
LES PAUL STANDARD

SLASH at first played replica sunburst-finish Les Pauls, built by local guitar-makers such as Kris Derrig or Max Baranet. Gibson made a deal with him in the late 80s, and from that point he played real Les Pauls. Gibson has issued a number of Slash signature models in more recent years.

Zu Beginn seiner Karriere spielte SLASH Les Paul-Kopien in einem Sunburst-Finish, angefertigt von lokalen Gitarrenbauern wie Kris Derrig oder Max Baranet. In den späten 1980er-Jahren schloss er einen Deal mit Gibson ab und spielte fortan originale Les Pauls. Seit den frühen 1990er-Jahren brachte Gibson insgesamt 12 Signature-Modelle auf den Markt.

GIBSON LES PAUL STANDARD

We've already seen two worn, played, and modified Les Paul Standards, the most famous and revered of the original Les Paul models. This one is in near-perfect original condition and shows how the guitar would have looked when it was new. The figured maple top – the "flame" according to guitar fans – is splendidly visible through the virtually unfaded red-and-yellow sunburst finish. The original tuners are intact – often the plastic tips will crumble with age – and the rosewood fingerboard and pearl makers show little signs of playing wear. The metal covers are still in place on the two humbucking pickups, and all the plasticware, including pickguard, knobs, selector disc, and pickup rings, are original and in good condition. It is, in short, a collector's dream. Just don't ask how much.

Zwei verschlissene und modifizierte Les Paul Standards haben wir bereits gesehen, die berühmtesten und meist verehrten Les Paul Originale. Dieses ist in nahezu perfektem und unverändertem Zustand und zeigt, wie diese Gitarre damals neu ausgesehen hat. Die Decke aus Ahorn – die „Flamme", wie Gitarrenfans sie nennen – ist durch das nahezu perfekte rot-gelbe „Sunburst"-Finish hervorragend zu erkennen. Die Original-Mechaniken sind noch intakt – oft lösen sich die Plastikspitzen mit der Zeit auf – und das Palisander-Griffbrett mit den Bundmarkierungen aus Perlmutt sieht aus wie neu. Der Metallabdeckung auf den zwei Humbucker-Pickups ist unversehrt. Das Schlagbrett, die Knöpfe, die Scheibe unter dem Pickup-Wahlschalter und die Pickup-Rahmen sind original und in gutem Zustand. Es ist, kurz gesagt, der Traum eines jeden Sammlers. Über den Preis reden wir besser nicht.

HAGSTROM P46 DELUXE

Albin Hagström set up his company in Sweden in 1925 to
import accordions, and from the 50s it produced guitars
with a number of brands, including Kent, Goya, and
Futurama as well as Hagstrom, for distribution at home
and abroad. The sparkle colour of the guitar pictured was
achieved with an unusual plastic finish, derived from
Hagstrom's experience with accordions and recalling
some of Gretsch's sparkling guitars of the 50s. It also had
a translucent plastic fingerboard and headstock. The four
single-coil pickups were grouped as two humbuckers, with
two roller wheels for volume and tone either side of a bank of
six pushbuttons: ACC(ompaniment) switched volume to the
roller below the pickups, and the others offered the pickups
in various combinations (including O, which switched them
all off). Hagstrom ceased guitar production in the early 80s,
but the company was revived in 2004.

*Albin Hagström gründete sein Unternehmen 1925
in Schweden, um Akkordeons zu importieren. In den
1950er-Jahren begann die Firma, Gitarren mit unterschiedlichen Markennamen herzustellen, u. a. Kent, Goya,
Futurama und Hagstrom, die in Schweden und international verkauft wurden. Die funkelnde Oberfläche der hier
abgebildeten Gitarre wurde mit einem ungewöhnlichen
Kunststoff-Finish erzielt, das Hagstrom von Akkordeons her
kannte und das an die Glitzergitarren von Gretsch aus den
1950er-Jahren erinnert. Das Griffbrett und die Kopfplatte
waren durchsichtig. Die vier Single-Coil Pickups waren zu
zwei Humbucker-Pickups gruppiert, mit zwei Rädchen für
Lautstärke und Ton über und unter einer Reihe von sechs
Druckknöpfen: ACC (kurz für Accompaniment) wechselte
die Lautstärke zu dem Rädchen unterhalb der Pickups, die
anderen boten unterschiedliche Pickup-Kombinationen
(darunter O, mit dem man alle ausschalten konnte). Anfang
der 1980er-Jahre stellte Hagstrom die Gitarrenproduktion
ein, das Geschäft wurde 2004 jedoch wiederbelebt.*

FUTURAMA

The British arm of the French Selmer company had a flagship store in London and distributed a variety of instruments using its own brands, one of which was Futurama. Guitars with the Futurama brand first appeared in the UK in the late 50s and were cheap electrics designed to offer a start for budding rock'n'rollers. Among the many British guitarists who began with a Futurama were George Harrison, Jimmy Page, and Albert Lee. The first Futuramas, like the guitar pictured, were made by Neoton in Prague, Czech Republic (part of Czechoslovakia at the time). In the early 60s, Selmer switched its supplier of Futurama guitars to the Hagstrom factory in Sweden, but by 1965 the brand had disappeared.

Der britische Arm der französischen Firma Selmer besaß in London einen Flagship-Store und verkaufte unterschiedliche Instrumente mit eigenen Markennamen – einer davon war Futurama. Futurama-Modelle kamen erstmals Ende der 1950er-Jahre in Großbritannien auf und waren billige E-Gitarren für angehende Rock'n'Roller. Zu den vielen britischen Gitarristen, die mit einer Futurama ihre Karriere begannen, gehören GEORGE HARRISON, Jimmy Page und Albert Lee. Die ersten Futuramas wurden, genau wie diese Gitarre, von Neoton in Prag (damals noch Tschechoslowakei) hergestellt. Ab Anfang der 1960er-Jahre ließ Selmer die Futurama-Gitarren von Hagström in Schweden produzieren, doch 1965 verschwand die Marke vom Markt.

1960– UNKNOWN MAKER FUTURAMA

GEORGE HARRISON plays a Futurama with The Beatles at the Top Ten club in Hamburg , in 1961, alongside bass player Stuart Sutcliffe.

Hier spielt GEORGE HARRISON seine Futurama zusammen mit den Beatles im Top Ten Club in Hamburg in 1961. Neben ihm sitzt der Bassgitarrist Stuart Sutcliffe.

NELS CLINE is the guitarist in Wilco, and he's an exploratory adventurer in solo work and with Sonic Youth's Thurston Moore. Cline's main guitar is a '59 Fender Jazzmaster that he describes as Frankensteined, with various modifications. He also plays Jerry Jones guitars, Crown and Hopf retro items, and a Jaguar.

NELS CLINE ist nicht nur der Gitarrist von Wilco, er ist auch Solo unterwegs und spielt mit Thurston Moore von Sonic Youth. Clines Hauptgitarre ist eine Fender Jazzmaster von 1959, die er wegen diverser Modifikationen als „Frankensteined" beschreibt. Er spielt auch Jerry Jones-Gitarren, Crown- und Hopf-Retrogitarren und eine Jaguar.

1961 – FENDER
JAZZMASTER

FENDER JAZZMASTER

Following the success of the Telecaster, Esquire, and Stratocaster, not to mention the Precision Bass and the Jazz Bass, Fender introduced a further solidbody guitar in 1958 with the upscale Jazzmaster. It had an enlarged headstock, a body with Fender's new offset-waist design, the first appearance of Fender's separate rosewood fingerboard, two big new-style single-coil pickups, a floating vibrato bridge, and an array of controls, including a small switch to select between preset rhythm and lead settings. Fender's custom colours of the period added an impressive sheen beyond the regular sunbursts and blondes: this Jazzmaster is finished in what Fender called burgundy mist metallic. Like almost all the colours Fender used, it was derived from the DuPont paints employed by the US car industry. Other original Fender colours included fiesta red, sonic blue, surf green, ocean turquoise, and firemist gold.

Nach dem Erfolg der Telecaster, Esquire, Stratocaster und nicht zuletzt des Precision Bass und Jazz Bass, führte Fender 1958 mit der hochwertigeren Jazzmaster eine weitere Solidbody-Gitarre ein. Sie hatte eine vergrößerte Kopfplatte und einen Korpus mit neuem Fender Offset-Waist Design (versetzte Taille). Zum ersten Mal tauchte Fenders separates Palisander-Griffbrett auf. Außerdem hatte die Jazzmaster zwei große, neue Single-Coil-Pickups, eine schwimmende Brücke und eine Vielzahl von Reglern, darunter ein kleiner Schalter, um zwischen voreingestelltem Rhythmus und Lead-Settings zu wählen. Die Farben von Fender aus dieser Zeit sorgten für einen besonderen Glanz, der über die sonst üblichen Sunburst- und Blonde-Töne hinaus ging. Das Finish dieser Jazzmaster nannte Fender „Burgundy Mist Metallic". Wie fast alle Farben, die Fender benutzte, stammte diese von DuPont, deren Lacke auch in der amerikanischen Automobilindustrie eingesetzt werden. Andere Original Fender-Farben trugen die Bezeichnungen Fiesta Red, Sonic Blue, Surf Green, Ocean Turquoise und Firemist Gold.

FENDER KURT COBAIN JAGUAR

A Jaguar was one of the guitars that Kurt Cobain played in Nirvana, and Fender recently re-created it, complete with unusual modified controls and DiMarzio pickups, for this realistic "Road Worn" reproduction. The Jaguar was Fender's first new electric of the 60s, with the same offset-waist body design as the recent Jazzmaster. The top-of-the-line Jag was the first Fender with 22 frets and a scale length of 24 inches, an inch and a quarter shorter than Fender's standard, making for an easier playing feel. It had a spring-loaded mute at the bridge that Fender optimistically thought players would prefer to manual methods, an extra set of lead-circuit switches added to Jazzmaster-style controls, and distinctive chromed control panels. The Jaguar was gone from the Fender line by 1975, while the Jazzmaster lasted until 1980. Both models have been reissued in various forms in more recent years.

2011 – FENDER
KURT COBAIN JAGUAR

Eine Jaguar war eine der Gitarren, die Kurt Cobain mit Nirvana spielte. Fender hat sie vor kurzem neu herausgebracht, mit ungewöhnlich veränderten Reglern und Pickups von DiMarzio, damit sie so aussieht, als hätte sie das ein oder andere Konzert auf dem Buckel. Die Jaguar war Fenders erste neue E-Gitarre der 1960er-Jahre, mit dem gleichen Offset-Waist-Korpus wie die neueste Jazzmaster. Die hochwertige Jag war die erste Fender mit 22 Bünden und einer Mensur von 24 Zoll, 1 1/4 Zoll kürzer als Fenders Standard, um das Spielen zu erleichtern. Sie besaß einen Federdämpfer am Steg (von dem Fender optimistischerweise dachte, Gitarristen würden diese Methode der manuellen vorziehen), „Lead Circuit"-Schalter zusätzlich zu den Reglern im Jazzmaster-Stil und verchromte Control Panels. 1975 strich Fender die Jaguar aus dem Programm, während die Jazzmaster bis 1980 weiter produziert wurde. Beide Modelle wurden vor einigen Jahren jedoch in verschiedener Form neu aufgelegt.

Nirvana's KURT COBAIN often played a Fender Mustang or Fender Jaguar, both of which were modified with humbucking pickups and some personal touches. Around the time of Cobain's death, he was developing a hybrid of the two models for Fender, who released the result as the Jag-Stang in 1996.

Nirvana-Frontmann KURT COBAIN spielte oft eine Fender Mustang oder Fender Jaguar. Bei beiden ließ er Humbucker-Pickups einbauen und kleinere Änderungen vornehmen. Kurz vor seinem Tod entwickelte er ein Hybrid aus zwei Modellen, das Fender 1996 als die Jag-Stang herausbrachte.

c. 1965 – DANELECTRO
BELLZOUKI 7020

1966 – DANELECTRO
GUITARLIN 4123

1967 – CORAL
SITAR

DANELECTRO BELLZOUKI 7020

Danelectro was started by Nathan Daniel in Red Bank, New Jersey, in the late 40s to make amplifiers, adding guitars from the late 50s. This Bellzouki was an early electric 12-string introduced around 1962 after a collaboration with Vinnie Bell, a busy New York session guitarist. Bell was apparently inspired by the music he'd heard in the 1960 movie Never On A Sunday and its title song, which featured the ringing sound of a traditional Greek bouzouki. The modern bouzouki is often electric and features four paired strings, sounding something like a 12-string guitar. The Bellzouki's unusual looks did not prove popular, however, and when the instrument did not sell well it was soon dropped from the Danelectro lines.

Danelectro wurde Ende der 1940er-Jahre von Nathan Daniel in Red Bank, New Jersey gegründet, der zunächst nur Verstärker baute, in den späten1950er-Jahren aber auch Gitarren produzierte. Diese 1962 eingeführte Bellzouki entstand in Zusammenarbeit mit Vinnie Bell, einem häufig gebuchten New Yorker Studiogitarristen, und war eine der ersten 12-saitigen E-Gitarre. Bell war offenbar vom Soundtrack und Titelsong des Films Never On A Sunday (1960) inspiriert, in dem eine traditionell griechische Bouzouki gespielt wurde. Die moderne Bouzouki ist oft elektrisch, besitzt vier Saitenpaare und klingt ähnlich wie eine 12-saitige Westerngitarre. Das ungewöhnliche Aussehen der Bellzouki kam jedoch nicht sonderlich gut an, und als das Instrument schlechte Verkaufszahlen schrieb, nahm Danelectro es bald wieder aus dem Programm.

JIMMY PAGE used a Danelectro Standard on-stage with Led Zeppelin for slide-playing on particular numbers. Danelectro made the two-pickup Standard 3021 model for about ten years from the late 50s, and Page's black-finish guitar had the brand's period coke-bottle headstock and lipstick-tube pickups.

JIMMY PAGE hat auf der Bühne mit Led Zeppelin bei bestimmten Stücken eine Danelectro Standard für Slides gespielt. Für einen Zeitraum von rund 10 Jahren produzierte Danelectro ab den späten 1950er-Jahren die Standard 3021 mit zwei Tonabnehmern. Pages schwarz lackierte Gitarre hatte den flaschenförmigen Kopf und Lipstick Tube-Tonabnehmer.

DANELECTRO GUITARLIN 4123

Danelectro, the New Jersey-based company set up by Nathan Daniel in the 40s, made a number of budget-price but effective guitars in the 50s and 60s. During the 50s it produced a number of models with the Silvertone brand for the Sears, Roebuck mail-order catalogue company. In 1958, having outgrown its original premises in Red Bank, the company moved to a new factory and offices in nearby Neptune. Shortly after, Danelectro introduced its short-horn Standard and Deluxe models, with laminated hardboard tops and vinyl-covered sides, and "lipstick tube" pickups. Jimmy Page later used a Standard 3021 for occasional slide work with Led Zeppelin. Next came the long-horn models, including the model 4123 shown here, also with lipstick pickups and featuring a white-to-bronze sunburst finish, an unusual long-horn lyre-shape body, and in this case no fewer than 32 frets.

Danelectro, in den 1940er-Jahren von Nathan Daniel in New Jersey gegründet, stellte in den 1950er- und 1960er-Jahren eine Reihe günstiger, aber effektiver Gitarren her. In den 1950er-Jahren produzierte das Unternehmen mehrere Modelle der Marke Silvertone für den Versandhandel Sears. 1958 war das Unternehmen so groß, dass es von seinem Sitz in Red Bank in neue Fabrik- und Büroräume nahe Neptune umziehen musste. Kurz darauf führte Danelectro die neuen Kurzhorn-Modelle Standard und Deluxe ein, mit laminierter Hartholzdecke, Vinyl beschichteten Zargen und „Lipstick Tube"-Tonabnehmern. Jimmy Page verwendete später eine Standard 3021 für gelegentliche Slides bei Led Zeppelin. Danach erschienen die Langhorn-Modelle, darunter die hier gezeigte 4123, ebenfalls mit Lipstick-Tonabnehmern und einem weiß-bronzefarbenen „Sunburst"-Finish, einem ungewöhnlichen Langhorn-Lyra geformten Korpus, und in diesem Fall sage und schreibe 32 Bünden.

CORAL SITAR

When MCA bought Danelectro in 1966, it introduced a new Danelectro-made brand, Coral, named after one of its record labels. The most unusual Coral instrument produced during the brand's short life was this electric sitar. After George Harrison used a real sitar on 'Norwegian Wood' in 1965, guitarists lined up to try the Indian instrument. The Coral Sitar was a relatively successful attempt to provide a sitar-like sound with a guitar's simpler playability. The key to its sitar imitation was an almost-flat plastic bridge, designed by Vinnie Bell (who also designed Danelectro's 12-string Bellzouki) to give a buzzy edge to the output. It also meant the Sitar was almost impossible to keep in tune. That did not stop its use on hits such as 'Green Tambourine' by The Lemon Pipers and 'Games People Play' by Joe South. This one is owned by Pink Floyd's David Gilmour.

Nachdem MCA Danelectro 1966 kaufte, wurde die neue Danelectro-Marke Coral gegründet, benannt nach einem von MCAs Plattenlabels. Das ungewöhnlichste Coral-Instrument, das während der kurzen Lebensdauer der Marke gebaut wurde, war diese E-Gitarre. Nachdem George Harrison für ‚Norwegian Wood' 1965 eine echte Sitar verwendet hatte, standen zahlreiche Gitarristen Schlange, um das indische Instrument selbst zu testen. Die Coral Sitar war ein recht erfolgreicher Versuch, einen sitarähnlichen Klang mit der einfachen Spielbarkeit einer Gitarre zu erzeugen. Die Ähnlichkeit zur Sitar lag an dem beinahe flachen Kunststoffsteg, designt von Vinnie Bell (der auch die 12-saitige Bellzouki von Danelectro entworfen hatte), um dem erzeugten Klang ein gewisses Summen zu verleihen. Deshalb war die Sitar allerdings auch nie ordentlich gestimmt. Trotzdem wurde sie für Hits wie ‚Green Tambourine' von den Lemon Pipers und ‚Games People Play' von Joe South verwendet. Dieses Exemplar gehört David Gilmour von Pink Floyd.

STEVE HOWE first used a Coral Sitar on the Yes album Close To The Edge in 1972. He occasionally used its specific sound with the band on stage, where it was bolted to a guitar "tree" that offered several guitars in playing position for fast changeovers during Yes's often marathon songs.

STEVE HOWE spielte auf dem Yes-Album Close To The Edge von 1972 eine Coral Sitar. Auch bei Konzerten mit der Band nutzte er gelegentlich ihren eigenwilligen Klang. Die Coral Sitar war mit zahlreichen anderen Gitarren an einem Gestell befestigt, damit Howe während der häufig langen Stücke schnell das Instrument wechseln konnte.

GIBSON SG STANDARD

Eric Clapton bought an SG Standard in the 60s to replace his Les Paul Standard, of which had already been stolen. He played the guitar pictured on stage in the late 60s with Cream, and he also used it in the studio during that period, notably to record the Disraeli Gears and Wheels Of Fire albums. He had a Dutch group of artists, The Fool, paint the guitar with an elaborate psychedelic scene. Todd Rundgren owned the guitar from 1974 to 2000, and it is now in a private collection.

Eric Clapton kaufte in den 1960er-Jahren eine SG Standard als Ersatz für seine Les Paul Standard, die ihm gestohlen worden war. Er spielte die hier abgebildete Gitarre Ende der 1960er-Jahren auf Cream-Konzerten und setzte sie in dieser Zeit auch für Studioaufnahmen ein, vor allem für die Alben Disraeli Gears und Wheels Of Fire. Eine holländische Künstlergruppe namens The Fool bemalte die Gitarre mit einer aufwändig psychedelischen Szene. Von 1974 bis 2000 war die Gitarre im Besitz von Todd Rundgren, heute ist sie Teil einer Privatsammlung.

1963 – GIBSON SG STANDARD

ERIC CLAPTON is most associated today with the Fender Stratocaster, but the instruments he used before he switched to the Strat around 1970 are the subject of deep analysis and heated debate by guitar fans. His pre-Strat electric choices included Telecaster, Les Paul, SG, Explorer, Firebird, and ES-335.

ERIC CLAPTON wird heutzutage vor allem mit einer Fender Stratocaster in Verbindung gebracht. Die Modelle, die er vor seinem Wechsel zur Strat um 1970 spielte, sind sehr umstritten von seinen Fans. Dazu gerhörten u.a. Telecaster, Les Paul, SG, Explorer, Firebird und ES-335.

FRANK ZAPPA played a number of guitars and, like many musicians, modified them to his own taste. He started in the Mothers Of Invention with a Gibson ES-5 Switchmaster and soon moved to SGs, and later he played Les Pauls and Strats. Zappa died aged 52 in 1993; 20 years later, Gibson issued a tribute "Roxy" SG.

FRANK ZAPPA spielte, wie viele andere Musiker auch, mehrere Gitarren und modifizierte sie nach seinem Geschmack. Er begann bei den Mothers Of Invention mit einer Gibson ES-5 Switchmaster und wechselte kurz darauf zu den SGs. Später spielte er Les Pauls und Strats. Zappa starb 1993 im Alter von 52 Jahren; 20 Jahre nach seinem Tod brachte Gibson ihm zu Ehren eine „Roxy" SG heraus.

GIBSON SG/LES PAUL CUSTOM

Here is another early SG/Les Paul, which combines the new SG sculpted-body design with the shortlived Les Paul markings: here we can see "Les Paul Custom" on a plate between the neck pickup and the end of the neck. During 1963, the Les Paul markings were dropped and the model would continue simply as the SG Custom. The main reason for the loss of Les Paul's name was because Paul did not want royalties from guitar sales tied up with his divorce from Mary Ford, and Gibson felt that Paul was a less valuable endorser with his popularity in decline. The Custom was an upscale model with three humbuckers, gold-plated hardware, and many luxurious appointments.

Dies ist noch eine frühe SG/Les Paul, bei der der neue SG geformte Korpus noch mit Les Paul Aufschrift versehen war. Hier steht „Les Paul Custom" zwischen Hals-Pickup und Halsende. 1963 wurde die Aufschrift Les Paul komplett weggelassen und stattdessen nur noch SG Custom verwendet. Hauptgrund dafür war, dass Les Paul keine Tantiemen aus Gitarrenverkäufen wollte, da er sich gerade von Mary Ford scheiden ließ. Darüber hinaus erschien er durch seine schwindende Popularität als Werbeträger nicht mehr geeignet. Die Custom war ein hochwertigeres Modell mit drei Humbucker-Pickups, vergoldeter Hardware und vielen luxuriösen Extras.

1961 – GIBSON
SG/LES PAUL CUSTOM

1961 – GIBSON
SG/LES PAUL STANDARD

GIBSON SG/LES PAUL STANDARD

Gibson introduced its SG design in 1961 to replace the original Les Paul solidbody models, using a new and highly sculpted double-cutaway body design. At first, the company continued to call them Les Pauls, and these early guitars with the new design are known as SG/Les Paul models, like the Standard pictured here – note the "Les Paul" on the truss-rod cover at the headstock. This example has the shortlived sideways-action vibrato that Gibson used on some guitars at the time, which required a different movement to the customary up-and-down vibrato. Gibson replaced the unit with its Vibrola during 1962. By 1963, the new-design guitars officially continued with the SG name alone, and they are still in production today.

1961 führte Gibson sein SG-Design ein, um die ursprünglichen Les Paul Solidbody-Modelle durch einen neuen, aufwändig geformten Korpus mit zwei Cutaways zu ersetzen. Zunächst bezeichnete Gibson die Gitarren weiterhin als Les Pauls. Diese ersten Modelle mit dem neuen Design werden auch SG/Les Paul genannt, wie diese hier abgebildete Standard – man beachte den „Les Paul"-Schriftzug auf der Abdeckung am Kopf. Dieses Modell verfügt über das damals nur kurzzeitig für einige Gitarren verwendete seitlich angebrachte Vibrato, das eine andere Handbewegung erforderlich machte als bei dem sonst üblichen Vibrato-Hebel. Gibson ersetzte das Bauteil 1962 durch sein Vibrola. Ab 1963 wurden die neuen Designs offiziell unter der Bezeichnung SG verkauft und werden bis heute hergestellt.

TONY IOMMI is best known for playing SG-Style guitars in Black Sabbath, including a much-used guitar that was built for him in the mid 70s by the guitar maker John Diggins (Jaydee) in Birmingham, England. Gibson issued an Iommi signature SG in 1998 and an Epiphone version in 2003.

TONY IOMMI ist vor allem für das Spielen von SG-Gitarren bei Black Sabbath bekannt. Eines der Instrumente ist eine viel gespielte Gitarre, die der Gitarrenbauer John Diggins (Jaydee) in Birmingham für ihn Mitte der 1970er-Jahre baute. Gibson brachte 1998 ein Iommi Signature-Modell SG und 2003 eine Epiphone Version heraus.

ROSETTA
THARPE

HANK MARVIN and his band The Shadows caused more British boys to form their own groups in the early 60s than anyone else. The bespectacled Marvin mostly played a Fender Stratocaster to aid his clean, melodic style, but for a brief period he used a UK-made substitute, the Burns Marvin.

HANK MARVIN und seine Band The Shadows inspirierten in den 1960er-Jahren mehr junge Männer in Großbritannien dazu, ihre eigene Band zu gründen als jede andere Band. Marvin spielte meistens auf einer Fender Stratocaster, die seinen klaren, melodischen Stil unterstrich. Für kurze Zeit lang spielte er auch auf einer in England gebauten Gitarre, der Burns Marvin.

1964 – BURNS MARVIN

BURNS MARVIN

Burns was the most successful British guitar maker of the 60s, and an endorsement in 1964 from Hank Marvin, the popular lead guitarist of The Shadows who usually plated a Stratocaster, did the brand no harm. The Marvin model combined Fender-like features and original ideas. Other key Burns models of the period included the Bison, Split Sonic, and Vista Sonic. Many a budding British guitarist started on a Burns, or on a guitar from other British brands of the period such as Vox or Watkins. Burns was bought by the US company Baldwin in 1965. The brand has had many comebacks since, and at the time of writing a variety of Burns models, almost all with a vintage vibe, are produced by Burns London Ltd.

Burns war der erfolgreichste britische Gitarrenbauer der 1960er-Jahre. 1964 wurde Hank Marvin, Lead-Gitarrist von den Shadows, der sonst immer eine Stratocaster spielte, Werbeträger der Marke. Das Marvin-Modell kombinierte fenderartige Züge mit eigenen Ideen. Andere wichtige Burns-Modelle aus dieser Zeit sind u. a. die Bison, die Split Sonic und die Vista Sonic. Viele britische Gitarristen starteten ihre Karriere mit einer Burns oder einer anderen britischen Marke aus dieser Zeit wie z. B. Vox oder Watkins. 1965 wurde Burns vom amerikanischen Unternehmen Baldwin übernommen. Die Marke feierte seitdem so manches Comeback. Verschiedene Burns-Modelle, fast alle im Vintage-Look, wurden bis zur Veröffentlichung dieses Buches von Burns London Ltd. hergestellt.

GUITAR ORGAN

VOX GUITAR ORGAN

The Vox brand may be better known on amplifiers, but at one time the original British company also applied it to guitars, some built at home, others in Italy. The experimental Guitar Organ had a bewildering set of controls, hardly surprising when the ambitious idea was to put the sound generators of a Vox Continental organ into a Phantom guitar. Vox wired the frets to tone modules in the body, and as a string touched a fret, the circuit was completed and a note sounded. Or at least, that was the theory. Few of the Guitar Organs were made, and few worked convincingly. It would not be until the guitar-synthesizer combinations that began in the 80s and the later developments in digital guitar modelling that convincing keyboard sounds and other voices were made reliably with a guitar.

Die Marke Vox ist für ihre Verstärker sicher besser bekannt, doch es gab eine Zeit, als das britische Unternehmen auch Gitarren herstellte, einige davon in Großbritannien, andere in Italien produziert. Die Regler der experimentellen Guitar Organ waren ziemlich verwirrend, was auch kaum verwunderlich ist, da sich Vox in den Kopf gesetzt hatte, die Klangerzeuger einer Vox Continental Orgel in eine Phantom-Gitarre zu verpflanzen. Vox verdrahtete die Bünde mit Tone-Modulen im Korpus, und wenn eine Saite einen Bund berührte, war der Kreislauf komplett und ein Ton erklang – so die Theorie. Es wurden nur wenige Guitar Organs hergestellt und kaum eine funktionierte anständig. Überzeugende Keyboard-Klänge und andere Stimmen wurden erst mit den Gitarre-Synthesizer-Kombinationen der 1980er-Jahre bzw. späteren Entwicklungen von Digitalgitarren-Modellen möglich.

IAN CURTIS is not remembered for his guitar playing, with the six-string duties in Joy Division mostly allocated to Bernard Sumner. But the singer was an occasional and (maybe) reluctant guitarist, using a few eye-catching instruments on stage, including a 60s Vox Phantom VI Special. Curtis died in 1980 aged 23.

IAN CURTIS, der Sänger von Joy Division, geht nicht für sein Gitarrenspiel in die Geschichte ein. Das übernahm zumeist Bandkollege Bernard Sumner. Der Sänger griff nur vereinzelt und eher zögerlich zur Gitarre, doch wenn, spielte er auffällige Modelle wie die Vox Phantom VI Special aus den 1960er-Jahren. Curtis starb 1980 im Alter von 23 Jahren.

STRATOCASTER

JIMI HENDRIX got his first Fender Stratocaster in 1966, possibly influenced by one of his heroes, Curtis Mayfield. At first, Hendrix used rosewood-fingerboard models, in sunburst, white, or black, and in his final years (1968 to '70) he played two maple-board models, one in white, the other in black.

Seine erste Fender Stratocaster kaufte sich JIMI HENDRIX 1966. Es ist gut möglich, dass er sich bei der Entscheidung von einem seiner Helden, Curtis Mayfield, beeinflussen ließ. Hendrix spielte zunächst auf Modellen mit Palisandergriffbrett in Sunburst, Weiß oder Schwarz. In seinen letzten Jahren (1968 bis 1970) spielte er zwei Modelle mit Ahorngriffbrett, die eine Gitarre in Weiß, die andere in Schwarz.

FENDER STRATOCASTER

Here is another example of Fender's custom colour guitars of the 50s and 60s, which provide many a collector's prized possession today. Some of the paints Fender used were from DuPont's Duco nitro-cellulose lines, such as this sonic blue example; others, for example lake placid blue metallic, were from DuPont's Lucite acrylic lines. The Stratocaster took a dip in popularity during the 60s, but the model's fortunes were revived later in the decade when Jimi Hendrix played Strats so spectacularly. The 70s then proved a Strat-filled decade, with players such as Eric Clapton, Jeff Beck, Curtis Mayfield, Ritchie Blackmore, Ernie Isley, and Mark Knopfler all employing this versatile instrument to great effect.

Dies ist ein weiteres Beispiel für Fenders bunte Custom-Gitarren der 1950er- und 1960er-Jahre, die von Sammlern heute wie Schätze gehütet werden. Einige der von Fender verwendeten Farben waren die Nitrocellulose haltigen Duco-Lacke von DuPont, wie zum Beispiel dieses Sonic Blue. Für andere Farben wie Lake Placid Blue Metallic wurden die Lucite-Acryllacke von DuPont verwendet. Während die Stratocaster in den 1960er-Jahren ein kleines Tal durchschritt, war das Comeback Ende des Jahrzehnts umso größer, als Jimi Hendrix mit Strat-Modellen spektakuläre Stunts auf der Bühne ablieferte. In den 1970er-Jahren war die Strat nicht mehr wegzudenken: Musiker wie Eric Clapton, Jeff Beck, Curtis Mayfield, Ritchie Blackmore, Ernie Isley und Mark Knopfler wussten dieses abwechslungsreiche Instrument wirkungsstark zum Einsatz zu bringen.

FENDER TELECASTER PAISLEY RED

This Telecaster evokes the 60s more than most thanks to an experiment with an unusual finish that Fender made in 1968 and 1969. The company's designers had fun applying self-adhesive wallpaper with a pink paisley or blue flower pattern, entirely visible thanks to a special see-through plastic pickguard. These shortlived models were in contrast to the view held by some collectors that once Fender was bought by CBS in 1965, the company's guitars became boring and predictable. Certainly there were some changes made by CBS that reflected badly on the guitars produced after 1965, but the Paisley Red and Blue Flower Telecasters were not among them.

Diese Telecaster ruft mehr als die meisten Modelle Erinnerungen an die 1960er-Jahre wach, dank eines Experiments mit einem ungewöhnlichen Finish, das Fender 1968 und 1969 produzierte. Die Designer des Unternehmens hatten viel Spaß, die Gitarren mit selbstklebender Folie mit rosa oder blauen Blumenmustern zu verschönern, die dank des durchsichtigen Plastik-Schlagbretts auch als Ganzes zu bewundern sind. Diese Modelle, die nicht lange hergestellt wurden, bildeten einen Kontrast zur Meinung einiger Sammler, Fender-Gitarren wären nach der Übernahme durch CBS im Jahr 1965 langweilig und vorhersehbar geworden. Sicher, CBS nahm einige Änderungen vor, die sich schlecht auf die Gitarren nach 1965 auswirkten, doch die Paisley Red und Blue Flower Telecasters gehörten nicht dazu.

JAMES BURTON has been one of the most influential Telecaster players of all time. He first came to attention with Ricky Nelson in the 50s, playing concise cameo solos, but his big break came when he joined Elvis Presley's band in 1969, where he used a psychedelic-finished Paisley Red Tele.

JAMES BURTON war einer der einflussreichsten Telecaster-Spieler aller Zeiten. In den 1950er-Jahren wurde er erstmals für seine prägnanten Soli bei Auftritten mit Ricky Nelson bekannt. Den großen Durchbruch hatte er jedoch 1969, als er Mitglied in Elvis Presleys Band wurde, wo er eine Paisley Red Tele mit psychedelischem Muster spielte.

GIBSON FIREBIRD V

With Fenders as popular as ever, Gibson looked for a competing design, even as its SG solidbody continued to sell. The result was the Firebird line, new for 1963, devised by American car designer Ray Dietrich. The four models were numbered I, III, V, and VII, each with different appointments but the same neck-through-body design, where the mahogany and walnut neck continues through to the end of the body, completed with added mahogany wings. They had a similar look to Fender's latest offset-waist body shape. The headstock featured six reverse-facing banjo-style Kluson tuners, and the V model had two mini-humbucking pickups and a Deluxe Gibson/Maestro Vibrola tailpiece. Sunburst was the standard finish, but Gibson offered ten optional finishes, including cardinal red, like this example. This first style of Firebird, made until 1965, is known as the reverse body thanks to its unusual shape.

Mit dem Erfolg der Fender-Gitarren wollte Gibson ein Konkurrenz-Modell auf den Markt bringen, obwohl sich die SG-Solidbodies weiter gut verkauften. Das Ergebnis: Die Firebird-Serie von 1963, entwickelt vom Detroiter Automobil-Designer Ray Dietrich. Die vier Modelle wurden I, III, V und VII benannt, mit jeweils unterschiedlichen Features, jedoch dem gleichen Design mit durchgehendem Hals (Neck-thru), d.h. der Hals aus Mahagoni und Walnuss verläuft bis zum Korpus-Ende, abgeschlossen durch angefügte Mahagoni-Flügel. Sie hatten Ähnlichkeit mit dem neuen Fender Offset-Waist Design (versetzte Taille). Der Kopf besaß sechs nach hinten zeigende Kluson-Mechaniken im Banjo-Stil, und das V-Modell besaß zwei kleine Humbucker-Pickups und einen Deluxe Gibson/Maestro Vibrola Saitenhalter. Das gängige Finish war „Sunburst", Gibson hatte jedoch zehn weitere Farboptionen im Angebot, darunter dieses Kardinalrot. Die erste Firebird, die bis 1965 hergestellt wurde, wird aufgrund ihrer ungewöhnlichen Form auch „Reverse Body" genannt.

GIBSON FIREBIRD I

It became clear to Gibson that sales of the first reverse-style Firebird were not matching the high production costs of these instruments, and in 1965 they were dropped from the line. The company issued a revised design, known now as the non-reverse type thanks to its slightly more conventional body shape. The new Firebirds had P-90 pickups on the cheaper models, such as this I finished in polaris white, and a more conventional Fender-like headstock with regular tuners, unlike the banjo types of the reverse Firebirds. Gibson dropped the complicated neck-through construction of the originals, relying instead on its conventional glued-in neck joint. The new Firebirds lasted in the Gibson line until they, too, were dropped in 1969.

Gibson erkannte, dass die Verkäufe der ersten reverse-Version der Firebird nicht die hohen Produktionskosten deckten, woraufhin sie 1965 aus dem Programm genommen wurde. Das Unternehmen brachte das Modell in abgeänderter Form heraus, heute auch non-reverse Version genannt, aufgrund seines etwas konventionelleren Korpus. Die neuen, günstigeren Firebird-Modelle besaßen Pickups vom Typ P-90, wie diese I in Polaris White, und einen konventionelleren fenderartigen Kopf mit üblichen Mechaniken anstatt den Banjo-Mechaniken der reverse-Firebirds. Gibson tauschte die komplizierte Neck-thru-Konstruktion der Originale gegen konventionelle verleimte Hals-Korpus-Übergänge. Die neuen Firebirds wurden bis 1969 produziert und anschließend ebenfalls aus dem Programm genommen.

GIBSON EDS-1275 DOUBLE 12

Double-neck electrics first appeared in the 50s from Stratosphere and Bigsby, and Gibson joined the club in 1958 with a pair of hollowbody double-necks. In 1962, a new solidbody Gibson version appeared, based on the company's new SG design. The idea is to offer the use of six-string and 12-string necks without having to change guitars, in live performance, although the price for this versatility is a heavy guitar that weighs on the shoulder. A rarer version was the EDM-1275, which offered a six-string guitar neck and a short "octave" or "mandolin" six-string neck. This example, finished in white rather than the more common cherry, is owned by Steve Howe, who used it onstage with Yes (and who changed the original tuners). Other famous users of Gibson double-necks included Jimmy Page, in Led Zeppelin, and Alex Lifeson, in Rush.

E-Gitarren mit Doppelhals gab es in den 1950er-Jahren zunächst nur von Stratosphere und Bigsby. 1958 trat Gibson dem Club mit zwei Hollowbody-Doppelhalsgitarren bei. 1962 kam eine neue Solidbody auf den Markt, die auf dem neuen SG-Design der Firma basierte. Musiker sollten bei Konzerten eine 6- und eine 12-saitige Gitarre spielen können, ohne das Instrument wechseln zu müssen. Nachteil ist das Gewicht, das schwer auf den Schultern liegt. Eine seltenere Version war die EDM-1275, mit einem 6-saitigen Gitarrenhals und einer kurzen oktavreinen bzw. einer "Mandolinen" Halsform mit sechs Saiten. Dieses Beispiel in Weiß statt dem sonst eher üblichen Kirschrot gehört Steve Howe, der die Gitarre bei Yes-Auftritten spielte und die Original-Mechaniken austauschte. Andere berühmte Nutzer von Gibson Doppelhals-Modellen waren u. a. Jimmy Page mit Led Zeppelin und Alex Lifeson mit Rush.

JOHNNY WINTER played his '63 Gibson Firebird since he bought it used for a few hundred dollars in the early 70s. Winter used other Firebirds and a few more guitars, but that original 'Bird', which he used mostly for slide, remained a favourite until his death in 2014 at the age of 70.

JOHNNY WINTER spielte eine 1963er Gibson Firebird, nachdem er sie Anfang der 1970er-Jahre für ein paar Hundert Dollar gebraucht gekauft hatte. Winter besaß noch mehr Firebirds und andere Modelle, doch diese Original-„Bird", die er meist für Slides einsetzte, blieb bis zu seinem Tod 2014 eine seiner Lieblingsgitarren. Er wurde 70 Jahre alt.

BRIAN JONES played a number of guitars in his short life, including a reverse-body Firebird in the mid 60s and this non-reverse Firebird VII, pictured on-stage here at an apparently security-conscious 1966 Stones date, just a few years before Jones's premature death in the summer of '69.

BRIAN JONES spielte während seines kurzen Lebens eine ganze Reihe unterschiedlicher Gitarren, darunter eine Reverse-Body Firebird Mitte der 1960er-Jahre und diese Non-Reverse Firebird VII. Das Foto stammt von einem Stones-Konzert von 1966, als die Band offenbar auf erhöhte Sicherheit setzte, nur drei Jahre bevor Jones im Sommer 1969 viel zu früh ums Leben kam.

ALEX
LIFESON

VENTURES MODEL

MOSRITE VENTURES MODEL

Mosrite began business in California in the late 50s, founded by Semie Moseley. The brand's big break came in the following decade with the Ventures Model. The Ventures were the biggest US instrumental guitar band, with US hits such as 'Perfidia' and 'Walk – Don't Run'. Moseley lent a guitar to Ventures guitarist Nokie Edwards, and the group and the guitar firm soon collaborated to design a signature model. A credit line for Mosrite on one of the group's album covers alone created an enormous demand for the new instrument, launched in 1963. This first style of Ventures model is known as the Mark I; a slightly later version, with simpler design, is known as the Mark II and was the type played by Johnny Ramone in the 70s.

Semie Moseley gründete Mosrite Ende der 1950er-Jahre in Kalifornien. Der große Durchbruch gelang der Marke im darauf-folgenden Jahrzehnt mit The Ventures, der damals erfolgreichsten Instrumental-Rock-Band in den USA mit Hits wie ‚Perfidia' und ‚Walk – Don't Run'. Als Moseley dem Ventures-Gitarristen Nokie Edwards eine Gitarre auslieh, kam es kurz darauf zur Kooperation und dem Design eines Signature-Modells. Durch Mosrites namentliche Nennung auf einem Albumco-ver der Band stieg die Nachfrage nach dem neuen Modell von 1963 enorm. Diese erste Version des Ventures-Modells heißt Mark I. Eine etwas spätere, einfachere Variante, die Mark II, wurde in den 1970er-Jahren von Johnny Ramone gespielt.

JOHNNY RAMONE was famous not only for his guitar sound that fuelled The Ramones but also for his unusual Mosrite guitars. He got his first, a blue Ventures Mark II, in the mid 70s, and when that was stolen in '77 he replaced it with a white Mark II. Ramone died in 2004 aged 55.

JOHNNY RAMONE war nicht nur für seinen Gitarrensound berühmt, der seine Band The Ramones antrieb, sondern auch für seine ungewöhnlichen Mosrite-Gitarren. Seine erste Mosrite, eine blaue Ventures Mark II, bekam er Mitte der 1970er-Jahre. Als sie 1977 gestohlen wurde, kaufte er sich eine weiße Mark II. Ramone starb 2004 im Alter von 55 Jahren.

LES PAUL DELUXE

GIBSON LES PAUL DELUXE

Despite the growing popularity of old guitars in the late 60s – which were by now called vintage guitars – Gibson did not act immediately to reissue its obsolete models that were causing most excitement: 50s Les Pauls, Flying Vs, Explorers, and so on. When it reintroduced old-style Les Pauls in 1968, it did not issue the one everyone wanted: the sunburst 50s model. It also managed to tangle wires with the release of another old-style Les Paul in 1969, which it named the Deluxe model. This had a sunburst finish and humbucking pickups – but mini-humbuckers, not the original types. Not a bad guitar, but not in correct original style. It wasn't until the 80s that Gibson grasped what was required, and in more recent years the company has made many reissue models that have gradually moved closer to the allure of those original 50s instruments.

Obwohl alte Gitarren Ende der 1960er-Jahre immer beliebter wurden – die zu dem Zeitpunkt bereits Vintage-Gitarren genannt wurden – ließ Gibson sich Zeit, ausgemusterte Modelle, die für neue Begeisterung sorgten, neu aufzulegen: Les Pauls aus den 1950ern, Flying Vs, Explorers etc. Als das Unternehmen 1968 Vintage-Les Pauls neu einführte, fehlte das entscheidende Modell, das alle wollten: das Sunburst-Modell aus den 1950er-Jahren. Außerdem gab es 1969 bei der Neuauflage einer weiteren alten Les Paul, dem Deluxe-Modell, ein Drähtegewirr. Die Deluxe hatte ein „Sunburst"-Finish und Humbucker-Pickups – allerdings kleine Humbucker und nicht die Originale. Keine schlechte Gitarre, doch eben nicht originalgetreu. Erst in den 1980er-Jahren verstand Gibson, was wirklich gefragt war. Seit einiger Zeit bringt das Unternehmen nun Neuauflagen heraus, die dem Reiz der Original 50er-Instrumente immer näher kommen.

ADAM GRANDUCIEL formed The War On Drugs with Kurt Vile in Philadelphia in 2005 and found fame with their second album, Slave Ambient, in 2011. Granduciel has a refined taste for retro guitars, favouring a '76 Les Paul Deluxe as his main stage axe and using instruments by Harmony, Burns, and Silvertone.

ADAM GRANDUCIEL gründete 2005 zusammen mit Kurt Vile in Philadelphia die Band The War On Drugs. Mit ihrem zweiten Album Slave Ambient von 2011 wurden sie berühmt. Granduciel hat eine Vorliebe für Retrogitarren, auf der Bühne spielt er hauptsächlich eine Les Paul Deluxe von 1976 sowie Instrumente von Harmony, Burns und Silvertone.

DAN ARMSTRONG SEE-THROUGH

KEITH RICHARDS has played almost as many guitars as there are Stones songs. His favourites in the early years included a Harmony Meteor, an Epiphone Casino, and a Gibson Les Paul Standard. He still loves Telecasters and Les Paul Juniors, but there have been oddballs, too, such as a see-through plastic Ampeg.

KEITH RICHARDS hat fast so viele Gitarren gespielt wie es Stones-Songs gibt. Seine Lieblingsgitarren aus den ersten Jahren waren eine Harmony Meteor, eine Epiphone Casino und eine Gibson Les Paul Standard. Er hat noch immer eine Vorliebe für Telecasters und Les Paul Juniors, spielte jedoch auch schräge Instrumente wie eine durchsichtige Ampeg aus Plastik.

AMPEG DAN ARMSTRONG SEE-THROUGH

Everett Hull set up Ampeg in New York in the 40s to make amplifiers and double-bass pickups. In the late 60s, Ampeg hired a local repairman named Dan Armstrong to design a new line of electric guitars. Armstrong carved bodies from blocks of clear plastic, intending to make the result distinctive as much as to exploit the sonic potential of the material. He also provided the instrument with six slide-in/slide-out pickups labelled Rock, Country, and Jazz, with a Treble and Bass variety of each. The imaginative See-Through guitar and its matching bass lasted little more than a year in production, brought down by conservative guitarists (Keith Richards excepted) and an expensive, time-consuming production process. Ampeg's instructions suggested that if the plastic body became scratched, the best way to repair it was to polish it with toothpaste.

Everett Hull gründete Ampeg in den 1940er-Jahren in New York, um Verstärker und Tonabnehmer für Kontrabässe herzustellen. Ende der 1960er-Jahre stellte Ampeg einen Mechaniker aus der Nachbarschaft namens Dan Armstrong ein, der eine Reihe neuer E-Gitarren entwerfen sollte. Armstrong schnitzte Korpusse aus durchsichtigen Kunststoffblöcken, um ihnen einerseits ein einmaliges Aussehen zu verleihen und andererseits, das klangliche Potential des Materials voll auszuschöpfen. Er verpasste dem Instrument außerdem sechs Slide-in/Slide-out-Tonabnehmer mit den Bezeichnungen Rock, Country und Jazz, mit je einer Treble- und einer Bass-Variante. Die fantasievolle See-Through und der dazu passende Bass wurden nur etwas mehr als ein Jahr hergestellt. Grund dafür waren konservative Gitarristen (mit Ausnahme von Keith Richards) und der teure, zeitaufwändige Herstellungsprozess. In Ampegs Gebrauchsanweisung stand, bei Kratzern sollte man den Plastikkorpus am besten mit Zahnpasta polieren.

VELENO ORIGINAL

John Veleno, an engineer and guitar teacher, began building his handmade carved-metal instruments around 1970, selling them individually to guitarists who passed through Florida on tour. His customers included Todd Rundgren, Lou Reed, Marc Bolan, Jeff Lynne, and Ace Frehley. The guitars were made almost entirely from aluminium, and the one pictured has a rare combination of three pickups and a gold anodised finish. It has Veleno's distinctive split "V" head-stock with a red jewel. One estimate of Veleno's production puts the number of Originals made between about 1970 and 1977 at a maximum of 185. Veleno also developed a small Traveller guitar and made two Egyptian "ankh"-shape guitars for Rundgren.

Der Ingenieur und Gitarrenlehrer John Veleno baute seine ersten handgefertigten Aluminiumgitarren um 1970. Er verkaufte sie einzeln an Gitarristen, die gerade durch Florida tourten. Zu seiner Kundschaft gehörten Todd Rundgren, Lou Reed, Marc Bolan, Jeff Lynne und Ace Frehley. Die Gitarren waren fast vollständig aus Aluminium gefertigt und das hier abgebildete Modell verfügt über eine seltene Kombination aus drei Tonabnehmern und einer golden anodisch oxidierten Oberfläche. Es besitzt Velenos charakteristisch geteilten „V"-Kopf mit einem roten Edelstein. Geschätzt stellte Veleno zwischen 1970 und 1977 maximal 185 Originals her. Er entwickelte auch eine kleine Traveller-Gitarre und baute für Rundgren zwei ägyptische „Ankh"-förmige Gitarren.

TODD RUNDGREN is best known as a songwriter, singer, and producer, but he's also a keen guitarist who has owned some interesting guitars over the years. Two of the most distinctive were the ex-Clapton SG Standard painted by The Fool, and two "ankh"-shaped metal guitars made for him by Veleno.

TODD RUNDGREN ist vor allem als Songschreiber, Sänger und Produzent bekannt. Er spielt aber auch ehrgeizig Gitarre und hat mit den Jahren ein paar interessante Modelle angesammelt. Die herausstechendsten waren die von The Fool bemalte Clapton SG Standard und zwei ‚Ankh'-förmige Metallgitarren, die Veleno für ihn angefertigt hat.

During KERRY KING'S early days in Slayer, he and fellow guitarist Jeff Hanneman mixed punk and metal to redefine thrash metal, and King developed his unique shrieking lead sound and superfast riffs. He has played B.C. Rich guitars from the start, and the company has issued a number of King signature models.

Die frühen Jahre der von KERRY KING und Jeff Hanneman gegründeten Band Slayer sind geprägt von einer Mischung aus Punk und Metal, die Thrash-Metal neu definierte. King entwickelte während dieser Zeit seinen eigensinnigen, schrillen Lead-Sound und superschnelle Riffs. Er spielte von Anfang an B.C. Rich-Gitarren, sodass das Unternehmen mehrere King Signature-Modelle herausbrachte.

1979 – B.C. RICH
MOCKINGBIRD STANDARD

B.C. RICH MOCKINGBIRD STANDARD

Bernardo Rico helped define the style of "pointy" metal-inclined guitars in his Los Angeles factories in the 70s and 80s. Rico played classical guitar at first, and when he started B.C Rich in the 60s he made acoustic guitars. But from the mid 70s, he developed his own electric style. Models followed like the through-neck Mockingbird shown here, as well as the ten-string Bich and other pointy devils such as the Warlock, Stealth, and Ironbird. Rico licensed his brand to Class Axe in 1989 and regained control in 1994, devising new models and revised versions of his classics in Hisperia, California. He died in 1999, after which B.C. Rich was sold to Hanser.

In den 1970er- und 1980er-Jahren half Bernardo Rico dabei, den Stil der spitz zulaufenden Metal-Gitarre in seinen Fabriken in Los Angeles mit zu definieren. Rico spielte zunächst klassische Gitarre, und als er B.C. Rich in den 1960er-Jahren gründete, baute er Akustikgitarren. Doch ab Mitte der 1970er-Jahre entwickelte er seinen eigenen E-Gitarrenstil. Es folgten Modelle wie die hier gezeigte Neck-thru Mockingbird, die zehnsaitige Bich und andere spitz zulaufende Teufelsgitarren wie die Warlock, Stealth und Ironbird. 1989 lizenzierte Rico seine Marke an Class Axe. 1994 übenahm er wieder selbst die Kontrolle und produzierte neue Modelle mit veränderte Versionen seiner Klassiker in Hisperia, Kalifornien. Nach seinem Tod 1999 wurde B.C. Rich an Hanser verkauft.

ICEMAN IC210

IBANEZ ICEMAN IC210

A leap forward for Ibanez innovation came with the angular Iceman, launched in 1975 and at first known, suitably, as The Flash. The new model was influenced by Gibson's Firebird and by Rickenbacker, but it marked the Japanese maker's first real stab at something fresh and original. In the early 70s, Ibanez was known for its copies of Gibson classics until legal action and the company's own inclinations brought a halt to that activity. The first Iceman models developed into the later IC210, like this one, with an unusual three-coil pickup and four-way tone switch. Paul Stanley of Kiss was the most famous Iceman player, and Ibanez issued a signature version for him in 1978, the PS10. Reissue Iceman models appeared first in the 80s and 90s and also in recent years.

In Sachen Innovation machte Ibanez einen Riesensatz nach vorn, als 1975 die kantige Iceman erschien. Das neue Modell, das passenderweise „The Flash" genannt wurde, war beeinflusst von Gibsons Firebird und von Rickenbacker, doch es war das erste wirklich frische und eigene Model des japanischen Gitarrenbauers. Anfang der 1970er-Jahre war Ibanez bekannt für die Nachahmung klassischer Gibson-Modelle, bis Gibson rechtlich dagegen vorging und Ibanez diese Aktivitäten sofort unterband. Die ersten Iceman-Modelle entwickelten sich zur späteren IC210 (siehe Bild), mit einem ungewöhnlichen Triple-Coil-Pickup und einem Vierweg-Tonschalter. Paul Stanley von Kiss war der berühmteste Iceman-Spieler, und Ibanez brachte 1978 mit der PS10 eine Signature-Version für ihn auf den Markt. Erste, neu aufgelegte Iceman-Modelle erschienen in den 1980er- und 1990er-Jahren sowie in jüngster Zeit.

PAUL STANLEY of Kiss has always favoured ostentatious guitars, in keeping with his band's outrageous image. Ibanez issued a signature model for him in 1978 based on the angular Iceman model, and the following year Stanley had Ibanez make a dazzling custom version with a cracked-mirror effect on the front of the body.

PAUL STANLEY hat immer schon auffällige Gitarren bevorzugt, die perfekt zum skandalösen Image seiner Band Kiss passten. Ibanez brachte 1978 ein Signature-Modell für ihn heraus, das auf dem eckigen Iceman-Modell basierte. Im Jahr darauf brachte Stanley Ibanez dazu, eine maßgefertigte Version mit dem Special Effect eines zerbrochenen Spiegels auf der Decke für ihn zu bauen.

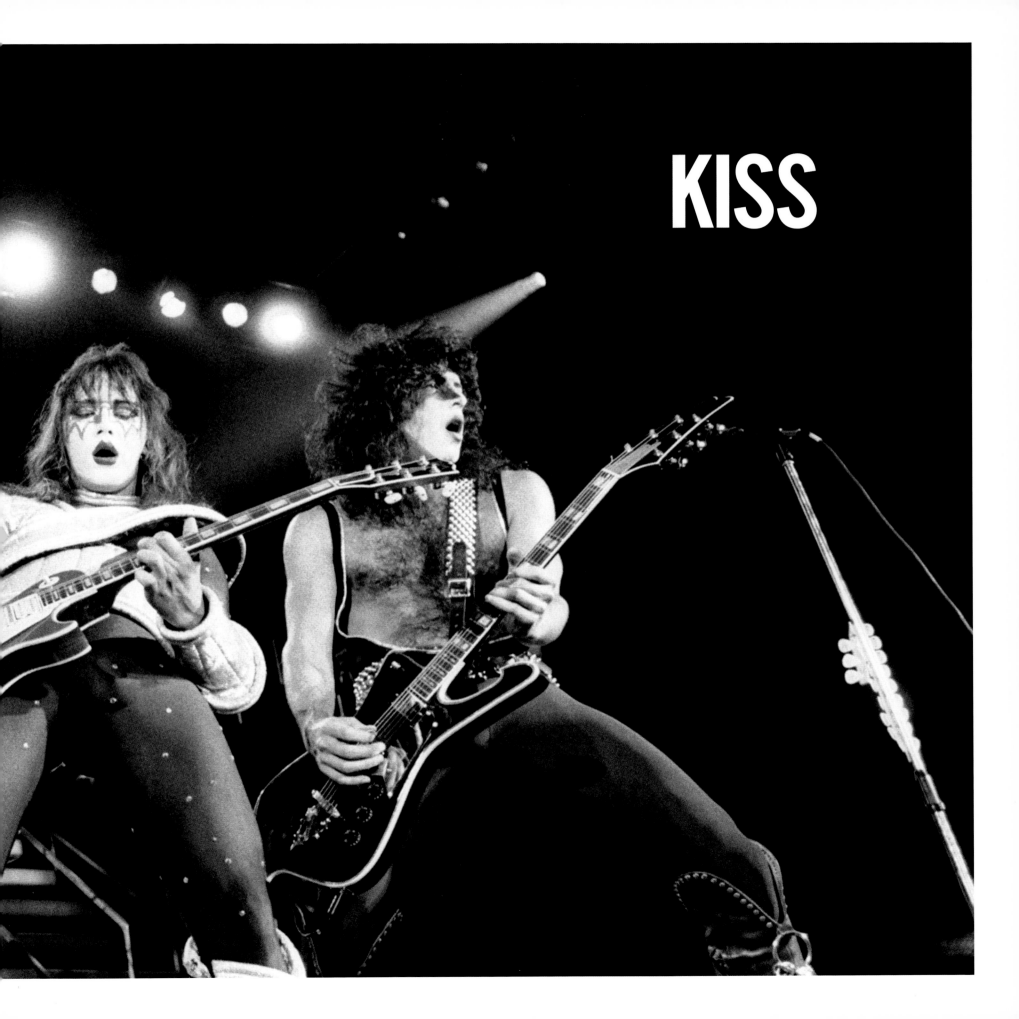

KISS

HAMER SUNBURST

Hamer was set up in Chicago in the mid 70s by a group of partners that included Paul Hamer and Jol Dantzig. Their first guitars were based on Gibson oldies and included the Standard, developed from the Explorer, and this Sunburst, introduced in 1977, which merged a Les Paul Junior (body shape), a Fender Telecaster (through-body stringing), and a sunburst Les Paul (woods, finish), adding new touches such as a pair of pickups from an up-and-coming maker called Larry DiMarzio. The Sunburst defined the outlook of Hamer, taking classic Gibson designs and reworking them for a fresh breed of guitar players. Hamer was sold in 1988 to Kaman, Ovation's parent company, and then to Fender when Kaman was sold in 2007. Fender closed Hamer five years later. Dantzig builds instruments today for his Jol Dantzig Guitar Design company in New England.

Hamer wurde Mitte der 1970er-Jahre in Chicago von einer Gruppe von Partnern gegründet, zu denen auch Paul Hamer und Jol Dantzig gehörten. Ihre ersten Gitarren entstanden in Anlehnung an alte Gibson-Modelle, u. a. die Standard (basierend auf der Explorer) sowie diese 1977 eingeführte Sunburst, bei der Elemnete einer Les Paul Junior (Korpusform), einer Fender Telecaster (Besaitung durch den Korpus) und einer Sunburst Les Paul (Hölzer, Finish) kombiniert wurden. Neu waren die Tonabnehmer eines neuen, aufstrebenden Herstellers namens Larry DiMarzio. Die Sunburst war das Modell, das Hamer definierte: klassische Gibson-Designs umgestaltet für eine neue Generation von Gitarristen. 1988 wurde Hamer von Ovations Muttergesellschaft Kaman übernommen, dann, als Kaman 2007 veräußert wurde, an Fender verkauft. Fender machte Hamer fünf Jahre später dicht. Heute baut Dantzig Instrumente für seine Firma Jol Dantzig Guitar Design in New England.

PRS CUSTOM

Paul Reed Smith's idea was to combine the best of Gibson and Fender in one solidbody instrument, and one of the first results from his new PRS company, founded in Annapolis, Maryland, 1985, was the Custom. It's still in production today alongside the other early model, the all-mahogany Standard. This Custom was the fifth guitar built by the new PRS operation, and it has the early control layout of volume, a five-way rotary pickup switch that offered Gibson-like thickness to Fender toppiness, and a "sweet switch" tone filter, as well as PRS's distinctive bird inlays. The mahogany/maple construction and fancy timber recalled classic 50s Les Pauls, while the through-body stringing and straightforward vibrato was drawn from the Fender rulebook.

Die Idee von Paul Reed Smith war, das Beste von Gibson und Fender in einem Solidbody-Instrument zu vereinen. Eines der ersten Produkte seiner Firma PRS, die er 1985 in Annapolis, Maryland gründete, war die Custom. Sie wird heute noch hergestellt, neben einem zweiten, früheren Modell – der Standard, komplett aus Mahagoni. Diese Custom war die fünfte Gitarre, die das Jungunternehmen PRS baute. Sie besitzt den frühen Lautstärkeregler, einen 5-Wege Drehschalter, der Gibsons satten und Fenders helleren Klang bot, sowie einen „Sweet-Switch"-Tonfilter und die für PRS typischen Vogel-Intarsien als Bundmarkierungen. Die Konstruktion aus Mahagoni/Ahorn und feinstes Holz erinnerten an die Les Pauls aus den 1950er-Jahren, während die Besaitung durch den Korpus und das direkte Vibrato klassische Fender-Merkmale waren.

RICK NIELSEN of Cheap Trick is an avid guitar collector and a notable Hamer endorser. The wildest instrument Hamer made for the whacky Illinois-born musician was a five-neck monster that Nielsen actually managed to play on-stage. It incorporated a 12-string, a fretless neck, and three six-string guitars, one with vibrato.

RICK NIELSEN von Cheap Trick sammelt leidenschaftlich gern Gitarren und hat eine Vorliebe für Hamer-Instrumente. Das verrückteste Modell, das Hamer für den exzentrischen Musiker aus Illinois gebaut hat, war eine Gitarre mit fünf Hälsen, die Nielsen tatsächlich auf der Bühne spielte. Das Modell bestand aus einer zwölfsaitigen, einer bundlosen und drei sechssaitigen Gitarren, eine davon mit Vibrato.

CARLOS SANTANA is a long-standing PRS player, ever since Paul Reed Smith first built him a guitar in 1980 in Smith's workshop in Annapolis, Maryland. PRS has since issued a number of Santana signature models, and they include guitars made in Korea as well as in the company's US factory.

CARLOS SANTANA spielt PRS-Gitarren seit Paul Reed Smith ihm 1980 die erste Gitarre in seiner Werkstatt in Annapolis, Maryland, gebaut hat. PRS brachte eine Reihe von Santana Signature-Modellen heraus, von denen manche in Korea und andere in der amerikanischen Fabrik des Unternehmens hergestellt wurden.

JACKSON RANDY RHOADS

Grover Jackson met Randy Rhoads in 1980 when Rhoads was a 24-year-old guitarist with Ozzy Osbourne. They designed a custom guitar together based on the general look and feel of the classic Gibson Flying V. A year or so later they collaborated again on a more radical variant of their design, with a notably offset body style. It was around this time that Grover, who had bought Wayne Charvel's parts business in 1978, began to use the Jackson brand for his guitars. With Rhoads's tragic death in an aircraft accident in 1982 and the subsequent interest in his unusual Jacksons, the first Jackson-brand production instrument appeared in 1983, the Randy Rhoads model. This example from that first year was the first built and was the first equipped with a Floyd Rose vibrato, which was quickly becoming the metal guitarist's dive-bombing trem system of choice.

Grover Jackson traf Randy Rhoads 1980, als dieser als 24-jähriger Gitarrist mit Ozzy Osbourne auf Tour war. Sie entwarfen gemeinsam eine Custom-Gitarre mit dem Aussehen und Spielgefühl einer klassischen Gibson Flying V. Etwa ein Jahr später kam es erneut zu einer Zusammenarbeit an einer radikaleren Variante ihres Designs, mit einer auffälligen Offset-Korpusform. In dieser Zeit begann Grover, der 1978 Wayne Charvels Ersatzteilgeschäft gekauft hatte, für seine Gitarren die Marke Jackson zu verwenden. Nach Rhoads' tragischem Flugzeugabsturz 1982 und dem anschließenden Interesse an ungewöhnlichen Jackson-Modellen, erschien 1983 mit dem Randy Rhoads Modell die erste produzierte Jackson-Gitarre. Dieses Beispiel aus dem Anfangsjahr war die erste, die je gebaut wurde. Sie besaß ein Floyd-Rose-Vibrato, das schnell zum bevorzugten Tremolo-System unter Metal-Gitarristen wurde.

DEAN Z

Dean Zelinsky started his Dean company in Evanston, Illinois, in 1977 with a trio of Gibson-influenced models: the Explorer-like Z, pictured here, the V, and the ML, which was a mix of the two. Most Deans featured a distinctive split headstock that harks back to Gibson's original (and at the time unused) design for the Explorer. Dimebag Darrell played a Dean ML before moving to Washburn instruments, but at the time of Darrell's murder in 2004, he and Zelinsky were working on the model that became the ultra-pointy Dean Razorback. Zelinsky left Dean in 1991, returned in 2000, and then left permanently eight years later. Dean continues in Tampa, Florida, and Zelinsky now heads DBZ in Houston, Texas.

Dean Zelinsky gründete seine Firma Dean in Evanston, Illinois im Jahr 1977 mit drei Gibson ähnlichen Modellen: die Explorer artige Z (siehe Bild), die V und die ML, eine Mischung aus beiden. Die meisten Deans besaßen eine auffällig gespaltene Kopfplatte, die auf Gibsons (damals nicht verwendetes) Original-Design für die Explorer zurückgriff. Dimebag Darrell spielte eine Dean ML bevor er zu Washburn-Gitarren wechselte. Kurz bevor Darrell 2004 ermordet wurde, arbeiteten er und Zelinsky gerade am Entwurf für die ultra spitz zulaufende Dean Razorback. Zelinsky verließ Dean 1991 und kehrte 2000 zurück, bis er acht Jahre später endgültig ausstieg. Dean baut heute noch Gitarren in Tampa, Florida, Zelinsky leitet DBZ Guitars in Houston, Texas.

JACKSON SOLOIST

Grover Jackson's brand came to symbolise the superstrat style of rock guitar that dominated the 80s. Grover joined Wayne Charvel's guitar-parts supply business in Asuza, California, in 1977, and a year later he bought the small firm. Charvel-brand guitars appeared in 1979. A few years later Grover began to use the Jackson brand, too, and the guitar shown is his first Soloist model and his first with a custom graphic. The Soloist evolved and became something of a template for the superstrat style, developed by Jackson, Charvel, Ibanez, Kramer, and others. There is no one superstrat design, but the general idea was to build on the classic Fender Stratocaster, adding more frets, deeper cutaways, an angled headstock, new pickup layouts, and a high-performance vibrato system, all aimed primarily at fast-gun players on the emerging shred/metal scene.

Grover Jacksons Marke wurde zum Symbol der Superstrat-Rockgitarre, welche die 1980er-Jahre beherrschte. Grover tat sich 1977 mit Wayne Charvels, Zulieferer für Gitarrenteile in Asuza, Kalifornien, zusammen. Ein Jahr später kaufte er die kleine Firma. Die ersten Gitarren der Marke Charvel erschienen 1979. Einige Jahre später begann Grover, auch den Markennamen Jackson zu verwenden. Die hier abgebildete Gitarre ist sein erstes Soloist-Modell und seine erste Gitarre mit eigener Grafik. Die Soloist wurde zur Vorlage für den Superstrat-Stil, den Jackson, Charvel, Ibanez, Kramer und andere entwickelten. Es gibt nicht nur das eine Superstrat-Design. Die Idee war, auf der klassischen Fender Stratocaster aufzubauen und diese mit mehreren Bünden, tieferen Cutaways, einem abgewinkelten Kopf sowie neu geformte Pickups und einem leistungsstarken Vibrato-System auszustatten – speziell ausgerichtet auf schnell spielende Gitarristen der aufkeimenden Shred/Metal-Szene.

DAVE MUSTAINE was in the original line-up of Metallica but was out before they made their first record. He formed Megadeth, who went on to great success, and he played Jackson V-style models, including the King V and various signature models. He moved to ESP in 2004 and two years later to Dean.

DAVE MUSTAINE gehörte zur Erstbesetzung von Metallica, verließ die Band jedoch noch vor dem ersten Album. Er gründete die ebenfalls erfolgreiche Band Megadeth und spielte auf Jackson V-Style Modellen, u.a. der King V und zahlreichen Signature-Modellen. 2004 wechselte er zu ESP und zwei Jahre später zu Dean.

1983 – JACKSON SOLOIST

PHIL COLLEN has been a guitarist in **Def Leppard** since he joined the band in 1982, and at first his main guitar was an **Ibanez Destroyer**, which had a similar body shape to Gibson's 50s Explorer. Since then, Collen has been a Jackson endorser, with a number of JC signature models to his name.

PHIL COLLEN ist seit 1982 Gitarrist bei Def Leppard. Seine wichtigste Gitarre war damals eine Ibanez Destroyer, die in der Form der Gibson Explorer aus den 1950er-Jahren ähnelt. Collen entwickelte später eine Vorliebe für Jackson-Gitarren. Mittlerweile gibt es eine Reihe JC Signature-Modelle, die seinem Namen Ehre machen.

BRIAN MAY SIGNATURE PRO

BRIAN MAY's guitar sound was at the centre of Queen and was quite different from anything else around. He enjoyed constructing exquisite, layered sound pictures in the studio, and live he was able to beam those pictures to ever-larger audiences. He has almost always used his home-made Red Special guitar.

Im Mittelpunkt der Band Queen stand BRIAN MAYs Gitarrensound, der sich so ziemlich von allem anderen abhob. Er liebte es, im Studio feinste, vielschichtige Klangbilder zu erschaffen, die er auf Konzerten Tausenden von Leuten präsentierte. Er spielte meistens auf seiner selbstgebauten Red Special.

GUILD BRIAN MAY SIGNATURE PRO

Queen guitarist Brian May and his father built his guitar, the famous Red Special, in 1964, and he's played it consistently throughout his career, along with replicas made by John Birch and others. The instrument has been reproduced a few times for commercial release, with Guild making the first copies, in 1984. The example shown – in green finish rather the original's red – is a later version that was closer to the original. It copied Red Special down to the same array of six pickup switches, providing on/off selection and phase switching for the repro pickups made by Seymour Duncan. Burns London produced a further copy in the early 2000s, and then May formed Brian May Guitars to produce the currently available model, the Brian May Special.

Queen-Gitarrist Brian May und sein Vater bauten diese Gitarre im Jahr 1964. Die berühmte Red Special spielte Brian während seiner gesamten Karriere, neben Repliken von John Birch und anderen. Das Instrument wurde einige Male für den kommerziellen Verkauf reproduziert, Guild stellte 1984 die ersten Exemplare her. Die hier abgebildete Gitarre (in Grün statt sonst Rot) ist eine spätere Version, die dem Original noch näher kam. Es war eine exakte Kopie der Red Special bis hin zur gleichen Anordnung von sechs Pickup-Schaltern zum Ein-/Aus-Schalten und einer Phasen-schaltung für Repro-Pickups von Seymour Duncan. Burns London produzierte Anfang der 2000er-Jahre eine weitere Kopie. Dann gründete May die Firma Brian May Guitars, um das derzeit erhältliche Modell herzustellen – die Brian May Special.

RICKENBACKER 355/12JL JOHN LENNON

The Beatles connection has always been important to Rickenbacker: John Lennon played a couple of the company's 325 models throughout most of the life of the band on stage and in the studio; George Harrison had a couple of 12-strings; and Paul McCartney sometimes used a Rick-enbacker bass for recording. The Californian firm issued a series of John Lennon signature models in 1989. There was a 325JL, which reproduced the guitar made for Lennon in 1964, and a long-scale version, the 355JL. The 355/12JL pictured was a long-scale version of the 320/12 that Lennon was given around the same time that Harrison got his 12-string, although Lennon rarely used his original. The pickguard has a repro Lennon signature and a self-portrait doodle.

Die Beatles-Connection war für Rickenbacker immer von großer Bedeutung: Auf der Bühne und im Studio spielte John Lennon fast die gesamte Beatles-Zeit über einige der 325er-Modelle. George Harrison besaß einige 12-saitige Gitarren, Paul McCartney verwendete einen Rickenba-cker-Bass für diverse Studioaufnahmen. Die Firma aus Kalifornien gab 1989 eine Reihe von John Lennon Signa-ture-Modellen heraus – die 325JL, eine Reproduktion der Gitarre, die Lennon 1964 anfertigen ließ, und die 355JL als Longscale-Version. Die hier abgebildete 355/12JL war eine Longscale-Version der 320/12, die Lennon zur gleichen Zeit geschenkt bekam als Harrison seine 12-String bekam, obwohl Lennon seine Original-Gitarre kaum spielte. Auf dem Schlagbrett sind die Unterschrift und ein gekritzeltes Selbstportrait von Lennon abgebildet.

JOHN LENNON's first American guitar was a Rickenbacker that he bought when The Beatles were playing a residency in Hamburg, Germany, in 1960. Rickenbacker later gave him some guitars, including a replacement 325 model for the road-weary original, and also a 12-string version, which proved awkward to play and he soon put aside.

JOHN LENNONS erste amerikanische Gitarre war eine Rickenbacker, die er erwarb, als die Beatles 1960 für einige Zeit in Hamburg lebten. Rickenbacker schenkte ihm später einige Gitarren, darunter ein 325-Ersatzmodell für das verschlissene Original und eine zwölfsaitige Version, die nicht wirklich gut spielbar war und die er deshalb schnell wieder weglegte.

MIKE RUTHERFORD, the Genesis bassist and guitarist, would often use a Rickenbacker or Shergold double-neck on stage, so that he could switch easily from bass to 12-string guitar during a song. He also played six-string guitar, and in the 80s he collaborated with the headless-guitar company Steinberger to design a new model, the GM.

MIKE RUTHERFORD, der Bassist und Gitarrist von Genesis, spielte bei Konzerten häufig eine Rickenbacker oder Shergold Doppelhalsgitarre, damit er während eines Songs leicht vom Bass zur zwölfsaitigen Gitarre wechseln konnte. Er spielte auch eine sechssaitige Gitarre, und in den 1980er-Jahren half er Steinberger, dem Hersteller von Gitarren ohne Kopfplatten, ein neues Modell zu entwerfen: die GM.

STEINBERGER GM4T

Ned Steinberger is best known for the mini-body headless bass guitars made from composite materials that he introduced in the early 80s, but Steinberger also produced six-string and 12-string guitars. Gibson bought Steinberger in 1987, and the GM line appeared shortly afterward, designed with help from the Genesis guitarist and bassist Mike Rutherford and the British guitar-maker Roger Giffin. As a contrast to the original almost body-less models, the GMs had real wooden bodies, but they retained the headless neck, with tuners incorporated into the bridge at the "wrong" end of the guitar, and active EMG pickups, in the popular 80s combination of bridge humbucker and two single-coils. Ned Steinberger today runs NS Design, best known for electric upright basses.

Ned Steinberger ist vor allem für seine aus Verbundstoffen gefertigten, kleinen Bässe ohne Kopfplatte bekannt, die Anfang der 1980er-Jahre eingeführt wurden. Doch Steinberger produzierte auch Gitarren mit sechs bzw. zwölf Saiten. 1987 wurde Steinberger von Gibson übernommen, kurz darauf erschien die GM-Serie nach den Entwürfen von Genesis-Gitarrist und Bassist Mike Rutherford und dem britischen Gitarrenbauer Roger Giffin. Im Gegensatz zu den ursprünglich fast korpuslosen Modellen, bestand der Korpus der GM aus Echtholz. Der kopflose Hals wurde bei-behalten, die Mechaniken in den Steg, am „falschen Ende" der Gitarre, eingebaut und aktive EMG-Pickups eingesetzt, in der in den 1980er-Jahren populären Kombination aus Humbucker und zwei Single-Coils. Ned Steinberger ist heute Geschäftsführer von NS Design, die vor allem für E-Kontrabässe bekannt sind.

1989 – RICKENBACKER
355/12JL JOHN LENNON

1989 – STEINBERGER
GM4T

FREDDIE
MERCURY

BRIAN
MAY

CHARVEL MODEL 4

The Charvel brand first appeared on guitars in 1979, following Grover Jackson's purchase of Wayne Charvel's guitar-parts supply business in California. An early Charvel appeared under the fast-moving fingers of Eddie Van Halen, which gave a great boost to the brand. When Charvel and its stablemate Jackson moved in 1986 to a joint venture with distributor IMC of Texas, a new, cheaper made-in-Japan line was launched, and some of the new models helped define the new superstrat style. This Model 4 has the style's favoured pickup layout of humbucker and two single-coils, high-performance locking vibrato system, angled headstock with locking nut, and a Strat-inspired body. Akai bought Jackson/Charvel in 1997 and dropped the Charvel brand, but Fender's acquisition in 2002 appeared to revive the name. Wayne Charvel ran several shortlived companies in the 80s and the Wayne brand in the late 90s.

Die ersten Charvel-Gitarren tauchten 1979 auf dem Markt auf, nachdem Grover Jackson Wayne Charvels Gitarren-Ersatzteilgeschäft in Kalifornien gekauft hatte. Eddie Van Halen spielte ein frühes Charvel-Modell und verhalf der Marke damit zu schneller Bekanntheit. Als Charvel und sein Partner Jackson 1986 ein Joint Venture mit IMC in Texas eingingen, brachte das Unternehmen eine in Japan produzierte Billig-Serie heraus. Einige dieser neuen Modelle halfen, den neuen Superstrat-Stil mit zu definieren. Diese Model 4 besitzt den für diesen Stil bevorzugten Humbucker-Pickup und zwei Single-Coils, ein leistungsstarkes „Locking"-Tremolo, eine abgewinkelte Kopfplatte mit Locking Nut und einen Stratocaster ähnlichen Korpus. Akai kaufte Jackson/Charvel 1997 und stellte die Marke Charvel ein. Fender übernahm das Unternehmen 2002 und verhalf ihr zu einem Comeback. In den 1980er-Jahren führte Wayne Charvel mehrere kurzlebige Unternehmen sowie die Marke Wayne Ende der 1990er-Jahre.

1986 – CHARVEL
MODEL 4

EDDIE VAN HALEN is a great guitar player: you only need to hear the solo on Michael Jackson's 'Beat It' to know that. In the early days, he liked to put guitars together from parts. The most famous result was his various striped "Frankenstein" guitars, which he used with Van Halen and for studio sessions.

EDDIE VAN HALEN ist ein großartiger Gitarrist: Man braucht sich nur sein Solo in ‚Beat It' von Michael Jackson anzuhören. In der Anfangszeit baute er gern Gitarren aus Einzelteilen zusammen. Am berühmtesten sind seine ‚Frankenstein'-Gitarren, die er mit Van Halen und bei Studioaufnahmen spielte.

CHARVEL SURFCASTER

One of the first signs of the 90s fashion for retro guitars came with Charvel's Surfcaster, launched in 1991. Makers found it convenient to look back to the best factors that made past instruments so distinctive and opted to use a patchwork of old-style features and knick-knacks to imbue "new" models with a suitably backwards-leaning vibe. The Surfcaster was a heady mix of design influences from the 50s, notably the lipstick pickups that recalled Danelectro, a Rickenbacker-like slash soundhole and triangular fingerboard markers, and a pearly pickguard that might have come from a vintage Fender. Many other electric brands took note of this early indication that retro could not only look good but also sound good and attract players.

Eines der ersten Anzeichen für die Retrogitarren-Mode der 1990er-Jahre war die Surfcaster von Charvel aus dem Jahr 1991. Gitarrenbauer pickten sich einfach die Elemente heraus, die Vintage-Instrumente so besonders machten. Also entschieden sie sich für eine Mischung aus Details und Merkmalen älterer Gitarren, um den „neuen" Modellen den entspannten Retrolook zu verleihen. Bei der Surfcaster traf ein Mix aus Design-Einflüssen der 1950er-Jahre aufeinander, insbesondere die Lipstick-Pickups, die an Danelectro erinnerten, ein Rickenbacker artiges Slash-Schallloch, dreieckige Bund-Markierungen und ein Schlagbrett aus Perlmutt, das von einer alten Vintage-Fender stammen könnte. Viele andere E-Gitarren-Marken deuteten die frühen Anzeichen richtig, dass Retro nicht nur gut aussehen, sondern auch vernünftig klingen und das Interesse von Musikern wecken konnte.

IBANEZ JEM777LG

The Japanese brand Ibanez made its big breakthrough among extreme rock players with the Steve Vai models, launched in 1987. Vai was a guitarist's guitarist who hit the big-time when he joined the new band of ex-Van Halen vocalist David Lee Roth. Vai's main guitar was a modified Charvel, and some elements of that and other Vai guitars made it to his new super-superstrat. The guitar was distinctive: it had colourful DiMarzio pickups in humbucker/single-coil/humbucker layout, a Monkey Grip body handle, Disappearing Pyramid inlays, a thin 24-fret neck (with top four frets scalloped), and Lion's Claw cutouts behind the Edge locking vibrato, to enable pull-ups. The debut JEM777 in Loch Ness Green was a limited edition of 777, which sold out almost immediately. More Vai signatures have followed, and the JEMs formed the basis for Ibanez's highly successful RG series of superstrats.

Der japanischen Marke Ibanez gelang der Durchbruch in der Rockszene mit Steve-Vai-Modellen, die 1987 auf den Markt kamen. Vai war Vollblutgitarrist und wurde als Mitglied von Ex-Van Halen-Sänger David Lee Roths neuer Band weltweit bekannt. Vais Hauptgitarre war eine modifizierte Charvel. Einige Elemente davon sowie anderer Vai-Gitarren wurden in der neuen Super-Superstrat integriert. Das Modell stach heraus: Es hatte bunte DiMarzio-Pickups im Humbucker/Single-Coil/Humbucker-Layout, einen Monkey Grip Body Handle, Disappearing-Pyramid-Inlays (Intarsien mit einer "verschwindenden" Pyramide), einen dünnen Hals mit 24 Bünden (die oberen vier Bünde ausgehöhlt) und Lion's Claw Cutouts hinter dem Locking-Tremolo von Edge, für besseres Hochziehen des Hebels. Die erste JEM777 in Loch Ness Green war eine limitierte Edition der 777, die fast auf der Stelle ausverkauft war. Weitere Vai Signature-Modelle folgten. JEMs bildeten die Grundlage für Ibanez' erfolgreichste RG-Serie an Superstrats.

STEVE VAI's break came in 1980 at age 20 when he joined Frank Zappa's band, and in '84 he replaced Yngwie Malmsteen in Alcatrazz. Vai's demonstrative and technically adept playing led to a place in David Lee Roth's post-Van Halen band in 1987 and to a subsequently successful solo career.

STEVE VAI feierte seinen Durchbruch im Jahr 1980, als er mit 20 Jahren Frank Zappas Band beitrat. 1984 nahm er den Platz von Yngwie Malmsteen bei Alcatrazz ein. Vais demonstratives und technisch versiertes Spiel verschaffte ihm 1987 einen Platz in David Lee Roths Post-Van Halen-Band und führte zu einer erfolgreichen Solokarriere.

1987 – IBANEZ
JEM777LG

JOE SATRIANI reached many ears with his spectacular album of 1987, Surfing With The Alien, and a year later he joined Mick Jagger's solo band for a world tour. He has gone on to a long and successful solo career, one of the few modern guitarists to make a mark with an emphasis on instrumental music.

Mit seinem spektakulären Album Surfing With The Alien von 1987 erreichte JOE SATRIANI ein großes Publikum. Ein Jahr später tourte er mit Mick Jaggers Soloband um die Welt. Satriani blickt auf eine lange und erfolgreiche Solokarriere zurück und ist einer der wenigen modernen Gitarristen, der mit Instrumentalmusik ein Zeichen setzen konnte.

IBANEZ JS2

Joe Satriani's signature guitars for Ibanez were based on a 540R model he played and experimented with and called Black Dog. Satriani's main requirement was for a relatively simple guitar. A trio of Satriani models were launched in 1990 and they underlined that simplicity: each had a dot neck, rosewood board, basswood body, Edge vibrato, two DiMarzio humbuckers, and a volume, tone, and three-way selector. There was the regular-finish JS1, the chrome-finish JS2, and the JS3, hand-painted by artist Donnie Hunt. The JS2's chrome finish proved impossible to produce consistently, and the model was quickly dropped, only returning on a plastic body for a 10th anniversary model, the JS10TH, in 1998.

Die Joe Satriani Signature-Gitarren für Ibanez basierten auf einer 540R, mit der er experimentiert hatte und die er Black Dog nannte. Satriani wollte vor allem eine recht simple Gitarre. 1990 kamen drei Satriani-Modelle auf den Markt, die genau diese Simplizität unterstrichen: jede hatte einen Hals mit Punkten als Bundmarkierungen, ein Griffbrett aus Palisander und einen Korpus aus Lindenholz, ein Edge-Vibrato, zwei Humbucker-Pickups von DiMarzio sowie einen Dreiweg-Schalter und Lautstärke- und Tonregler. Es gab das reguläre Finish JS1, das Chrom-Finish JS2 und das JS3, handbemalt vom Künstler Donnie Hunt. Das Chrom-Finish der JS2 konnte allerdings nicht lange produziert werden, also wurde das Modell schnell wieder aus dem Programm genommen. 1998 tauchte es zum 10-jährigen Jubiläum noch einmal auf dem Plastikkorpus der JS10TH auf.

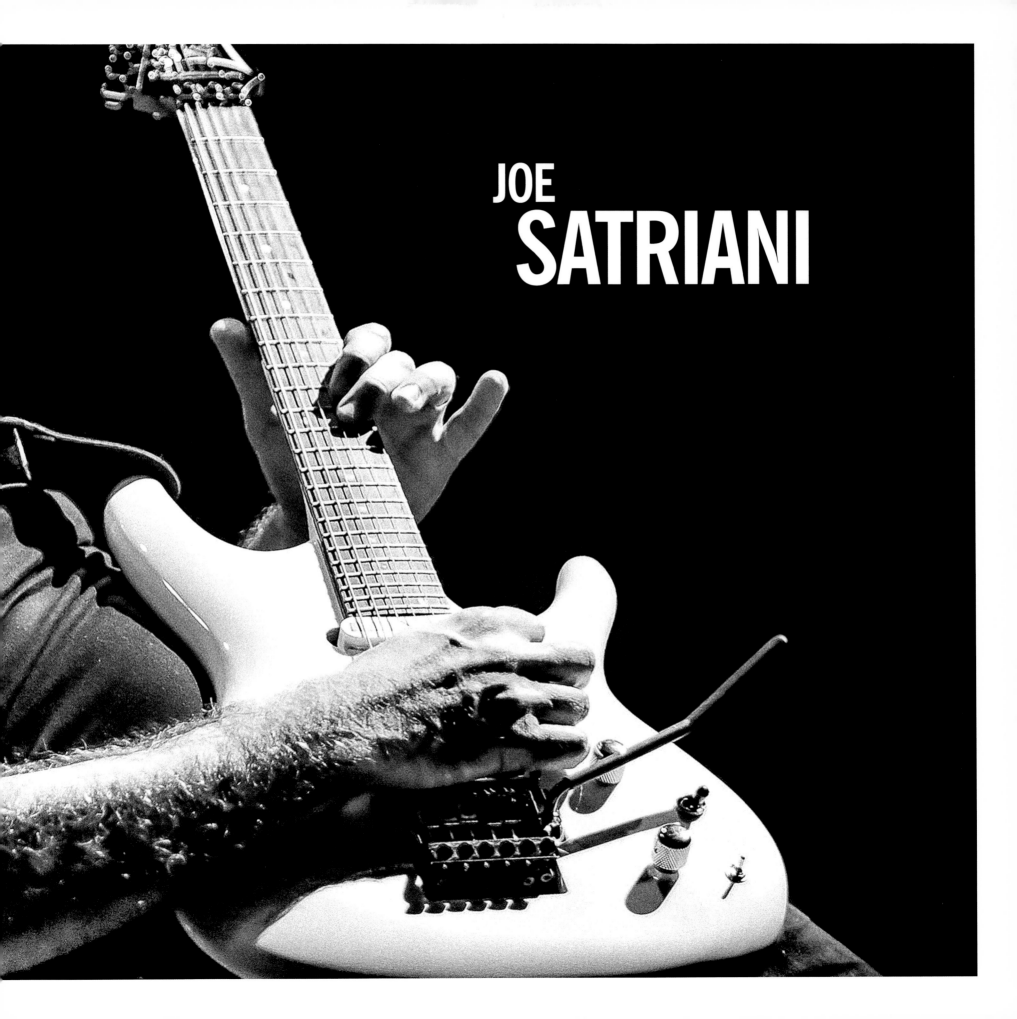

FENDER ERIC CLAPTON STRATOCASTER

Fender introduced its first signature models in the late 80s, two Stratocasters named for Eric Clapton and Yngwie Malmsteen. Clapton had discovered that his faithful old bitser Strat, Blackie, was coming to the end of its useful life, and he began talking to Fender about a modern replacement. After much to-ing and fro-ing with prototypes and neck shapes and active circuitry, the final design went on sale in 1988. It had Fender's new Lace Sensor pickups, a midrange-boosting circuit, a blocked-off vintage-style vibrato, and a repro of Clapton's signature on the end of the headstock. Many signature Stratocasters have followed the Clapton and Malmsteen guitars, including models named for Jeff Beck, Ritchie Blackmore, Dick Dale, David Gilmour, Buddy Guy, Mark Knopfler, John Mayer, Bonnie Raitt, Nile Rodgers, and Stevie Ray Vaughan.

Seine ersten Signature-Modelle führte Fender Ende der 1980er-Jahre ein, zwei Stratocaster benannt nach Eric Clapton und Yngwie Malmsteen. Clapton musste feststellen, dass seine treue alte Bitser-Strat Blackie allmählich ausgedient hatte und bat Fender um einen modernen Ersatz. Nach einigem Hin und Her mit Prototypen, Halsformen und aktiver Schaltung ging das finale Design 1988 in den Verkauf. Es besaß Fenders neue Lace Sensor Pickups, einen MidBoost-Schalter, ein blockiertes Vintage-Vibrato und eine Reproduktion von Claptons Unterschrift am Kopfplattenende. Nach den Modellen Clapton und Malmsteen folgten noch viele weitere Signature-Stratocasters, darunter solche mit den Namensgebern Jeff Beck, Ritchie Blackmore, Dick Dale, David Gilmour, Buddy Guy, Mark Knopfler, John Mayer, Bonnie Raitt, Nile Rodgers und Stevie Ray Vaughan.

ALBERT LEE was a confirmed Fender Telecaster player for much of his career, and he played one on many of his classic recordings with Emmylou Harris, Eric Clapton, and others, and on his influential solo cut 'Country Boy'. In more recent years he has worked on new instrument designs with Music Man.

ALBERT LEE spielte während seiner Karriere lange Zeit auf einer Fender Telecaster, unter anderem auf seinen klassischen Alben mit Emmylou Harris, Eric Clapton und anderen Künstlern. Auch in seinem wohl bekanntesten Song ‚Country Boy' spielt er eine Tele. In den letzten Jahren arbeitete er mit Music Man an neuen Instrumentendesigns.

MUSIC MAN ALBERT LEE

Leo Fender left Fender a few years after it was bought by CBS in the mid 60s, and in 1972 he set up Music Man with a couple of ex-Fender colleagues. Music Man produced some fine guitars, including the StringRay and Sabre models. Leo left and founded G&L, and in 1984, Music Man was bought by Ernie Ball, best known for guitar strings. Production moved to the Ernie Ball HQ in San Luis Obispo, California. The first new guitar was the Silhouette, designed by Dudley Gimpel and guitarist Albert Lee, with a compact body and a distinctive headstock with four tuners one side and two the other. Lee's own signature model appeared in 1993 with an unusually angular body design, three pickups, and that distinctive headstock. Music Man's later signature models included guitars named for Steve Lukather, Steve Morse, and John Petrucci.

Leo Fender verließ Fender wenige Jahre nachdem CBS das Unternehmen Mitte der 1960er-Jahre übernommen hatte. 1972 gründete er Music Man mit einigen ehemaligen Fender-Kollegen. Music Man baute hervorragende Gitarren, darunter die StringRay und die Sabre. Leo verließ das Unternehmen und gründete G&L. 1984 wurde Music Man von Ernie Ball gekauft, einer bekannten Marke für Gitarrensaiten. Produziert wurde fortan in der Ernie Ball Zentrale im kalifornischen San Luis Obispo. Die erste neue Gitarre war die Silhouette, entworfen von Dudley Gimpel und Gitarrist Albert Lee. Sie besaß einen kompakten Korpus und eine charakteristische Kopfplatte mit vier Mechaniken auf einer Seite und zwei auf der anderen. Lees eigenes Signature-Modell erschien 1993 mit einem ungewöhnlich verwinkelten Korpusdesign, drei Pickups und dem gleichen besonderen Kopf. Zu den späteren Signature-Modellen von Music Man gehörten Gitarren benannt nach Steve Lukather, Steve Morse und John Petrucci.

JEFF BECK came to fame with The Yardbirds in the 60s and quickly became a star. He is renowned today as one of the greatest guitarists of our times. Beck has played various instruments over the years, including Teles and Les Pauls, but now he's a confirmed Stratocaster man, complete with Fender signature model.

JEFF BECK wurde in den 1960er-Jahren mit den Yardbirds berühmt und war schnell ein Star. Er gilt heute als einer der größten Gitarristen unserer Zeit. Beck griff über die Jahre zu zahlreichen Instrumenten, darunter Teles und Les Pauls. Heute spielt er ausschließlich Stratocaster und besitzt sein eigenes Fender Signature-Modell.

RITCHIE BLACKMORE emerged in the late 60s with Deep Purple, responsible for one of the most famous riffs of all time in 'Smoke On The Water'. He is a guitar stylist with a taste for classical-leaning melodic invention set in heavy rock, later playing on his own solo outings, primarily with Rainbow.

RITCHIE BLACKMORE trat in den späten 1960er-Jahren mit Deep Purple erstmals in Erscheinung und erfand für 'Smoke On The Water' einen der berühmtesten Riffs aller Zeiten. Er ist ein Gitarrenkünstler mit einem Hang zu klassisch angelehnten Melodien im Heavy Rock Bereich. Später spielte er für eigene Soloprojekte, überwiegend mit Rainbow.

1994 – PRS
MCCARTY MODEL

2003 – PRS
TREMONTI SE

PRS MCCARTY MODEL

Ted McCarty ran Gibson during its 50s heyday, and PRS's McCarty Model, launched in 1994, was the first to bear his name – it was later applied also to PRS's line of hollowbody guitars. The McCarty Model built on previous PRS solidbody models, especially the Dragon of 1992, and on Paul Reed Smith's evolving theories about the development of the modern electric guitar, and it was developed with help from guitarist David Grissom. Compared to earlier PRSs, it had covered humbuckers, a slightly thicker mahogany back and thinner headstock, lighter tuners, a three-way pickup switch, and different pickup specs. For some players, it shifted PRS a little closer to the classic feel and sounds of 50s Gibson Les Pauls.

Zu Hochzeiten von Gibson in den 1950er-Jahren leitete Ted McCarty die Geschäfte, und das McCarty Modell von PRS, das 1994 auf den Markt kam, war die erste Gitarre, die seinen Namen trug – später wurde er auch für die Hollow-body-Gitarren von PRS verwendet. Das McCarty-Modell basierte auf älteren PRS Solidbodies, vor allem der Dragon von 1992, sowie auf den Theorien von Paul Reed Smith über die Entwicklung der modernen E-Gitarre. Entwickelt wurde sie mit Hilfe von Gitarrist David Grissom. Im Vergleich zu früheren PRS-Modellen besaß dieses verdeckte Humbucker-Pickups, ein etwas dickeres Rückenteil aus Mahagoni, eine dünnere Kopfplatte, leichtere Mechaniken, einen Dreiweg-Pickup-Schalter und verschiedene Pick-up-Optionen. Für einige Gitarristen rutschte PRS damit mehr in die klassische Ecke, vergleichbar mit Gibson Les Pauls aus den 1950er-Jahren.

PRS TREMONTI SE

The key PRS solidbody models so far had been the Custom, Standard, and McCarty Model, all with the company's accustomed double-cutaway body shape. A new single-cutaway model appeared in 2000, logically named the Singlecut. Gibson thought it was too close to the design of its classic Les Paul and took legal action, which was finally settled in 2006 with a win for PRS. Mark Tremonti of Creed and Alter Bridge was only the second artist to score an endorsement deal with PRS, after Carlos Santana, and his take on the Singlecut first appeared in 2001. The guitar pictured is a Tremonti signature from PRS's budget SE line, the US company's first instruments made in Korea.

Die bisher prominentesten PRS-Solidbodies waren die Custom, Standard und die McCarty, alle mit der firmenüblichen Korpusform mit Double Cutaway. Ein neues Modell mit Single Cutaway erschien im Jahr 2000 und hieß logischerweise auch Singlecut. Gibson war der Meinung, sie wäre dem Design der klassischen Les Paul zu ähnlich und ging gerichtlich dagegen vor. 2006 gewann PRS den Prozess. Mark Tremonti von Creed und Alter Bridge war erst der zweite Künstler, der nach Carlos Santana einen Werbevertrag mit PRS abschloss. Seine Version einer Singlecut kam 2001 auf den Markt. Die hier abgebildete Gitarre ist eine Tremonti aus PRS' günstigerer SE-Serie, die das US-Unternehmen erstmals in Korea herstellen ließ.

MARK TREMONTI built on his success as a shredder with taste in Creed and then Alter Bridge to become a well known endorser of PRS guitars, helping with the development of the company's singlecut solidbody design. A native of Detroit, Tremonti made his first solo album, All I Was, in 2012.

MARK TREMONTI machte als Shredder-Gitarrist mit Geschmack Karriere in der Band Creed und später bei Alter Bridge. Tremonti, der ursprünglich aus Detroit stammt, ist ein bekannter Werbeträger für PRS-Gitarren. Er unterstützte das Unternehmen bei der Entwicklung eines Singlecut Solidbody-Designs. Sein erstes Soloalbum, All I Was, nahm Tremonti 2012 auf.

WASHBURN NUNO BETTENCOURT N-8

Washburn is a famous old American brandname that lives on today as a modern, international manufacturer of all kinds of guitars. George Washburn Lyon was an associate in Chicago's big Lyon & Healy operation, founded in 1864, and provided the brandname for most of the flattop acoustic guitars produced by the company. Various business changes led to Washburn's ownership by Fretted Industries from the 70s, and the brand soon began to appear on Japanese-made electric guitars. Washburn's signature models for Extreme guitarist Nuno Bettencourt typify the 90s guitar scene, with versions made in the United States, Japan, and Korea. This US Custom Shop double-neck has six and 12-string necks, with the 12-string's second set of tuners behind the bridge, a mix of Seymour Duncan and Bill Lawrence pickups, and a single volume control with neck-split switch and pickup selector.

Washburn ist eine geschichtsträchtige US-amerikanische Marke, die heute als moderner, internationaler Hersteller unterschiedlichster Gitarren weiterlebt. George Washburn Lyon war ein Partner des 1864 gegründeten Chicagoer Herstellers Lyon & Healy. Nach ihm waren die meisten Akustik-Flattops benannt, die die Firma produzierte. Geschäftliche Veränderungen führten dazu, dass Washburn in den 1970er-Jahren von Fretted Industries übernommen wurde und der Name kurz darauf auf in Japan produzierten E-Gitarren prangte. Washburns Signature-Modelle für Extrem-Gitarrist Nuno Bettencourt waren typisch für die Gitarrenszene der 1990er-Jahre. Unterschiedliche Versionen wurden in den USA, in Japan und Korea hergestellt. Diese Doppelhalsgitarre aus dem US Custom Shop besitzt Hälse mit sechs und zwölf Saiten, mit einem weiteren Mechanik-Set für eine 12-saitige Gitarre hinter der Brücke, einem Mix aus Seymour Duncan und Bill Lawrence Pickups sowie einen einzelnen Lautstärkeregler mit Neck-Split-Schalter und Pickup-Wahlschalter.

PARKER NITEFLY

Parker began as a partnership between guitar maker Ken Parker and electronics expert Larry Fishman. Financed by Korg, the firm began producing instruments in 1993, based near Boston. The Fly models employ a radical construction, featuring extra-thin lightweight wooden bodies strengthened by a composite carbon and epoxy material that forms a thin "external skeleton" around the wood. Necks are similarly made, and the guitars generally combine sounds from "acoustic" piezo pickups and conventional magnetic "electric" pickups. Korg and Parker parted ways in 2000, and US Music Corp of Illinois bought the brand three years later. Fishman runs his Fishman Transducers company, making popular devices for acoustic amplification, and Parker makes guitars under the Ken Parker Archtops banner.

Parker begann als Partnerschaft von Gitarrenbauer Ken Parker und Elektronikexperte Larry Fishman. Mit finanzieller Unterstützung von Korg stellte die Firma 1993 nahe Boston erste Gitarren her. Die Fly-Modelle sind außergewöhnlich gebaut, mit einem extra-dünnen, federleichten Korpus aus Holz, gestärkt durch ein Epoxid/Carbon-Gemisch, das ein dünnes „Außenskelett" um das Holz bildete. Der Hals war ähnlich gebaut, und die Gitarren erzeugten einen Klangmix aus „akustischen" Piezo-Pickups und konventionellen magnetischen Elektro-Pickups. Korg und Parker trennten sich im Jahr 2000, drei Jahre später wurde die Marke von der US Music Corp of Illinois gekauft. Fishman leitet heute seine erfolgreiche Firma Fishman Transducers und stellt Geräte zur akustischen Verstärkung her. Parker baut Gitarren unter dem Banner Ken Parker Archtops.

1999 – WASHBURN
THE DIME CULPRIT CP2003

WASHBURN THE DIME CULPRIT CP2003

Dimebag Darrell rose to fame with Pantera, and his favourite guitar was a Dean ML guitar, which he won in a talent contest at a music store in Dallas, Texas. A friend refinished the contest guitar in blue and added lightning-bolt graphics. Dimebag moved to the Washburn brand in the mid 90s as Dean battled with business problems, and he began playing instruments that were of a similar design to the ML. This is one of the Culprit signature models that Washburn released, complete with the ML's Explorer-meets-V shape, this time with a rather more sliced look to the outlines. Dimebag was back with Dean, working on a design that would become the ultra-pointy Dean Razorback, before his untimely death in 2004.

Dimebag Darrell wurde mit Pantera berühmt. Seine Lieblingsgitarre war eine Dean ML, die er bei einem Talentwettbewerb eines Musikladens in Dallas gewonnen hatte. Ein Freund lackierte die Contest-Gitarre blau um und verzierte sie mit Blitz-Symbolen. Mitte der 1990er-Jahre wechselte Dimebag zur Marke Washburn, als Dean mit geschäftlichen Problemen zu kämpfen hatte. Er begann Gitarren zu spielen, die der ML vom Design her ähnelten. Dies ist eines der Culprit Signature-Modelle, die Washburn auf den Markt brachte. Sie besaß die Explorer-trifft-auf-V Form der ML, diesmal allerdings mit etwas angeschnitteren Umrissen. Dimebag kehrte zu Dean zurück und bastelte an einem Design für die spätere, ultra spitz zulaufende Dean Razorback, bevor er im Jahr 2004 vorzeitig verstarb.

DIMEBAG
DARRELL

FENDER '72 TELECASTER DELUXE

In the 70s, Fender put humbucking pickups on some new Telecaster models, reacting to a popular modification made by some guitarists. None were especially popular at the time and they did not last long. Come the late 90s, and these older models were rediscovered, not least because Thom Yorke of Radiohead was seen regularly with a 70s two-humbucker Telecaster Deluxe. The band's huge popularity helped along the new-found hipness of the humbucker'd Tele. Bands such as Snow Patrol, Coldplay, Gomez, and Maroon 5 were drawn to the look and feel and sound of a Tele with one or more humbuckers. Fender soon reissued some of the old models to meet the demand, aiming to improve on the sometimes unreliable originals. The new/old Teles included this Deluxe, the f-holed Telecaster Thinline, also with two humbuckers, and the Telecaster Custom, with neck humbucker and regular bridge pickup.

In den 1970er-Jahren stattete Fender einige neue Telecaster-Modelle mit Humbucker-Pickups aus und reagierte damit auf eine Abänderung, die unter Gitarristen sehr beliebt war. Zu der Zeit verkaufte sich keine der Gitarren sonderlich gut, so dass sie schon bald aus dem Programm genommen wurden. Ende der 1990er-Jahre wurden diese älteren Modelle neu entdeckt, nicht zuletzt weil Thom Yorke von Radiohead regelmäßig eine Telecaster Deluxe aus den 1970er-Jahren mit zwei Humbucker-Pickups auf Konzerten spielte. Der Riesenerfolg der Band machten die Telecaster mit Humbuckern zum ersten Mal populär. Bands wie Snow Patrol, Coldplay, Gomez und Maroon 5 fühlten sich vom Look, der Spielbarkeit und dem Klang einer Telecaster mit einem oder mehreren Humbucker-Pickups angezogen. Fender stillte die Nachfrage mit der Neuauflage einiger älterer Modelle und versuchte, die Schwachstellen der bisweilen unzuverlässigen Originale zu beheben. Zu den neuen alten Teles gehören u. a. diese Deluxe, die Telecaster Thinline mit F-Loch (ebenfalls mit zwei Humbucker-Pickups) und die Telecaster Custom, mit Humbucker in der Hals-Position und regulärem Steg-Pickup.

2005 – FENDER
'72 TELECASTER DELUXE

2010 – GIBSON
ERIC CLAPTON 1960 LES PAUL AGED

GIBSON ERIC CLAPTON 1960 LES PAUL AGED

The Les Paul remains an attractive instrument to many players today and has stood up to the new ideas, the new materials, the new electronics, and all the rest that makers have thrown at the electric guitar since this classic was designed back in the 50s in Kalamazoo, Michigan. Gibson, now located in Nashville, has had two changes of owner since then, but it is well aware of the value of its oldest solidbody guitar. Its Custom Shop creates upscale modern takes on the vintage idea, such as this signature Eric Clapton model that strives to re-create the guitar – long since lost to history – that Clapton used in 1966 to record the classic John Mayall "Beano" album.

Die Les Paul ist für viele Gitarristen auch heute noch attraktiv und konnte sich gegenüber den neuen Designs, neuen Materialien, neuer Elektronik etc. behaupten, mit denen Gitarrenbauer E-Gitarren ausstatten, seit dieser Klassiker in den 1950er-Jahren in Kalamazoo, Michigan entwickelt wurde. Gibson, mittlerweile mit Sitz in Nashville, wechselte seitdem zwei Mal den Besitzer, kennt den Wert der ältesten Solidbody jedoch ganz genau. Der Gibson Custom Shop entwickelt noch hochwertige, moderne Versionen des alten Vintage-Designs, wie z. B. diese Eric Clapton Gitarre, die dem (längst verschollenen) Original möglichst nahe kommen soll, das Clapton 1966 für die Aufnahme des Albums ‚Blues Breakers' (auch ‚Beano' genannt) mit John Mayall verwendete.

THOM YORKE in particular and Radiohead in general enjoyed widespread popularity from the late 90s, and the band's fondness for Telecasters – especially the models from the 70s and 80s fitted with humbucking pickups – did much to revive interest in these instruments among other open-minded indie and alternative bands.

THOM YORKE und Radiohead im Allgemeinen feierten Ende der 1990er-Jahre große Erfolge. Die Tatsache, dass die Bandmitglieder eine Vorliebe für Telecasters hatten – insbesondere für die Modelle mit Humbucker-Tonabnehmern aus den 1970er- und 1980er-Jahren– verstärkte das wiederaufkeimende Interesse an diesen Instrumenten, vor allem bei aufgeschlossenen Indie- und Alternative-Bands.

Back in the mid 60s, ERIC CLAPTON played a sunburst Gibson Les Paul Standard on John Mayall's classic "Beano" album. The guitar was stolen soon afterward and has never been recovered, and it has since achieved legendary status among guitar fans. Gibson issued a limited-edition repro of the instrument in 2010.

Mitte der 1960er-Jahre spielte ERIC CLAPTON eine Sunburst Gibson Les Paul Standard auf John Mayalls Albumklassiker ‚Beano'. Die Gitarre wurde kurz darauf gestohlen und ist nie wieder aufgetaucht. Unter Gitarrenfans ist sie legendär. Gibson brachte 2010 eine Reproduktion der Gitarre in limitierter Auflage heraus.

ALEXI LAIHO GREENY

ALEXI 'WILDCHILD' LAIHO is singer and lead guitarist with Finland's Children Of Bodom, and he's rated among metal fans for his melodic invention and speedy riffing. At first he endorsed Jackson Randy Rhoads-style guitars, but in 2003 he moved to an alliance with ESP, with whom he now has a number of signature models.

ALEXI 'WILDCHILD' LAIHO ist Sänger und Leadgitarrist bei Children Of Bodom aus Finnland. Er wird von Metal-Fans für seine erfinderischen Melodien und seine schnellen Riffs geschätzt. Zunächst spielte er vorwiegend auf Jackson Randy Rhoads-Gitarren, 2003 wechselte er jedoch zu ESP und hat mittlerweile mehrere eigene Signature-Modelle.

ESP ALEXI LAIHO GREENY

ESP, or Electric Sound Products, began as a small custom shop at the back of a Tokyo music store in 1975, established by Hisatake Shibuya. His early guitars were copies, but he began to develop original takes on traditional models around the time ESP opened its first overseas office, in New York City, ten years later. The main business for the US arm at first was copies and superstrats, but custom shop specials and signature guitars followed, as well as production models, including a signature V for Kerry King. ESP added a second-tier budget brand, LTD, in 1996. This ESP signature model for Alexi Laiho of Children Of Bodom features an extreme V shape and Laiho's favoured skull decoration, Floyd Rose vibrato, and simple volume control and boost switch.

Electric Sound Products, kurz ESP, begann 1975 als kleiner Custom-Shop im Hinterhof eines Musikladens in Tokio. Die ersten Gitarren von Gründer Hisatake Shibuya waren ausschließlich Kopien, doch zehn Jahre später, als ESP seine erste Auslandsfiliale in New York eröffnete, begann er, eigene Versionen von traditionellen Modellen zu entwickeln. Das Kerngeschäft des amerikanischen Ablegers bestand zunächst in der Produktion von Kopien und Superstrats, später folgten Sonderanfertigungen und Signature-Gitarren sowie Serienproduktionen, u. a. von der Signature V für Kerry King. 1996 gründete ESP die preisgünstigere Zweitmarke LTD. Dieses Signature-Modell von ESP für Alexi Laiho von Children Of Bodom besitzt eine extreme V-Form und Laihos geliebten Totenkopf als Verzierung, ein Floyd Rose Vibrato, einen einfachen Lautstärkeregler und Boost-Schalter.

ESP SNAKEBYTE SW

The Japanese ESP company continued to develop its guitar lines through its US offices during the 90s, and late in that decade Gibson took legal action over the body shapes which it said copied some of its classic models. A settlement was reached in a US court in 1999, and the agreement stated that ESP would not use the shape and appearance of any of Gibson's Explorer, Flying V, SG, and Les Paul series guitars, but that specific revised versions would not infringe Gibson's trademark rights. ESP has an impressive list of mostly metal-inclined signature models for the likes of Gus G (Ozzy Osbourne), Jeff Hanneman (Slayer), and Michael Wilton (Queensrÿche), but the company's biggest endorsers are Kirk Hammett and James Hetfield of Metallica, whose signature guitars include this Snakebyte model for Hetfield, as well as Truckster and Iron Cross models, and a number of KH models for Hammett.

Die japanische Firma ESP entwickelte in den 1990er-Jahren weiterhin Gitarrenserien über ihre Filiale in den USA. Kurz vor dem Milleniumswechsel ging Gibson wegen Nachahmung von Korpusformen der klassischen Modelle gerichtlich gegen ESP vor. 1999 kam es vor einem US-Gericht zur Einigung, wonach ESP nicht länger die Form oder das Aussehen jedweder Gibson Explorer, Flying V, SG oder Les Paul verwenden durfte, bestimmte überarbeitete Versionen jedoch nicht gegen das Markenrecht von Gibson verstoßen würden. ESP verfügt über eine beeindruckende Ansammlung hauptsächlich metallastiger Signature-Modelle, u. a. für Gus G (Ozzy Osbourne), Jeff Hanneman (Slayer) und Michael Wilton (Queensrÿche). Die größten Werbeträger der Firma sind jedoch Kirk Hammett und James Hetfield von Metallica, zu deren Signature-Gitarren auch dieses Snakebyte-Modell für Hetfield gehört sowie die Truckster und Iron Cross Modelle sowie einige KH-Modelle für Hammett.

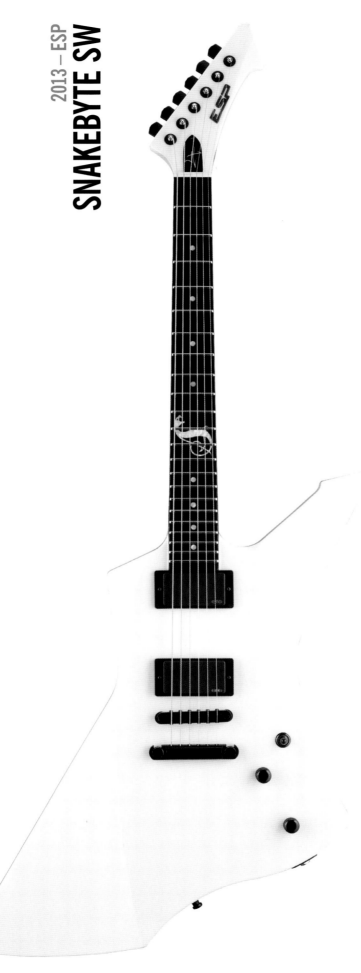

Metallica carved much of the modern metal template, working hard in the 80s to build their success and defining a genre with Master Of Puppets in 1986. JAMES HETFIELD (rhythm) and Kirk Hammett (lead) have worked their way through an arsenal of pointy guitars, and today they play and endorse a line of ESP models.

Metallica hat die moderne Metal-Musik und das Genre durch ihre hart erarbeiteten Erfolge in den 1980er-Jahren stark mitgeprägt, u.a. mit dem Album Master Of Puppets aus dem Jahr 1986. JAMES HETFIELD (Rhythmus) und Kirk Hammett (Lead) haben sich durch ein ganzes Arsenal an spitz zulaufenden Gitarren gespielt. Heute sind sie Werbeträger einer Serie von ESP-Modellen.

LINE 6 JAMES TYLER VARIAX JTV-69

Sound modelling was a new technology applied to guitar playing at the start of the 2000s. This now widespread idea is based on the storage and recall of digital re-creations of classic guitar and amp sounds. The California-based Line 6 brand was started by Marcus Ryle and Michel Doidic, formerly designers at Oberheim, which made effects and synthesizers. Line 6 was an innovator in creating digital software models and at first offered its Vetta amps and Pod boxes. It launched a modelling guitar, the Variax, in 2003, with onboard modelled sounds. This JTV-69 is one of a line of Variax guitars designed by the California high-end guitar maker James Tyler and produced by Line 6, and it offers access to 28 modelled sounds, from sitar and acoustic guitar to a range of electric styles, as well as 11 alternative tunings.

Sound-Modellierung war eine neue Technologie, mit der Gitarristen Anfang der 2000er-Jahre zu experimentieren begannen. Dieses mittlerweile geläufige Konzept basiert auf dem Speichern und Wiederaufrufen digitaler Neukreationen von Klängen klassischer Gitarren und Verstärker. Die in Kalifornien ansässige Marke Line 6 wurde von Marcus Ryle und Michel Doidic gegründet, die davor für Oberheim tätig waren, ein Unternehmen, das Effekte und Synthesizer herstellte. Line 6 war ein Vorreiter in der Erstellung digitaler Software-Modelle. Sie verkauften zunächst Vetta-Verstärker und Pod-Boxen, bis 2003 die Modelling-Gitarre Variax auf den Markt kam, die andere Gitarrentypen simulieren konnte. Diese JTV-69 ist eine von mehreren Variax-Gitarren, die der renommierte Gitarrenbauer James Tyler aus Kalifornien baute und von Line 6 produziert wurde. Sie kann 28 verschiedene Instrumente nachahmen, von Sitar über Akustikgitarre bis hin zu verschiedenen E-Gitarre und 11 alternativen Tunings.

2013 – LINE 6
JAMES TYLER VARIAX JTV-69

FENDER DELUXE STRATOCASTER HSS IOS

Along with Gibson's Les Paul, the Fender Stratocaster and Fender's other early solid-body design, the Telecaster, still dominate the electric guitar landscape today. In 1954, Leo Fender launched the Stratocaster from his small factory in Fullerton, California, and offered just one model well into the 70s. At the time of writing, Fender offers 62 Stratocaster models, made in its factories in the USA and Mexico and those of its overseas suppliers, aiming to provide a Strat for any kind of player who wants one. This model with iOS connectivity is the latest attempt to connect guitar and computer – or smartphone or tablet – for recording, editing, monitoring, and so on. We must wait to gauge its success. Meanwhile, and on any guitar you happen to pick up, guitarists will continue to enjoy the decades-old pleasure of strings on frets and the sweet, sweet guitar music that tumbles forth.

Neben der Les Paul von Gibson dominieren die Fender Stratocaster und Fenders anderes frühes Solidbody-Design, die Telecaster, noch immer die heutige E-Gitarren-Landschaft. 1954 baute Leo Fender seine erste Stratocaster in seiner kleinen Fabrik in Fullerton, Kalifornien, und verkaufte bis spät in die 1970er-Jahre ausschließlich ein Modell. Derzeit gibt es 62 Stratocaster-Modelle von Fender, die die Firma in ihren Produktionsstätten in den USA und Mexiko herstellt sowie die seiner ausländischen Lieferanten, um möglichst jedem den Zugang zu einer Strat zu ermöglichen. Dieses Modell mit iOS-Konnektivität ist der neueste Versuch, eine Gitarre an Computer, Smartphone oder Tablet anzuschließen, für Aufnahmen, Schnitt, Monitoring, usw. Ob das Modell Erfolg hat, lässt sich noch nicht sagen. Derweil genießen Gitarristen mit jeder Gitarre, die sie in den Händen halten, das Glücksgefühl vieler Jahrzehnte, wenn Saiten auf Bünde treffen und diesen wunderbaren Klang erzeugen.

2014 — FENDER

DELUXE STRATOCASTER HSS iOS

BONNIE RAITT is well known to fellow guitarists as a great blues and slide player, and she enjoyed wider fame following her bestselling Nick Of Time album in the late 80s. Raitt's favourite guitar is a '65 Strat she calls Old Brown, and Fender issued a signature model in 1995.

BONNIE RAITT gilt unter Kennern als großartige Blues- und Slide-Gitarristin. Mit ihrem Hitalbum Nick Of Time wurde sie Ende der 1980er-Jahre weltberühmt. Raitts Lieblingsgitarre ist eine Strat von 1965, die sie selbst „Old Brown" nennt. Fender brachte 1995 ein Signature-Modell heraus.

**MICHAEL
JACKSON**

ENNIFER
BATTEN

CHAPTER 04
INFORMATION

GUITAR INDEX

JOSÉ RAMÍREZ
1A
Page 28

LINE 6
J. T. VARIAX JTV-69
Page 170

LOWDEN
0-25
Page 58

LOWDEN
0-25
Page 58

MANZER
PIKASSO II
Page 59

MARTIN
STAUFFER-STYLE
Page 13

MARTIN
0-42
Page 14

MARTIN
N-20
Page 33

MARTIN
D-28
Page 42

MARTIN
D-18
Page 43

MARTIN
D-45
Page 43

MARTIN
D12-45
Page 56

MARTIN
000-42ECB
Page 56

MARTIN
OM-42
Page 56

MOSRITE
VENTURES MODEL
Page 136

MUSIC MAN
ALBERT LEE
Page 158

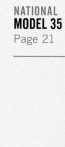

NATIONAL
STYLE O
Page 20

NATIONAL
MODEL 35
Page 21

OVATION
ADAMAS 1687
Page 54

PAGÉS
SIX-COURSE GUITAR
Page 12

PARKER
NITEFLY
Page 162

PRS
CUSTOM
Page 145

PRS
MCCARTHY MODEL
Page 160

PRS
TREMONTI SE
Page 160

RICKENBACKER
360/12
Page 96

ARTIST INDEX

A

ALLMAN, DUANE
Page 105

ARMATRADING, JOAN
Page 55

ATKINS, CHET
Page 32, 84, 95, 109

AUERBACH, DAN
Page 69, 92

B

BAEZ, JOAN
Page 14, 16

BARRUECO, MANUEL
Page 37

BATTEN, JENNIFER
Page 172

BEAM, SAMUEL
Page 60

BECK, JEFF
Page 85, 130, 158, 159

BELL, VINNIE
Page 123

BENSON, GEORGE
Page 42, 91

BENSUSAN, PIERRE
Page 58

BERRY, CHUCK
Page 78

BETTENCOURT, NUNO
Page 162

BETTS, DICKEY
Page 105

BLACKMORE, RITCHIE
Page 5, 130, 158, 159

BONAMASSA, JOE
Page 116

BREAM, JULIAN
Page 27

BRYANT, JIMMY
Page 109

BUCKLEY, TIM
Page 51, 52

BURRELL, KENNY
Page 73, 77

BURTON, JAMES
Page 42, 131

C

CHRISTIAN, CHARLIE
Page 70

CLAPTON, ERIC
Page 57, 89, 105, 113,
124, 130, 158, 167

CLINE, NELS
Page 120

COBAIN, KURT
Page 121

COCHRAN, EDDIE
Page 84

COLLEN, PHIL
Page 147

CROSBY, DAVID
Pages 42, 44, 95

CURTIS, IAN
Page 129

D

DALE, DICK
Page 158

DARRELL, DIMEBAG
Page 146, 163, 164

DAVIES, DAVE
Page 113

DE LUCIA, PACO
Page 8, 18

DOUGLAS, JERRY
Page 21

E

**EVANS, DAVID HOWELL
(„THE EDGE")**
Page 113

EVERLY, DON
Page 32, 49, 84

EVERLY, PHILIP
Page 32, 49, 84

F

FRIPP, ROBERT
Page 107

G

GALLAGHER, NOEL
Page 86

GALLUP, CLIFF
Page 85

GARLAND, HANK
Page 82

GATTON, DANNY
Page 103

GILMOUR, DAVID
Page 5, 49, 108, 123, 158

GRANDUCIEL, ADAM
Page 137

GREEN, FREDDIE
Page 73, 74

GREEN, GRANT
Page 87

GREEN, PETER
Page 114

GRISSOM, DAVID
Page 160

GUTHRIE, WOODY
Page 46

GUY, BUDDY
Page 158

H

HALL, JIM
Page 77

HAMMETT, KIRK
Page 169

HARRISON, GEORGE
Page 28, 48, 79, 80, 95,
96, 119, 123, 148

RECOMMENDED ALBUMS

01

ANDRÉS SEGOVIA
THE ART OF SEGOVIA
Deutsche Grammophon 471 697-2
2002 compilation

THE BEATLES
A HARD DAY'S NIGHT
1964, Parlophone PMC 1230

BERT JANSCH
ROSEMARY LANE
1971, Transatlantic Records TRA 235

COLDPLAY
PARACHUTES
2000, Parlophone 7243 5 27783 2 4

DAVID CROSBY
CROSBY, STILLS & NASH
1969, Atlantic cs 19117

ELVIS PRESLEY
THE SUN SESSIONS
RCA Victor APM1-1675
1976 compilation

THE EVERLY BROTHERS
IT'S EVERLY TIME
1960, Warner Bros. Records – W 1381

IRON & WINE
OUR ENDLESS NUMBERED DAYS
2004, Sub Pop SP 630

JANIS IAN
BETWEEN THE LINES
1975, Columbia PC 33394

JERRY DOUGLAS
TRAVELER
2012, eOne Music FOM-CD-21

JOAN ARMATRADING
SHOW SOME EMOTION
1977, A&M Records AMLH 68433

JOAN BAEZ
VOL.2 & IN CONCERT
1961, Hoodoo Records 263450

JOHN RENBOURN
THE HERMIT
1976, Transatlantic Records TRA 33

JOHN WILLIAMS
GUITAR CONCERTOS
1968, Columbia M3X 31508

JONI MITCHELL
BLUE
1971, Reprise Records MS 2038

JULIAN BREAM
PLAYS GRANADOS & ALBÉNIZ
1990, RCA Red Seal ARC1-4378

LEO KOTTKE
6 & 12-STRING GUITAR
1969, Takoma C-1024

LYLE LOVETT
PONTIAC
1988, Ariola 259 497

MANUEL BARRUECO
SOMETIME AGO
1994

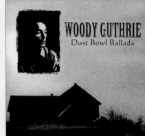

MICHAEL HEDGES
AERIAL BOUNDARIES
1984, Windham Hill Records WH-1032

PACO DE LUCÍA
ENTRE DOS AGUAS
1983, Philips 814 106-1

PAT METHENY
STILL LIFE (TALKING)
1990, Geffen Records GFLD 19196

PETE SEEGER
WE SHALL OVERCOME
1963, CBS BPG 62209

PIERRE BENSUSAN
INTUITE
2001, Favored Nations FN2130-2

RODRIGO Y GABRIELA
RODRIGO Y GABRIELA
2006, ATO Records ATO0030

SON HOUSE
FATHER OF FOLK BLUES
1965, Columbia CL 2417

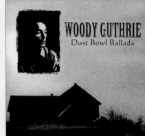

WOODY GUTHRIE
DUST BOWL BALLADS
1940, RCA Victor P-27 and P-28

02

B.B. KING
LIVE AT THE REGAL
1965, Ace CH 86

THE BEATLES
REVOLVER
1966, Parlophone PCS 7009

BIG BILL BROONZY
TROUBLE IN MIND
Smithsonian Folkways SFW CD 40131
2000 compilation

THE BLACK KEYS
RUBBER FACTORY
2004, Fat Possum Records 80379-2

THE BYRDS
MR. TAMBOURINE MAN
1965, Columbia CS 9172

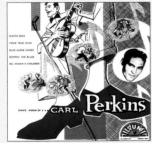

CARL PERKINS
**DANCE ALBUM OF
CARL PERKINS**
1957, Sun Record Company LP-1225

CHARLIE CHRISTIAN
**THE GENIUS OF THE
ELECTRIC GUITAR**
1987 compilation, Columbia CJT 40846

CHET ATKINS
FINGER-STYLE GUITAR
1956, RCA Victor LPM-1383

CHET ATKINS
WORKSHOP
1961, RCA Victor LSP-2232

CHUCK BERRY
BERRY IS ON TOP
1959, Chess LP 1435

CLIFF GALLUP
BLUEJEAN BOP!
1956, Capitol Records 2 C 064-82077

COUNT BASIE & HIS ORCHESTRA
APRIL IN PARIS
1957, Verve Records 825 575-2

CREAM
GOODBYE
1968 RSO – 823 660-2

CROSBY, STILLS, NASH & YOUNG
DÉJÀ VU
1970, Atlantic – SD 7200

DIRE STRAITS
BROTHERS IN ARMS
1985, Warner Bros. Rec. 9 25264-2

DJANGO REINHARDT
SWING DE PARIS
2003, Proper Records PROPERBOX 53

EDDIE COCHRAN
SINGIN' TO MY BABY
1957, Liberty LRP 3061

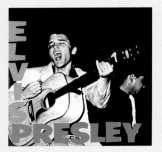

ELVIS PRESLEY
ELVIS PRESLEY
1956, RCA Victor LPM-1254

GEORGE BENSON
BREEZIN'
1976, Warner Bros. Rec. BS 2919

GRANT GREEN
FEELIN' THE SPIRIT
1963, Blue Note BLP 4132

GRANT GREEN
IDLE MOMENTS
1964, Blue Note BLP 84154

HANK GARLAND
JAZZ WINDS FROM A NEW DIRECTION
1961, Columbia CL 1572

HOWARD ALDEN
SWEET AND LOWDOWN: OST
1999, Sony Classical CD 89019

JIM HALL
CONCIERTO
1975, CTI Records CTI 6060

JOHN MCLAUGHLIN
EXTRAPOLATION
1969, Marmalade 608 007

KENNY BURRELL
GUITAR FORMS
1965, Verve Records 825 576-2

KENNY BURRELL
MIDNIGHT BLUE
1963, Blue Note Records BLP 4123

MUDDY WATERS
THE BEST OF MUDDY WATERS
1958, Chess LP 1427

NEIL YOUNG
AFTER THE GOLD RUSH
1970, Reprise Records ⯑RS 6383

OASIS
(WHAT'S THE STORY) MORNING GLORY?
1995, Creation Records CRE CD 189

SUZANNE VEGA
SOLITUDE STANDING
1987, A&M Records SP-5136

T-BONE WALKER
THE COMPLETE CAPITOL / BLACK & WHITE RECORDINGS
Capitol Records CDP 7243 8 29379 2 0
1995 compilation

TEN YEARS AFTER
UNDEAD
1968, Deram DES 18016

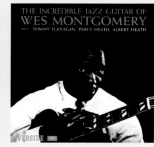

WES MONTGOMERY
FULL HOUSE
1962, Riverside Records RLP 434

WES MONTGOMERY
THE INCREDIBLE JAZZ GUITAR OF WES MONTGOMERY
1960, Riverside Records RLP 12-320

ALBERT LEE
SPEECHLESS
1986, MCA Records 253 005-1

THE ALLMAN BROTHERS
AT FILLMORE EAST
1971, Capricorn Records SD 2-802

BOB MARLEY (THE WAILERS)
BURNIN'
1973, Island Records SMAS-9336

BONNIE RAITT
NICK OF TIME
1989, Capitol Records – CDP 7 91268 2

BUDDY HOLLY
THE "CHIRPING" CRICKETS
1957, Brunswick BL 54038

CHEAP TRICK
IN COLOR
1977, Epic PE 34884

CHILDREN OF BODOM
FOLLOW THE REAPER
2008, Spinefarm Records SPI99CD

THE CLASH
LONDON CALLING
1979, CBS 88478, CBS Clash 3

CREAM
DISRAELI GEARS
1967, RSO – 823 636-2 YH

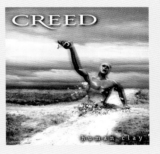

CREED
HUMAN CLAY
1999, Wind-Up – 60150-13053-2

DANNY GATTON
REDNECK JAZZ EXPLOSION
1978, NRG Records NLP9-2916

DAVID BOWIE
EXCERPTS FROM OUTSIDE
1995, Music On Vinyl MOVLP500

DEF LEPPARD
ADRENALIZE
1992, Bludgeon Riffola 510 978-2

DEREK & THE DOMINOS
LAYLA AND OTHER ASSORTED LOVE SONGS
1970, ATCO Records – SD 2-704

DIXIE CHICKS
TOP OF THE WORLD TOUR LIVE
2003, Columbia – C2K 90794

ELVIS PRESLEY
ON STAGE
1970, RCA Victor – LSP-4362-2

ERIC CLAPTON
JOHN MAYALL BLUES BREAKERS WITH ERIC CLAPTON
1966, Deram 844 827-2 (1966)

EXTREME
PORNOGRAFFITTI
1990, A&M Records 75021 5313 2

FLEETWOOD MAC
THEN PLAY ON
1969, Reprise W7 – RSLP 9000

FRANK ZAPPA
HOT RATS
1970 Bizarre Records RS 6356

FREDDIE KING
LET'S HIDE AWAY AND DANCE AWAY
1961, King Records (3) 773

JEFF BECK
BLOW BY BLOW
1975, Epic PE 33409

JENNIFER BATTEN
TRIBAL RAGE: MOMENTUM
1997, Mondo Congo Records MCR-0123

JIMI HENDRIX
AXIS: BOLD AS LOVE
1967, Track Record 613 003

JIMMY BRYANT & SPEEDY WEST
TWO GUITARS COUNTRY STYLE
1954, Capitol Records T 520

JOE BONAMASSA
LIVE FROM THE ROYAL ALBERT HALL
2010, J&R Adventures PRAR92340

JOE SATRIANI
SURFING WITH THE ALIEN
1987, Relativity 88561-8193-1

JOHNNY WINTER
SECOND WINTER
1969, Columbia KCS 9947

KING CRIMSON
IN THE COURT OF THE CRIMSON KING
1969, Island Records – ILPS 9111

THE KINKS
ARE THE VILLAGE GREEN PRESERVATION SOCIETY
1968, Pye Records NPL 18233

KISS
LOVE GUN
1977, Casablanca Records NBLP 7057

LED ZEPPELIN
LED ZEPPELIN II
1969, Atlantic 588198

LES PAUL
THE LEGEND & THE LEGACY
1991, Capitol DPRO-79082

MEGADETH
RUST IN PEACE
1990, Capitol Records 068 79 1935 1

METALLICA
MASTER OF PUPPETS
1986, Vertigo 838 141-1

MERLE TRAVIS
THE MERLE TRAVIS GUITAR
1956, Capitol Records T 650

NIRVANA
NEVERMIND
1991, DGC – DGCD-24425

OZZY OSBOURNE
BLIZZARD OF OZZ
1981, Jet Records JETLP 234

PANTERA
COWBOYS FROM HELL
1990, ATCO Records 7 91372-2

QUEEN
SHEER HEART ATTACK
1974, EMI – EMC 3061

RADIOHEAD
OK COMPUTER
1997, Parlophone – NODATA 02

THE RAMONES
RAMONES
1976, Sire SASD-7520

THE ROLLING STONES
AFTERMATH
1966, Decca SKL 4786

THE ROLLING STONES
EXILE ON MAIN ST.
1972, Rolling Stones Records COC 69100

RUSH
MOVING PICTURES
1981, Anthem Records (2) ANR-1-1030

SANTANA
SUPERNATURAL
1999, Arista 19080 1

SEX PISTOLS
NEVER MIND THE BOLLOCKS HERE'S THE SEX PISTOLS
1977, Virgin V 2086

THE SHADOWS
GREATEST HITS
1963, Columbia 33SX 1522

SISTER ROSETTA THARPE
THE GOSPEL OF THE BLUES
2000 compilation, MCA Records
B0000533-02

SLAYER
REIGN IN BLOOD
1986, Def Jam Recordings GHS 24131

STEVE VAI
PASSION AND WARFARE
1990, Relativity 88561-1037-2

TIM BUCKLEY
HAPPY SAD
1969, Elektra EKS-74045

TODD RUNDGREN
HERMIT OF MINK HOLLOW
1978, Bearsville BRK 6981

U2
THE JOSHUA TREE
1987, Island Records 90581-1

VAN HALEN
VAN HALEN
1978, Warner Bros. Rec. BSK 3075

VINNIE BELL
WHISTLE STOP
1963, Verve Records V6-8574

THE WAR ON DRUGS
LOST IN THE DREAM
2014, Secretly Canadian SC310

WILCO
YANKEE HOTEL FOXTROT
2002, Sundazed Music LP 5161

YES
THE YES ALBUM
1971, Atlantic 2400 101

IMPRINT:

ISBN: 978-3-943573-11-4
Copyright © 2014 by Edel Germany GmbH, Hamburg / Germany
Music copyright see music credits. All rights reserved.
No part of this publication may be reproduced in any form
without the prior written permission of the publisher.

EDITORIAL DIRECTION: Jos Bendinelli Negrone
PROJECT COORDINATION: Gabrielle Berlin
TEXT: Tony Bacon
TRANSLATION & PROOF-READING: Margit Sander, Ruth Frobeen
GRAFIK DESIGN & ART DIRECTION: Seidldesign
LAYOUT: Alexander Mertsch
PHOTO CREDITS: All pictures from Getty Images, unless stated otherwise.
Page 37, Manuel Barrueco: Courtesy of Stephen Spartana
Page 58, Pierre Bensusan: Courtesy of David Bevan /AliveNetwork.com

All guitar images are from Backbeat & Jawbone, London (www.jawbonepress.com).
The following key identifies who owned which guitar at the time of photography, by page number.
Multiple images on one page are listed left to right or top to bottom. **10**, **11**, **12** Robert Spencer;
13 Martin, Steve Howe; **14** Hank Risan; **15** Scott Chinery; **19** Russell Cleveland; **20** anonymous,
Scott Chinery; **21** Graeme Matheson; **24** Malcolm Weller; **25** Raymond Ursell; **26** Russell
Cleveland, Yoshi Serizawa; **28** Juan Teijeiro; **29**, **31** Russell Cleveland; **32** Gibson, Michael Wright;
33 Mandolin Bros; **36** Russell Cleveland; **37** Raymond Ursell; **39**, **40** Scott Chinery; **42** Martin;
43 Scott Chinery, Martin; **46** Adrian Lovegrove; **47** Scott Chinery; **48** George Harrison; **49** David
Gilmour; **50** Music Ground; **51** Steve Howe; **54** Tim Fleming; **56** Scott Chinery, House Of Guitars;
58 House Of Guitars; **59** Scott Chinery; **60** House Of Guitars; **61** Taylor; **63**, **64**, **65** House Of
Guitars; **70** Adrian Ingram, Scott Chinery; **71** Richard Chapman; **72**, **73** Scott Chinery; **76** Gruhn
Guitars, Scott Chinery; **78** Scot Arch; **79** Larry Wassgren; **82**, **83** Scot Arch; **84** Chet Atkins; **85**
Jeff Beck; **86** Scott Chinery; **87** Scott Chinery, Mike Slubowski; **88** Scot Arch; **89** Eric Clapton,
Scott Chinery; **90** Gibson, Adrian Lovegrove; **91** Tony Bacon; **94** Paul Day, John Reynolds, Gary
Dick; **96** George Harrison; **97** Paul McCartney, Guitar & Bass; **102** Country Music Hall Of Fame,
Gruhn Guitars, Brian Fischer; **104** Gruhn Guitars, Mike Slubowski; **105** Mike Slubowski; **106**
David Noble, **107** Scott Chinery; **108** Scott Chinery; **109** Paul Day; **110** David Noble; **111** Paul
Unkert; **112** Scott Chinery, Eric Clapton/Christie's, Dave Brewis/Rock Stars Guitars; **114** Gary
Moore; **115** Jimmy Page, Scott Chinery; **118**, **119** Paul Day; **120** Scott Chinery; **121** Fender; **122**
Michael Wright, Paul Day, David Gilmour; **124** David Noble; **125** David Noble, Todd Rundgren;
128 Paul Midgeley; **129** Paul Day; **130** Scott Arch; **131** Adrian Hornbrook; **132** Scott Arch,
Steve Ostromogilsky, Steve Howe; **136** Clive Kay; **137** Bruce Bowling; **138** Michael Wright;
139 Don Clayton; **140**, **141** Paul Day; **144** Andrew Large; **145** PRS; **146** Robert Witte, Michael
Wright; **147** Robert Witte; **148** Guild; **149** Rickenbacker, Steve Howe; **152** Michael Wright; **153**
Lars Mullen; **154**, **155** Hoshino; **158** Paul Midgeley, Paul Day; **160** Gareth Malone, PRS; **162**,
163 Guitar & Bass; **166** Fender, Gibson; **168**, **169** ESP; **170** Line 6; **171** Fender.

Special thanks to:
Joe Satriani, Ian Gillan, Mick Brigden, John Dee, Ara Tadevosyan,
Drew Thompson, Ulf Zick, Michael Putland, John Pambakian,
Bernd Hocke and René Valjeur.

Produced by optimal media GmbH, Röbel / Germany
Printed and manufactued in Germany
earBOOKS is an imprint of Edel Germany GmbH
For more information about earBOOKS
please visit www.earbooks.net

THE ROLLING STONES during the production of the
music video for "Respectable" in New York, 1978.

*THE ROLLING STONES während des Videodrehs zu
„Respectable" in New York, 1978.*